MAGIC CARPET RIDE

Quarry Press
Pop Music and Culture Books

NEIL YOUNG: DON'T BE DENIED
by John Einarson

ENCYCLOPEDIA OF CANADIAN ROCK, POP & FOLK MUSIC
by Rick Jackson

SOME DAY SOON: PROFILES OF CANADIAN SONGWRITERS
by Douglas Fetherling

CALLING THE SHOTS: PROFILES OF WOMEN FILMMAKERS
by Janis Cole and Holly Dale

JOHN KAY

MAGIC CARPET RIDE

JOHN KAY & JOHN EINARSON

QUARRY PRESS
ROCKS!

*To the women in my life —Elsbeth, Jutta and Shawn —
as well as the countless friends and supporters who through
their letters and words of encouragement helped me get
through some of the tough times in my life.*

John Kay

The publisher acknowledges the financial assistance of The Canada Council, the Ontario Arts Council, the Department of Canadian Heritage, and the Ontario Publishing Centre.

Canadian Cataloguing in Publication

Kay, John
    Magic carpet ride: the autobiography of John Kay and Steppenwolf

ISBN 1-55082-108-3

    1. Kay, John   2. Rock musicians — Biography.
I. Einarson, John, 1952– .   II. Title.

ML420.K39A3 1994   782.42166'092   C94-900602-5

Design consultant: Keith Abraham.
Printed and bound in Canada by Webcom Limited, Toronto, Ontario.

Published in Canada, the United States of America, and the United Kingdom by **Quarry Press, Inc.,**
P.O. Box 1061, Kingston, Ontario K7L 4Y5.

CONTENTS

INTRODUCTION

I know my share of history
How hard it is to be free from
Wearing masks that turn to skin
Hiding what you could've been
Ride with me, baby
Until the end of the day

RIDE WITH ME, 1971

Born *To Be Wild*. The song is a symbol of the 1960s, a timelessly appealing image of freedom, long hair tossed in the wind, straddling a motorcycle, engine revved full throttle, riding off in search of America. *Born To Be Wild* became an instant hit upon its release in 1968, a rallying cry for American youth, the perfect song for that eventful summer before the Chicago riots and the assassinations of Robert Kennedy and Martin Luther King — and the perfect sound track for the counterculture flick *Easy Rider*. The song has appeared in virtually every movie, film, documentary, or retrospective of that tumultuous decade, its opening snare drum crack enough to give it away immediately, evoking memories of an era when personal freedom and adventure seeking were legitimate goals for a generation.

The song refuses to die. More than twenty-five years later it's still heard every hour of every day in every city across North America, still selling in the hundreds of thousands. Whenever it comes on your car radio you cannot ignore it, your arm involuntarily lurching to crank up the volume control. It's one of those songs that just can't be appreciated at low volume — it's no holds barred, take no prisoners rock 'n' roll at its rawest. Every novice band cut its teeth on it in a thousand garages; it's a rock 'n' roll rite of passage. And each year for the past twenty-five years, tens of thousands of people throng to hear John Kay and Steppenwolf perform the song live, to recapture the spirit of *Born To Be Wild*. It's a motley crew of aging hippies, Vietnam vets, bikers old and new, young heavy metal freaks seeking the source, and paunchy middle - aged parents often with their kids in tow. They sit politely throughout the set, appreciative applause for the newer material and lesser known Steppenwolf tracks, saving their energy for the finale. They all know why they're there. So does John Kay. He knows what that song means to them and to him. It's the song that has kept him on the road touring successfully for almost three decades. It's paid for his sprawling, secluded retreat in the hills of Tennessee. It's the song that is most immediately identified with his image, the black leather and sunglasses, the growling voice and menacing delivery.

Then comes the knock-out punch three song finale: the hypnotic organ of *Magic Carpet Ride*, the power chording of *Born To Be Wild*, and finally those four drug-drenched opening chords that slide into *The Pusher*. Bang, bang, bang; one, two, three. The audience, to a person, is on its feet, shouting each line, fists slamming into the air, as if it brings them some kind of mass spiritual release, a catharsis. It's an amazing sight, this oddball mix of fans dreaming of a bygone era. No band wants to follow that combination, none can, except maybe The Rolling Stones.

As he leaves the stage, guitar held aloft in triumph, John Kay knows he's given them their money's worth. They got what they came for. Next year, when he passes through their area again, they'll be back to be a part of the moment all over again. "Born To Be Wild" once more.

Symbols have played an integral role in shaping John Kay's life. As a teenager growing up in West Germany, handicapped by poor eyesight, his daydreams were filled with symbols of America: Cowboys and Indians, Coca-Cola, James Dean, Little Richard, and rock 'n' roll music. Cardboard guitar in hand in front of his mother's tailoring mirror miming to records in a language he couldn't understand, young Joachim Fritz Krauledat longed to live in America. His subsequent success in the music world as the founder and leader of Steppenwolf was built around symbols. The black leather and macho swagger created an identifiable image that sold millions of records worldwide. The symbol of a motorcycle and the lyrics "Get your motor running, head out on the highway" in *Easy Rider* became synonymous with the Steppenwolf name. His ever-present sunglasses became a symbol of youthful alienation from society. Few knew that John was legally blind and wore those shades out of necessity, not fashion. His socially-conscious lyrics in songs like *The Ostrich, Don't Step On The Grass, Sam*, and *Monster* became symbols for the counterculture and precursors of environmental consciousness. Those same lyrics also became an obvious target for the political establishment and drew the public ire of the White House in 1969, only serving to further John's stature as a spokesperson of the American youth culture.

There have been other symbols, not so positive for John. The symbol of the wolf, an image he built up, exploited by unscrupulous agents and former bandmates who ran the Steppenwolf legacy into the ground in the late 1970s. Determined to restore the band's reputation, John launched a costly counteroffensive, costly financially and personally as he set out on the road for up to eleven months of the year, reconquering old territory and winning new fans.

And there is another symbol, more powerful and compelling, that shaped John Kay. It sits on the shelves in his study on the lower level of his private sanctuary, his retreat from the months and years on the road. It's a comfortable home, finely furnished, floor to ceiling windows that catch the warm southern sun in the morning over the lake, well-organized because he expects that of everything around him. His eyesight deficiencies dictate that; he couldn't live any other way. It's there on the shelves among the many books and records he has collected and not far from a photo album of faded black and white snapshots from a time he barely knew and of a young man in a uniform he never met.

On those shelves rests a piece of the Berlin Wall. He carved it out with his own hands a few years back, carefully packed it, and brought it home to Tennessee. Its prominent position on the shelf is not for the benefit of friends or to impress guests. It serves as a brick and mortar epitaph to what might have been, to what his life might have become if he and his mother had not escaped East Germany back in the summer of 1948 in the midst of the Berlin Blockade that set Cold War tensions between East and West racing. Although they fled the barbed wire years before the Berlin Wall was erected, it has always served as a symbol, not only to John but to all Germans, of freedom lost and a people divided.

There is a very different man behind the sunglasses, black leather and growling voice. John Kay the rock star and John Kay the man are two different people. He has successfully crafted an image, but the real John Kay, not the one who sings of heavy metal thunder and magic carpet rides, is a thoughtful, articulate and intensely private individual. Though many of his best known songs reek of macho chauvinism and hedonistic pleasures, he has remained married to the same woman for twenty-seven years and is the father of a grown daughter. A devoted family man, John worked hard to create as normal a life for his family as possible living in the rock 'n' roll fast lane of sixties and seventies Los Angeles. He has stepped back from the spotlight several times throughout his lengthy career in order to keep his family life in perspective.

During the heyday of Steppenwolf, John lived life to the fullest, indulging in all the recreations available to someone of his calibre in the rock 'n' roll pantheon. But there is another side to him. He credits an innate sensitivity towards women from being raised almost exclusively by his mother whose nurturing and daring decisions early in his life allowed him the freedom to become what he is today. His close relationship with his wife, Jutta, has been his source of inner strength.

It has been a long, tough road for John Kay, truly a magic carpet ride from political oppression in Eastern Europe to freedom, success, conflict, and personal triumph in North America. John has proven time and again that he is a survivor. This book is the record of John Kay's ride to freedom. Ride with him.

John Einarson

John Kay in concert, 1970.

Billboard on Sunset Strip, 1968.

The original band (clockwise from lower left): Goldy McJohn, Rushton Moreve, Michael Monarch, Jerry Edmonton, and John Kay.

ONE

RENEGADE

Crossing the line in the dead of night
Five years old and on the run
"This ain't no game boy, don't make a sound
And watch that man with the gun"
Say a prayer for the ones we leave behind
Say a prayer for us all
Come take my hand and hold on tight

The Wall, 1990

"*P*ack your rucksack, Joachim. We're going on a trip." That was all my mother told me the night we escaped from East Germany. She had obviously planned this for some time but feared telling a four-year-old who, unaware of the need for secrecy, might blab it all about. One had to keep silent about these matters because of the Communist Party members in town. To communicate this in any way, even by telephone or letter, was out of the question. I'm certain she told the Kranz family, our benefactors in Arnstadt whom I called Onkel Hugo and Tante Else, and sought Hugo's advice while considering the move. But she didn't dwell on the risks involved. Once she set her mind to something, that was that. Since my eyesight problem was diagnosed, she knew that the only way I would ever get proper medical attention and the kind of diet I needed to improve my eyes was in the West. "If that's what the boy needs" — she acted out of a sense of practicality. I don't ever recall her saying that she was afraid that night. To this day she's rarely reflected on what might have happened.

The Iron Curtain already existed in a physical sense because the border was ringed with barbed wire and patrolled by Russian soldiers. The *Volksarmee* did not as yet exist, or if so, it did not yet patrol the border.

That night, my mother packed a small suitcase with some clothes, my father's ring, and a few photos of him she had brought from Tilsit. I packed what few things I had in my rucksack, not knowing where we were bound. Strangely, one of the things I included was a little glass Santa Claus Christmas tree ornament which, for some reason at the time, was important to me. She bid farewell to the Kranz family; it was not easy saying goodbye. They had been our family for four years, the only family I knew.

I vaguely recall we took a train as far as Eisenach near the border. Once there, we went to a house where we were joined by a dozen or so others. My Aunt Ida, recently reunited with my mother after several years in a Russian work camp, accompanied my mother and me on our escape. At the house we were met by two brothers who were to be our guides to freedom. My mother gave them what she had saved from sewing alterations in Arnstadt. A truck came for us and we rode in the back to the boundary line. I remember huddling in our group, hunkering down, waiting on the East German side. I had a cold and a cough. One of the guides took me aside. "Stifle yourself, boy, and do what you are told! The border guards have guns and will shoot you if they hear you cough." To me the whole thing was an adventure. I had no idea what was happening. I don't know if my mother ever weighed the possibility of being shot. At best she probably figured that because they were women and children, they would be taken prisoner and most likely sent home. Whatever the consequences, there was no turning back now.

We crossed near the Hartz Mountains south of Brunswick and Hannover. I remember seeing search lights moving, though I don't recall seeing the towers. One guide took off down the line to cut the barbed wire. The men were separated from the women and children and crossed the line first. At the time, I didn't understand why the men went ahead, but thinking about this years later I surmised that the men were likely serving as decoys. It was a very bright night, and in the moonlight the ground looked like sand to me. As the women passed under the wire, one of the guides took me by the hand and led me through. As I crouched I could hear a commotion, then gunfire, maybe a machine gun burst. "Hurry, hurry, hurry, just keep running!" implored our guide. We made it under the severed wire and ran as far and as fast as we could go to freedom. What happened to the men is a mystery to me. Whether any or all or none of them made it through, I have no idea to this day.

I remember that night fairly well, and have thought of it many times over the years. My mother's decision that night changed my life forever.

My birthplace would be hard to find,
It changed so many times,
I'm not sure where it belongs.
But they tell me the Baltic Coast was full of amber,
And the land was green before the tanks came.

RENEGADE, 1970

East Prussia, the place of my birth, no longer exists on any map, swallowed up under the terms of Nazi Germany's surrender in 1945. The northern portion was absorbed by the former Soviet Union into the republic of Byelorussia with the southern territory placed under the Polish flag. East Prussia had been a province of Germany prior to 1914, but although still German territory, was arbitrarily separated from Germany proper under the terms of the Versailles Treaty following World War I. That action was, however, a minor irritant compared with much harsher terms enacted on the defeated Germany. Though East Prussia remained under German authority, it was isolated from 'the fatherland' by the Polish Corridor and the free city of Danzig, a bone of contention for many Germans.

Populated by German-speaking residents, East Prussia was a rural outpost, at times amid hostile neighbors, the Russians and the Poles. The province was bordered to the northwest by Lithuania, a nation carved from Russian control after World War I. During that war, the Russians had fought their way into East Prussia, burning everything in their wake before being routed by German Field Marshall Von Hindenburg. With the loss of Lithuania and the humiliation by Von Hindenburg, the Russians harbored some resentments in that vicinity. The Poles, on the other hand, eyed East Prussia with a certain amount of concern. They viewed it as a potential springboard for German aggression against Poland as well as a desirable Baltic seaport.

The East Prussian inhabitants considered themselves staunchly German, separated physically though not spiritually from the fatherland. Isolated from the mainstream of German life, they saw themselves as unique, an independent-spirited, self-reliant people who took great pride in their Prussian ancestry. A century and a half earlier, Prussia had been transformed under the Hohenzollern Dynasty from a poor, agricultural peasant society into one of the leading military powers of Europe. Its armies were considered the best disciplined on the continent and its people industrious and obedient to the Prussian Princes who ruled them. Their quest for expansion in the late 1800s resulted in halting Napoleon III's eastern advances and in the eventual unification of Germany under Prussian rulers. Prussians continued to rule Germany until the end of World War I. With the rise of a little Austrian shit named Adolf Hitler to the position of Reichschancellor of Germany in 1933, Prussian influence declined. However, their sense of self-importance to Germany remained strong.

East Prussians, in turn, were viewed by the main body of Germans as 'those rural types out there,' hayseeds, provincial in their outlook. They were, nonetheless, Germans, and when Adolph Hitler came to power in 1933 and began building the Third Reich, reuniting "Ostpreussen" or East Prussia to Germany proper was declared a priority of German nationalism. That nationalist fervor ultimately resulted in the German assault on Poland on September 1, 1939, ushering in World War II. With the fall of Poland, East Prussia was once again a physical part of Germany for five brief years during the war. It was during this period and under these circumstances that I, Joachim Fritz Krauledat, was born in the town of Tilsit, East Prussia, along the Niemen River near the Lithuanian border. About the only thing the town is known for is a flavor of cheese named Tilsit. Like East Prussia itself, Tilsit no longer exists, destroyed, captured, and renamed Sovetsk by the Soviets in 1945.

As a result, I don't have a homeland with an extended family because we were all displaced by the war. I left Tilsit as an infant in my mother's arms. What she left behind was bombed into oblivion by the Red Army in late 1944 during their race to Berlin. There is nothing left that was ours, mine. Even the name of the town has been changed. I can't take my daughter to my hometown and point to this street and say, "Your great grandfather lived here." Or point to another spot and say, "This is the corner where your grandfather and grandmother first met." At an early age I asked my mother who in our family was still alive, who was who one generation ago and where did I come from? It was difficult for her to explain in a way that, I as a child, could understand. Over the years I met various relatives and was able to piece together some roots, but it's a far cry from, "This is who you are and this is where you come from." It's as though someone took a family photograph and there were all these empty spaces. Every two out of three would be blank like some Hollywood B movie where the image fades then disappears. But we were no different than many thousands of other families after the war. When you're surrounded by that degree of loss you can hardly view your own lot as being the exceptionally tragic one. There were plenty of families much worse off than ours.

The first mental image of my life, the earliest concrete thing I can recall that I considered mine, was a tiny room above a tannery in a courtyard you entered through an archway along a narrow old cobblestone street. This was my first real home and would remain so from the time I was a few months old until age four, a tannery in the small town of Arnstadt, in what became the German Democratic Republic or East Germany. During that period my whole world was my mother and the Kranz family, Hugo, Else, and their niece Helga. They virtually adopted my mother and I as surrogate relatives in the dying months of World War II. These four people were, as far as I knew then, my only family.

I never had the opportunity to know my father. He died somewhere in the Baltic region fighting the Russians two months before I was born. All I know of him is what my mother told me once I was old enough to ask who he was. When I did ask about my father, she showed me a handful of photographs of him in his uniform, one of the few things we took with us when we left Tilsit. His name was Fritz Krauledat, of Lithuanian background, the name abbreviated from the Lithuanian "Krauledeites." He was born March 17, 1913 in the rural community of Absteinen. Because the village was so close to the Lithuanian border, there was a lot of intermingling of the two groups. I know little about his early years before he met my mother. He was the oldest of nine children raised on a small farm. Centuries earlier the Huns and the Mongols who swept through Eastern Europe left behind portions of their disintegrating armies in retreat. These Asians intermarried with the locals so there are a lot of high cheek bones and almond eyes in that part of the world, physical traits I seem to have inherited from my father. In many ways I resemble him physically, tall and dark, but whether I have any of his habits of character, I do not know.

My mother recalls my father as an affectionate man, never uncomfortable or reluctant to show his love for her. I'm sure he would have been the same with me had he been given the chance to know me. I believe my mother and father genuinely loved one another and enjoyed being together. They would probably have led long, happy lives together and had more children had a twisted individual named Adolph Hitler not spoiled their plans. All I know of his family was that they were considered poorer than my mother's family and she took some heat from her mother when she married him. My maternal grandmother felt my mother was marrying below her station.

Centuries ago, German knights marched into the East Prussian region and parceled out land grants to their friends who in turn set up a feudal system. This kept the region very rural, agricultural, and isolated, a very spartan existence for the inhabitants. Eventually many of the farmers purchased the land for themselves. Like most Germans of the time, these simple rural folk embraced Lutheranism after the Protestant Reformation. During the 1700s, over twenty-thousand French Protestant Huguenots, fleeing persecution at the hands of Roman Catholics, settled in the region of East Prussia. A century later, descendants of French Huguenots who had earlier escaped to Austria took up offers of free land in East Prussia and, like the Lithuanians, intermarried with the locals. My mother's family were descendants of those Austrian Huguenot settlers. Her maiden name was Zimmermann, her father being German. But her mother (my maternal grandmother) was born a Kendler, from the French name Chandler, which meant candlemaker. Because of her Huguenot-Austrian background, my mother's mother always saw herself above the common East Prussian folk.

Elsbeth Zimmermann, my mother, was born September 27, 1913, in the little village of Malissen in East Prussia, one of seven children born to a moderately successful farm family. She's an energetic person, friendly, cordial and likes people. Growing up on a farm as the oldest daughter, she learned to accept responsibility early in her life. At times stubborn and strong-willed, she's always been very practical-minded and gone her own way, the rest of the world be damned. She can be a very determined person; whatever she wants to do, she goes after it. Nothing slows her down and woe be it to anyone who runs afoul of her. She'll let you have it with both barrels. I've found some of these characteristics in me: don't cross me. I do forgive but I don't forget. Somewhat overbearing at times, she's most often right. These qualities, developed early, served her well and prepared her for the rocky road that, unbeknown to her, lay ahead. When I think what she endured in her life, the hand fate dealt her, I'm amazed she has maintained such a positive outlook. But she was never someone who permitted whatever life handed her to crush her spirit. Where there's life, there's hope. She really lived that adage. Her ability to laugh and find joy in life got her through some difficult times. Her demeanor came from that attitude. She is a very courageous woman, but she doesn't see herself that way.

We all tend to elevate our mothers to sainthood as a result of the nurturing, childrearing and self-sacrifice they generally exhibit in the eyes of their siblings. My mother would not distinguish herself from the countless others who, because of the war had only two choices: make the best of the situation handed to you or just spiritually and physically let the world trample you and be a passive victim. My mother was sometimes angry or would cry when something hurt her but she never, ever permitted her troubles to dampen her spirit for long.

During World War I the Russians pushed across the Niemen River into East Prussia, destroying everything in their path including my maternal grandfather's farm. They were forced to flee westward until the Russians themselves were pushed back. My mother recalls her father rebuilding their farm and suffering hard times immediately following the war. That experience however did not prejudice her against Russians. Russian prisoners captured during their withdrawal were allocated to farmers in the region to help rebuild. They were given room and board and most had no desire to return home after the Bolshevik Revolution, happy to be working. She witnessed these Russian workers as a young girl and found them hardworking and honest. It would not be the last time she would encounter Russians.

Because Malissen was a small farming community, my mother traveled to the nearby village of Peschicken to attend school. There, as a young girl, she met my father who also attended that school. Growing up in nearby communities, they saw each other frequently during social functions but did not become romantically involved until she moved to Tilsit. Her recollections of the years after World War I were pleasant enough, going to country dances and lots of companionship with friends and relatives. Early in her life my mother learned to be a very good seamstress. It is a skill that has served her well all her life. From the time she left home as a young woman, wherever she lived she has never been unemployed long. After completing her schooling, Elsbeth moved from the farm to Tilsit, the nearest town of any consequence, to pursue her trade. She also wanted to be out from under the scrutiny of her mother who was more preoccupied with appearances and upward mobility. Arriving in Tilsit, Elsbeth rented a room and, through word of mouth, found work almost immediately as a seamstress and tailor.

By his late teens, my father determined that farming was not his future. The traditional practice of dividing the land among the children, as had often been done since the days of feudalism, hadn't left enough land for everyone. His plan was to one day have his own trucking firm. Growing up on a farm, he was well acquainted with machinery and seeing the future in mechanized farming, thought it would be a worthwhile endeavor to operate a trucking service in the rural community. However, he lacked sufficient income and education to facilitate that dream. He saw his opportunity when the German army came calling for him in 1936.

Despite the Versailles Treaty's prohibiting such activity, the remilitarization of German was already in full swing when my father was drafted. After the wholesale slaughter of World War I, the Allied powers refused to believe there could ever be another war in Europe, never realizing that the seeds of the next conflict were firmly planted in that 1919 Treaty. Sensing their weakness or at least probing for it, Hitler proceeded to violate each and every tenet of the Treaty with no opposition. During his term of duty, my father, stationed with the Eleventh Division North Baltic mounted artillery regiment in East Prussia, decided to become a career soldier, thus enhancing his chances for advancement. He planned to serve out his twelve years, retire, and with a sufficient pension launch his trucking firm. It was a good plan that got sidetracked a few years later with the German invasion of Poland.

By the time he was drafted, Fritz had married Elsbeth and taken an apartment in Tilsit. To this day my mother still speaks of him in a way that indicates their relationship was very special. He was the great love of her life. Since he was stationed in a garrison near Tilsit, she saw my father often in the years before the outbreak of the war.

I don't know whether my father believed in the Nazis and their ideals but based on what I was told and what my mother's attitude towards the Nazis was, I don't think he did. He was drafted before the military establishment became tainted by the infusion of Hitler's fanatics. Soldiering was considered an honorable profession in that part of the world prior to World War II, especially in East Prussia with its military heritage. Under those circumstances, my father's service in the military was quite normal. You do your service and go home, only he saw it as an opportunity to further his goals.

My father must have sensed that war clouds were on the horizon, though he apparently rarely spoke of it with my mother. He rose to the rank of "Oberwachmeister" (Brigade Sergeant Major), the senior non-commissioned officer. His regiment was a horse-drawn artillery unit, a remnant of the First World War when cavalry and horses still presented a dashing image and mobility. But they were an anachronism with the advent of the *blitzkrieg,* the highly mechanized lightning warfare Germany was about to unleash. Dashing no longer mattered; horses were no match for tanks. I remember my stepfather telling me how when he was in the German army they had rounded up the remnants of a whole company of Polish cavalry that had been decimated. Apparently these poor bastards had foolishly gone up against German tanks with drawn swords, believing their own officers' propaganda that the tanks weren't real, merely cardboard. With the invasion of Poland in the fall of 1939, my father's regiment saw combat there and in 1940 he was in France. He came home briefly between those campaigns and both times he was wounded. My mother always spoke with great fondness of those times when he returned. They would go on excursions up to Koenigsberg, a very beautiful city in East Prussia near the Baltic Sea, renamed Kaliningrad by the Soviets after the war.

For my mother, the war was distant. Far from the center of power in Berlin, she viewed the Nazi party people who came out from there to the villages with a jaundiced eye. There were Nazi party members in every community but they had a stigma attached to them. For those living in Tilsit, there was no pounding of cannons or air raid sirens wailing. Their only contact with the war itself in the early years were the husbands, brothers, or sons coming home. Like my father, most avoided talking about the war. My mother has reasonably good memories of the early war years because she was isolated from the day to day activity of the war until near the end. Under-informed and disconnected from where it was all happening, people went about their lives. However, they were doomed to become the first Germans to bear the onslaught of the Russian army when it finally came at them.

My mother doesn't have any warmth for Hitler and what was going on in Germany at that time, viewing Hitler's actions, the senselessness and insanity he caused, as the acts of a twisted individual. Her life, if not ruined, was certainly altered in a major way along with the lives of millions of others who suffered considerably worse. She definitely holds the Nazis responsible for what happened in East Prussia and her having to flee her home. It was Hitler who forced the Russians into the war by attacking them. She doesn't blame the Russians for what happened to her life. But she stopped reminiscing about those events many years ago.

In June of 1941, Hitler launched Operation Barbarossa, his ill-fated attack on the Soviet Union and my father was sent off to the Russian Front. I have photographs of him in Russia, one of him sitting and writing a letter to my mother, horses all around. He came home on leave a few times, the last visit being around Christmas of 1943. When he left he knew my mother was pregnant with me. By then the Russians had launched their massive counteroffensive after the German failures at Stalingrad and Leningrad and were pushing German forces back, inflicting horrific losses. In March, 1944, one month before my birth, my mother received notification that my father had been killed at Pleskau, somewhere in the Baltic States east of Tilsit. It was a standard notice of a heroes death in battle; she was never informed of how he died. For my mother, eight months pregnant and alone, the news was devastating. It remains to this day the hardest thing that she has faced in her life, the death of the one she loved. Everything else that happened to her since she just took in stride. Nothing was ever able to replace him. My mother has always contended that my eyesight problem (I'm legally blind) was a direct result of the trauma she endured on learning of the death of my father.

I was born on April 12, 1944 in Tilsit. By then, the war was still distant but getting closer each day. When I was three or four months old my mother decided to visit my father's mother in the village of Stallopoen. My father's father had died earlier and with the family having lost several sons in the war, the two women could console each other during their time of grieving. Although I obviously met my paternal grandmother then, I was far too young to have any recollections of her. I did meet her years later when she visited us in West Germany and I loved her instantly. She was this big, rotund, earthmother type, born on a farm, with a wonderful sense of humor, very loving. She was the kind of person who would smother you with affection. From her and my father's sister whom I met later as well, I got a sense of what my father would have been like.

It must have been in July or August of 1944 that we traveled to my grandmother's because while we were there, my mother received a letter from a neighbor in Tilsit. The letter warned her not to return because the Russians were approaching the Niemen River bordering East Prussia and Lithuania. Tilsit had already experienced heavy artillery shelling. The letter said that there was nothing for my mother and I to come home to. With the Red Army advancing at great speed through the Baltic States, the Germans became more desperate to defend their territory. As the Eastern Front was being shattered, Hitler had moved his headquarters from Obersolzberg to East Prussia in July. Over twenty-five German divisions, three hundred and fifty thousand men, had been destroyed by the Russian advance through Byelorussia, the biggest loss inflicted on the German army in the Eastern campaign and one from which they could not recover. The Germans were throwing everything they had into defending East Prussia, the fiercest fighting being along the Niemen. By October, however, the Red Army's General Cherniakhovsky and the Third Byelorussian Army crossed the Niemen, setting foot for the first time on German soil. Tilsit fell to the Russians within days. The mass exodus of Germans fleeing westward from the Baltics in the wake of the Russian advance had begun. By April 1945, East Prussia had vanished from the map.

So instead of returning eastward, my mother reasoned, "All I have left is my child and this suitcase. If the Russians are coming this way, I'm going further west." Leaving my paternal grandmother, she boarded a train with no specific destination in mind, just heading west. To the best of my knowledge none of the two families had anyone residing in Germany itself prior to the end of the war. She left everything behind in Tilsit: furnishings, household goods, memorabilia. All she had was what she had brought with her — some clothes and a few photographs of my father. I was still a baby in her arms. She had been issued a travel permit for the trip to

Stallopoen as a war widow to visit family members anywhere in Germany. It was not specific as to destination or length of visit so she used it for this trip. I had an ear infection at the time and cried for much of the trip. The train route crossed the former Polish Corridor into Germany, traveling south west until forced to halt at the little town of Arnstadt in the province of Thuringen, southwest of Leipzig. Arnstadt, located in an historic area with rolling hills, tight little winding roads, a wooded region dotted by old castles, small towns and villages, was only a few miles from the Wartburg, the castle where Martin Luther had translated the Bible into German.

It was night time when the train pulled into Arnstadt. The conductor announced that as a result of bombed out tracks down the line they could go no further. Apparently the Germans had a USO kind of service during the war years, for the majority of people traveling were predominantly soldiers coming to and from the various fronts. At every station were volunteers serving hot meals and drinks. When my mother and I got off the train at Arnstadt, we were greeted by a couple of volunteers, one of whom was Mrs. Else Kranz. She was an older woman who had already lost two sons in the war. "Do you need a place to stay?" she asked. Mrs. Kranz and her husband operated a tannery and had a spare room in their home, previously occupied by one of their sons. My mother accepted, and we ended up staying with the Kranz family for four years. It was my first real home, the room I shared with my mother above the tannery. And the Kranz family — Hugo, Else, and their young niece Helga — became my surrogate family. They were older and had already raised their children so were able to share their experience with my mother. This was important for her because she no longer felt she was on her own. She had support.

The tannery had been built in the 1400s in a town that traced its history back almost a thousand years. Largely untouched by the rapid industrialization of Germany in the twentieth century, it was a typical medieval burgh — cobblestone streets, ancient half timbered houses, and farms spread around the town. Having no industrial base or strategic value, the town was spared any destruction and bore no visible signs of the war.

As the war drew to a close my mother thought she had eluded the Russians. The town was lucky to have escaped the revenge

Russian troops exacted on other German communities — looting, raping, mass arrests, and executions. By the time the Russians had arrived in Berlin, they were enacting a reign of terror. Fortunately, it was the Americans who were the first Allies to arrive in Arnstadt. Tense at first, not knowing what, if any, resistance to expect, the Americans came in at nightfall with their tanks and proceeded to machine gun every window in town. The terrified townsfolk huddled on their floors until the shooting ceased. The overly anxious Americans soon discovered no one was shooting back. There wasn't a German soldier to be found in town. Needless to say, the townsfolk were less than gracious to their 'liberators' since there was nothing to liberate them from. A few days later, my mother, upon finding an American chocolate bar placed in my pram by a GI, promptly threw it away in anger. With the arrival and establishment of American authority, there was, however, a feeling that the war was over and they could now get on with their lives again.

Not so. In July, 1945 at Potsdam in Germany, the Allied leaders, having vanquished Hitler and Nazi Germany, determined the restructuring and rebuilding of Europe, including the partitioning of Germany into four zones of occupation. A few months earlier, in April, American and Russian forces had met for the first time at Torgau on the Elbe River, more than a hundred miles east of Arnstadt. According to the agreements reached at Potsdam, the Americans were forced to withdraw westward to beyond the Werra River, leaving Arnstadt in the hands of the Russian administration. The American troops withdrew and a Cossack regiment soon moved in. But there was no retaliation, no pillaging, raping, or looting. The transition of authority was peaceful. My mother recalled their behavior as exemplary, respectful, and polite. She speaks well of the Cossacks stationed there and their interactions in the community and at the tannery. Tall, handsome, boots polished, they always conducted themselves as gentlemen.

This is where I had the first memories of my life, living in Arnstadt. By and large, they're warm recollections as a result of the wonderful family I had and the feeling of sanctuary they offered my mother and me. It was my whole world, she and I in that little room above the tannery. Shortly after we arrived, my mother did what she always did everywhere else throughout her life, she started sewing. With a town full of people unable to afford new clothes and with nothing new available after the war, they needed their existing wardrobes altered. She was kept busy. Meanwhile, I got on with growing up. In my early years I did not see very many men in their prime. Germany had lost a generation to the war. The Cossacks, however, were men in their twenties and early thirties. I observed them as they came in and out of the tannery regularly to barter food for leather to make boots and saddles.

That food was greatly valued because we were living on food stamps which provided us with whatever was available locally — in our case a lot of fish, mainly herring. We had fish all the time, endlessly — fried, battered, grilled, stewed. To this day I avoid fish because I had it up to my nose as a kid. There was also an abundance of fruit trees throughout the countryside. Every spring the townspeople would take their ladders and pilfer the fruit that grew along the roads — plums, cherries, apples, pears — to supplement the limited rations and endless servings of herring.

I played out on the street with a few neighborhood kids but mainly with the boy next door named "Gert." Hugo would often let me hang around while he worked in the tannery. The Cossack soldiers who came in to do business had things on their backs which I thought were violins or other instruments. But Hugo carefully explained to me that these were not violins but tommy guns. One day a couple of Cossack officers came to the tannery to barter. Hugo, having just completed tanning some hides, had chemicals on his hands, and before greeting the officers and shaking their hands, walked over to a basin on the wall and washed up. He then approached the officers and extended his hand to them. Observing my uncle's action, they then went over to the basin and washed their hands, thinking it was some sort of local custom to clean one's hands before greeting a guest. I thought at the time, "What a great thing to do." I was so taken by their humanity. There they were, the occupiers, having vanquished the Nazis, they could take whatever they wanted, but they were polite enough to observe what they perceived as a local custom.

I used to go on little trips around town with Uncle Hugo or my mother. On one such excursion, I became separated from my mother. She finally discovered me standing in an intersection in the center of the town. There was a police woman perched on a little pillar in the middle of the intersection directing traffic, which in itself was rather ludicrous since few people had cars, and if they did, there was so little gasoline available due to rationing. She must have been directing bicycles or something but there I was standing beside her crying my eyes out having lost my mother. I also remember my mother taking me to the Wartburg Castle, either by train or bicycle, and seeing a beautiful ornate coach that some baron used to ride in.

What I recall most from those years, though, is that at around age three and a half something triggered an interest in my father. I do not recall what brought it on, nor does my mother, but one night in our little room I asked her where he was. To her credit, she avoided the kinds of things some parents say to young children in this situation, like, "Your Daddy's living with the angels in heaven." She told me, on a level I could understand for my age, he was gone, died in the war, and would never be back. That moment was devastating to me for I felt a great sense of loss, which in hindsight is somewhat odd because I had never seen or met him. She had a handful of photos that she showed me for the first time that night. I'm sure had I asked she would have shown them to me earlier, but she did so now to help me come to terms with this revelation. Seeing a real human face and at the same time being told that this person whom I just met is gone forever caused me my first real pain. We cried for a very long time, and whenever my father's name came up or my thoughts turned to him it would trigger another flood of tears. That became a defining moment in my life.

It's the greatest pain I have had to suffer. To this day, recalling that night still disturbs me. It was only much later in life that I realized every time I felt emotional pain, for myself or others, I was revisiting that moment in my life. As far as I'm concerned, my first conscious moment on this planet was that night.

I have never felt any great anger in my life for not having a father. I have, however, felt sadness, not only for my own loss but to an equal extent for my mother because I saw the great sorrow it caused her. The closest I ever came to knowing my father was when my paternal grandmother came to visit us in Hannover and stayed with us in our apartment. She was a hefty farm woman with a great sense of humor who baked some terrific fruit pies for me. But I never saw her again. After I had reached a stage in my life where I was living in a nice house in the canyons of Los Angeles, surrounded by the spoils of my success, so to speak, I began to compare my father's life with mine. He went from meager beginnings into love, marriage, hard work, responsibility, then a bullet in the head. He was deprived of the joy of seeing his son grow up. When I think about what he missed, I appreciate what I have even more. My success in aiming high and reaching my goals probably gave my mother more satisfaction than anything else in her later life. In her quiet moments, she probably said to the spirit of my father, "I did alright, didn't I?" She sees many qualities in me that were my father's; I think she wanted to raise me to be like him. And I think she is pleased with the outcome.

I also realized at some point in my life that everything I ever learned about "men" things, like sports, hitching up a horse, or using power tools, I gleaned from books or people who passed through my life. I was very much shaped as a whole person by my mother. I viewed my world through a more sensitive perspective than the more typical brash male attitude. I was affected by her values — her sensitivity to what is proper conduct and her empathy for others. In my better moments I am usually sensitive to the difficulties or experiences of people. I attribute that to my mother's touch. Had my father been around I probably would not have gotten away with some of the things I did when I was a teenager, like skipping school, hanging out in pool halls, avoiding responsibilities, being lazy. He might very well have said: "Guitar? Rock 'n' roll? Hey, you're thirteen years old, you're half blind, you don't speak English, what are you going on about? Finish school and learn a trade." If he had been around I might not be where I am today.

Within our first few years in Arnstadt, my mother noticed that I would squint a lot and that I couldn't see very well. When I was in my pram, if the sun was directly in my eyes I would cry; when she put a little sheet over the canopy to keep the sun out, I would stop crying. So she suspected something was afoot. The town was too small to have any specialists, so she took me to a doctor in the nearby town of Erfurt. There, the doctor told her I had a sight deficiency and prescribed some little round glasses which I wore from early on. She has a photograph of me, one of the earliest shots in which I'm wearing little round John Lennon glasses which were tinted for the sun. I was born color blind and extremely light sensitive. Whereas normal vision is considered to be 20/20, my vision is 20/200, which is the definition of legally blind. I can see but not very far. This doctor also told my mother that the chances of my sight improving might be increased by a more nutritious and balanced diet. What my mother read between these words was that I needed to get to the West where things had normalized enough that food was in regular supply and more diversified. Stories were already filtering back to East Germany by 1948 about the rebuilding and improved quality of life in West Germany. Shortly thereafter, she decided that she was going to get us out of East Germany. Improved nutrition for my eyesight was the immediate benefit that attracted her.

After the war, Germany had been divided into four zones of occupation administered to the west by the Americans, British, and French and to the east, the largest zone, by the Soviets. While the western Allies sought to rebuild West Germany into an economic power as a buffer to communist ambitions in Europe, the Soviets exerted their control over the East through a military build-up and German Communist puppet governments. The Soviets were busy dismantling East German factories and hauling off to the USSR whatever industrial machinery they could get their hands on. Given that their zone was largely agricultural and that they were spiriting away any industrial capability along with its skilled operators and technicians, it's no wonder that East Germany was much slower to recover from the war than the West. Under the Marshall Plan, the United States pumped billions of dollars into revitalizing the West German economy. By the late forties, West German shops were already stocked with a wide variety of foods, manufactured goods, and some luxury items. Rationing remained in place much longer in the East than in the West.

Besides the economic competition, the two superpowers waged an ideological war as well. Each proclaimed a unified German nation as their goal but molded in their own likeness. Realizing that they could not control reunification, the Soviets began to resist it, blocking measures like a single German currency. Compounding this dilemma was the fact that deep inside the Soviet zone was Berlin, also divided into zones of occupation with a free Western sector. In an attempt to flex their muscles and up the ante in the Cold War, the Soviets sealed off all access to West Berlin by rail or road in 1948. The Americans retaliated with the Berlin Airlift, a year long drop of supplies, delivering thousands of tons of food, medical supplies, and fuel to the beleaguered West Berliners. In an attempt to consolidate their efforts into a national identity, the Americans supported the creation of a democratic, free enterprise German Federal Republic in May 1949. In October of that same year, the Soviets countered with the creation of the German Democratic Republic. The boundary between the two became known as the Iron Curtain. It was during this period that my mother decided to escape.

We were by no means unique or alone. With the recovery of East Germany bogged down under the Soviets and the reins tightening over the people, the exodus of East Germans to the West grew from a trickle to a stream and eventually to a flood. By 1949, tens of thousands were fleeing each month. Over a decade later in 1961 the Soviets erected what became the symbol of division and oppression to all Germans, the Berlin Wall. But by then, my mother and I were already safely on the other side.

Not long before we left, my great aunt Ida Kendler had found her way to Arnstadt. She had been stuck in East Prussia at the end of the war and was subsequently deported to Russia to work in a forced labor camp. There she made uniforms until her release in 1948, whereupon she came to stay with us. There must have been some contact made for her to know where we were. She was the first actual relative that I met. Simultaneous to her arrival, my mother somehow received word that her younger brother Alfred and older brother Willy, who had both been in the German army and may have been prisoners, were now settled in West Germany. With news that there was family on the other side, coupled with my need for an improved diet, my mother and Aunt Ida were now more than ever determined to make their way to the West. Besides, the various freedoms my mother had always enjoyed were gradually disappearing in East Germany. Never one to bite her tongue, she might have gotten herself into trouble speaking her mind.

It was too difficult for us to get to West Berlin to be airlifted out. We were closer to the border of West Germany. Through Frau

Arndt, the matriarch of the town, my mother learned of a means of escape. She had done some alterations for Frau Arndt at her home. The Arndt family were the leading members of the community; in fact, the town had been named after them. On a summer's night a few weeks later, we fled Arnstadt with a suitcase and the clothes on our backs to start a new life in West Germany. Like most things in my life, I never looked back.

I've never really told my mother my feelings about her or thanked her for what she risked for me. I've been meaning to tell her in a letter for some time now but perhaps this song says it best:

> *I remember I was barely four,*
> *When Mama told me "Daddy's Gone . . . died in the war.*
> *He won't be home again."*
> *I never knew him, a picture's all I had.*
> *Mama raised me all by herself through good and bad.*
> *Somehow she bore the pain.*
> *She's the one who believed in me,*
> *Always knew when to let me be.*
> *Showed me how to keep wrong from right.*
> *She was there for me day and night.*
> *I know just what I am, oh I'm no shining knight.*
> *But I believe I'm a better man,*
> *For the women in my life.*

FOR THE WOMEN IN MY LIFE, 1993

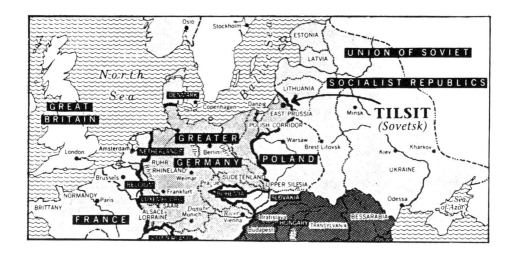

Northern Europe in 1941 (above), and "Germany" after the war.

My father at age 16.

My mother and father (on leave from the war) at home in Tilsit, 1940.

Postcard notification of my father's death in action on the Russian Front, 1944.

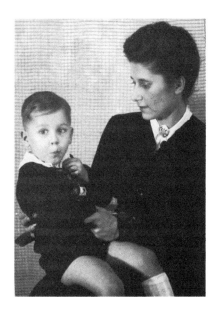

My mother and I after fleeing to Arnstadt (top left).

My friend "Gert" and I (with glasses) in front of his grandfather's clock shop, two doors down from our tannery home (top right).

The Kranz Tannery on the Ober Weibe in Arnstadt (left). Hides were worked on in the courtyard and dried into leather on the rails above. We lived upstairs on the right.

TWO

RAISED IN THE RUINS

I was raised in the ruins, mama
'Til I was thirteen
Every day I heard the radio
Every night I had the same old dream
To sing my song
And watch my name in lights
If you wanna see your dream come true
Honeychild, you gotta get right down and fight

LIVE YOUR LIFE, 1977

I don't remember what happened after we ran from the border, but my mother told me that we first went to the Friedland Refugee Camp somewhere not far from where we crossed. There, West German authorities accepted refugees and awarded us citizenship. My mother was registered as a war widow, and I was given a small stipend because I was classified as a half orphan. I continued to receive this stipend until I was thirteen.

After no more than a day at the refugee camp we set off to make contact with some of my mother's family already in the West — her brother Willy in Hannover and her mother and brother Alfred on a small farm near West Kirchen in Westphalia, southwest of Hannover. The majority of the surviving family members on both sides had made their way to West Germany, the latest by about 1950, though both of my grandfathers were dead by then.

Hannover was a city steeped in history. A century earlier it had been the capital of the province of Prussia and boasted dozens of beautifully designed buildings. Some, like the elaborate city hall with a pond behind it where I first learned to skate, survived the war. Many did not. The city is located along the Leine River surrounded by rich farmland and serves as the commercial center for the region. It was an industrial city with rubber, chemical, machinery and car manufacturing. Because it had a fair amount of industrial activity geared to the war effort, the city had the hell bombed out of it. Entire residential areas were left in ruins, the devastation so extreme that whole districts were bulldozed and new grids and streets were drawn. You could walk for blocks and blocks and see all newly built apartments, most constructed to absorb the refugees like us who had been displaced and had no housing in the town. Because of its industrial base, the city was able to rebuild and recover fairly quickly after the war. By the time we arrived, Hannover was already starting to find its feet.

After surveying her job prospects in Hannover, my mother took me to visit my grandmother and my uncle Alfred and his wife Inge in West Kirchen. They were renting a little plot of land outside of the village with a simple country house, more like a shed, which they had refurbished into living quarters. They grew their own vegetables and had a chicken coop and as a result were better off than most people on food stamps. The visit was not only to say hello (she hadn't seen them since the war) but to leave me there while she established herself in Hannover. Once settled and working, she would return for me.

I recall this being the next most painful experience of my short but already eventful life, being separated from my mother for the first time. It was a terribly traumatic period. To this day I'm uncertain how long it was, nor can my mother recall, but it must have been at least a month or two. For me it felt like an eternity. My mother told me not to worry, that it wasn't forever, and she would be back soon. She was my whole world. Without her I felt lost for the first time in my life.

By early winter of 1948, the two of us were back together in Hannover. We moved into a building on Dachenhausenstrasse in an area that had not been as badly damaged as other sections of the city. There was a fairly elaborate building, four or five stories high, constructed before the First World War, formerly occupied by well-to-do families. They had lived in extensive apartments with stables in the back yard for horses and carriages. The top floor of the building consisted of a series of attics where the servant staff had lived. My mother managed to rent one of these. It was about sixteen feet by twelve feet, with a slanted roof and a skylight that opened out. There was a bomb crater, a hole about wagon wheel size, that had been repaired with new plaster. It was just one room with a bathroom down the hall shared by the other attics. We had a bed that we shared and a chair or two. Later my mother bought a table with chairs as well as a chest of drawers. A few weeks after we moved in Aunt Ida moved into an adjacent attic. She was a seamstress, too, and my mother had told her there was plenty of work to be found in Hannover.

I remember Christmas 1948 in that attic in Hannover and celebrating it in the true sense of the occasion because of my reunification with my mother. I recall walking with her in Hannover and seeing decorations in shop windows. The shops were not exactly overflowing with goods, but, by comparison with East Germany, it was absolutely Babes in Toyland to this wide-eyed little kid. There were Christmas trees with lights and tinsel, confectionery treats, cakes and toys. I was absolutely amazed. My mother bought a little Christmas tree that we put on our table and decorated with real wax candles, tinsel, and a few ornaments. One of the things that made the journey from the East was the little glass Santa Claus ornament that I still own to this day. We put that on our tree that first Christmas in the West. Every year since, it has been on our Christmas tree.

That first Christmas in Hannover, I had two presents: a box of Playdough-like sticks of colored clay, and a book. Each page had a head on top and like the Ten Little Indians, one head would disappear with each page. I was absolutely beside myself with joy. My mother recalls that I skipped around the table with the little tree on it and sang something to the effect that I was so happy. I was the happiest kid in that building at least. I had my mother back with me, we had our own place with our own tiny Christmas tree, we had decent food regularly, and I had some toys to play with. What more could a four-year-old possibly want?

Reflecting on those early years in Hannover and Christmas time, I remember our second Christmas there while still living in the attic. One of the wealthy women my mother worked for said to her, "Our children are home now so why don't you bring your boy over next time you come and we'll have a little Christmas get-together." I walked into their home and there was this enormous Christmas tree. I had no idea private homes would have trees that size. I had only seen them that big in the public square. The tree was hung with dozens of candy canes and fancy ornaments and sparkling presents were all around it. This was the first time I had come in contact with any wealth. Still, I wouldn't trade the memories of our first Christmas in Hannover for anything. They have stayed with me throughout my life and make each new Christmas all the more special to me. Perhaps because of those memories I have always tried to make the holiday season a warm and joyous time in our little family, wherever we are.

In order for my mother to work on a daily basis, she put me into a pre-school day care located at the edge of one of the large city parks with acres and acres of woods and a zoo at the far end. They cut a swath right at the edge of the woods and built two or three long barrack like buildings for the center. Although operated by the Swedish Red Cross, it was staffed by German women. Working women dropped off their kids, usually by taking the street car, and picked them up after work.

There I was, five years old, legally blind, a house key around my neck, taking the street car with my monthly pass from my home to the day care center, staying there until my mother came to pick me up. There were many latch-key kids like me in postwar Germany because so many mothers had to work, either because they were single parents or the family needed two incomes. It was an accepted thing. All I remember of the day care was that the food was repetitious, unspeakably vile concoctions that looked and tasted like wallpaper paste, a different flavor each day.

One afternoon, after my mother had picked me up at the day care and we were walking along the edge of the park toward the street car, I saw my first black man, an American soldier. He looked enormous to me. My astonishment at seeing a black person was obvious to him so he stopped for a moment and gave me a big smile. He spoke to me (I have no idea what he said because I didn't speak English) and bent over to pat me on the head before going on his way. Later, when I was eight or nine, my mother and I went to see a German film entitled *Toxi*, a story about a little German mulatto girl, an offspring of a black American soldier and a German woman. The story was about how this girl Toxi was shunned. Most of the kids accepted her but some adults had their racial prejudices. It was all presented within the context of postwar German society. I remember so well the end of the story. It was Christmas time and Toxi had been living in a foster home with a German family. When it came time for the children to play a role in the Christmas play, the shepherd and the three wise men and all that, little Toxi decided she wanted to be a shepherd. So one of the white kids put on blackface to be the Moor, Belthezar or whomever, and Toxi put white make-up on to be a shepherd. The climax of the scene came when her father appeared to claim his daughter whom he had never seen and take her back to America. He walked in and went straight for the child with the black face. Toxi cried out, "No, it's me!" My heart went out to her as kids do toward someone who's unfairly treated. I fell in love with that little mulatto girl.

After living in the attic for some time, the sister of my Uncle Willy's wife Leni, her name was Tuta, and her husband Robert some-how also wound up in Hannover. They set out to convert what had been the stables into living quarters. Robert hired a couple of men to do the renovations, one of them being an ex-prisoner of war recently released from Russia named Gerhard Kyczinski. He was a mason by trade and he and his partner began turning this bombed out barn into living space.

Since my mother and I lived on the fourth floor, Tuta would ask her to lower down a jug of water to the workers because they had no water down there. One way or another, my mother got to talking with Gerhard. She learned that he had been married before the war and had two daughters but was now divorced. He was raised in the Pommern region near the Oder River right at the Polish border. After four years as a prisoner in Russia, he had come to West Germany in search of work as a mason, bricklayer, anything, when Tuta and Robert hired him.

In what seemed like a relatively short period, a few months as best I can recall, my mother and Gerhard decided to get married. During his time in the Russian prison camp, his wife had taken up with another man. When he returned, she wanted nothing to do with him and promptly divorced him. It must have left a fairly substantial scar on his psyche. After surviving the horrors of a Russian prison, near starvation, enduring unspeakable conditions, probably the one thing that kept him going was the thought of seeing his wife and children again one day. I'm sure it was quite a blow to him when he returned to find she had no interest in seeing him. I feel for the man because of what he endured.

When she told me she was thinking of getting married, I was excited. I wanted a father and I'm sure my positive response likely pushed her to proceed with her plans. I envied kids who had fathers, although there weren't all that many of them after the war. I remember my mother telling me that I had come home dejected after some kids had said, "You can't play with us because you don't have a father."

In August of 1950, Elsbeth Krauledat married Gerhard Kyczinski. The marriage was a sensible arrangement. My mother was a very practical person. But in no way was this uncommon after the war. There were thousands of women, alone with children, who made such decisions, including my wife's mother. There was little romantic spark between them, though my mother deserved that kind of happiness in her life after what she had been through. But she never permitted that to make her one of those quietly suffering, 'accept-your-lot-in-life,' downtrodden persons. She always looked good, she dressed well, everything in life interested her, she enjoyed the company of others, and remained optimistic.

My relationship with my stepfather was tentative at the beginning. It's not that we disliked each other, it's just that I never accepted him as an authority figure. He was a good man, though, didn't drink to excess, run around with other women, neglect his family or blow his paycheck. He was fine in his normal behavior. He loved to play a German card game called Skat which almost every German male knows how to play and most of them are intense about it. Usually on the weekends, Friday or Saturday nights, a group of the neighborhood men would get together, have a few drinks and play Skat either at a nearby pub or in their homes. Every fourth week or so they would meet at our place after we had moved to our new apartment. Gerhard would send me out for beer. A nine-year-old boy buying beer seems strange to North American society but in the neighborhood everybody knew one another so the store-keeper would know that I was buying it for my stepfather.

I used to watch them play and listen to their stories of the war. Some of them had been prisoners in Russia. Rather than dwelling on the sheer human resources required to survive, they focused their stories on those things that were amusing. Occasionally, there were insights into how gruesome it could be. Gerhard once spoke about how people would sneak a crust of bread under their shirt and in the quiet of the barracks lying on their bunks would eat it. Sometimes people would keep a little stash to barter with. One time, a prisoner was caught stealing food from another and the other prisoners killed him by quietly suffocating him. Gerhard also held some respect for his Russian guards, pointing out that they were almost all from the rural areas, many illiterate and naive. They were almost as badly off as the prisoners so they felt a common bond with them. Those stories really stuck with me as a kid. Gerhard took a job with the Brinkmann tobacco company delivering their products to the outlying areas of the city. He drove a truck and sometimes took me on his rounds. Because we were now a family, we became eligible for one of the new refugee dwellings being built in the destroyed areas of the city, very plain but nevertheless

very livable apartment buildings. Within a short time, one was allocated to us and our quality of life changed for the better. I remember going to see the apartment before we moved in; it seemed enormous compared to our attic. Located on the top floor of a four-story
building, it featured a bathroom, a hallway, a large kitchen, small
living room, and one bedroom. My parents took the bedroom and I
slept in the living room. At first it was sparsely furnished because
we didn't have much, but my stepfather was very good at carpentry
and made some furniture. The move was uplifting for us. We were
no longer considered displaced people; we now had a home. We
stayed in that apartment, 35 Kronenstrasse, from late 1950 until we
emigrated to Canada in 1958.

Once we moved into the new apartment, I became part of a
group of neighborhood kids. We would spent much of our time
exploring and playing in the ruins which surrounded the area of
our apartment buildings. A half a block away from where we lived
had been an army garrison complex with dormitories and a big
exercise area as well as an enormous above ground bunker that was
so massive it could not be blown up after the war. I believe it stands
to this day. There was a scrap metal dealer nearby who would pay
us a few coins for any scrap metal we could dig up or pull out of the
ruins. We would try to find pipes or anything made of metal, but
this wasn't too wise because the government hadn't had the time
or manpower to sift through every ruin for unexploded bombs or
grenades. There was a lot to poke around in and there were stories
all over Germany of kids losing hands or eyes after finding unexploded grenades or bombs that hadn't been diffused.

Soccer was king in Germany then, still is. Next to our apartment building was an open area about the width of a soccer field.
With some chalk we drew imaginary goal posts on the sides of the
buildings. I couldn't play very well during the daylight hours if it
was very sunny because my eyes are so light sensitive that I had to
squint even with my dark glasses on. When it got to be dusk, however, my eyes would open up. I was more like a cat or an owl at
night; I could see a lot with very little light. Then I could play soccer much better and hold my own with the other kids. But kids
being kids, they soon discovered my weakness.

One time I received the honor of making an eleven metre

penalty kick from some kid acting as the self-appointed referee that day. While I was being distracted by someone else in cahoots with this clown, he took a half brick that had been laying on the sidelines, just small enough to hide behind the ball. All the other kids could see what was going on but I didn't have a clue. I came running at the ball as fast as I could and WHAM, hit it with my right foot, propelling both the ball and the brick into the air. The front of my foot was in pain so I pulled it out of my shoe and it looked like the hands of that James Bond character Oddjob, all level and flat. I tried chasing the culprit but he was a good runner and knew if he could get past a certain point, I couldn't see him. That night it dawned on me: this incident must be revenged. I may not be able to see but that doesn't mean my mind is impaired.

Days went by and the offender kept his distance from me. I never let on that I was harboring any ill will. He started coming closer and closer. I was talking to some of the others kids, so he figured it was safe enough for him. That's when he got the surprise of his life. After I finished talking to his sidekick, I turned to him and said, "And as for you . . ." BAM, I decked him. His buddies were all taken aback. "That's for what you did to me five days ago. Just remember this, if you mess with me you might be able to out run me but I will remember and sooner or later I will get even." From then on I had a degree of respect among my age group and we all got along pretty well.

It had been a practical joke at my expense and what I learned from it was that there are times when you just have to bide our time and wait. You just have to say to yourself, "Right now is not the moment." If you let your emotions govern you and fly off the handle, you make matters worse. You're better off just marking it down, remembering who did what, and the opportunity will come when you will see to it that this does not go unpunished. I have an explosive temper if someone aggravates me. I've learned over the years to control it more but I've had my moments. The outbursts wouldn't ever last long but they were intense and I have been known to put my fist through one or two walls.

There was a movie theater a short distance from our place featuring what was considered kid's fare: mostly Gene Autry movies dubbed into German. Thank goodness it wasn't subtitles because with my eyes I wouldn't have been able to read them. To see Gene Autry and Gabby Hayes speak German never struck me as very funny until years later while on a trip with my wife (who is also from Germany) to Europe. We saw *Butch Cassidy and The Sundance Kid* dubbed into Italian with "Ciao Bootch" and all that. We were cackling through the whole thing. The Italians thought we were nuts, but we were simply recalling all those dubbed in movies we watched as kids.

One winter my stepfather, who had always demurred to my mother regarding Christmas presents for me, bought me a pair of ice skates. I was thrilled to receive them, touched more by the fact that he had bought me something himself than just the idea of the skates themselves. He gave me my first skating lesson, taking me to the little frozen pond behind the city hall for my first tentative steps. Feeling a bit bold, I struck out on my own and the next thing I knew I woke up in my bed at home. Apparently I lost my balance, and hit my head on the ice. Gerhard immediately brought me home on the streetcar and, feeling a little groggy, I was put to bed. I likely suffered a mild concussion but this did not deter me from returning to the ice several times with friends. We would get some hockey sticks and go to the Maschsee, an artificial lake across town, to play.

On two occasions my mother and I took holiday trips to the Baltic resort town of Travemuende not far from Kiel, a very popular vacation spot with white beaches and fancy hotels. It was just the two of us and we stayed in a little bed and breakfast house. We spent two weeks by the sea and I took to the Baltic Sea like a duck to water. It was very shallow warm water, very little in the way of wave action. Later when we went back the second time and I was older, my mother let me rent one of those little kayaks with a double paddle. I went out too far and didn't have the strength or stamina to fight the riptide. I started drifting toward the East German border which was marked in the water with buoys. I was beginning to panic when all of a sudden this creature popped out of the water next to me, a man with a face mask and snorkel. I had never seen the like before. He turned out to be a West German lifeguard and was not at all pleased about having to swim the better part of a mile to catch me. Meantime, I was in the riptide getting further away as he swam towards me. He read me the riot act as he paddled me all the way back to shore. I still remember how scared I was about drifting into East Germany.

Not too long after moving to the new apartment, my mother enrolled me in first grade at a nearby elementary school. It was an older building, within walking distance of home, that had survived the war. As was the custom when you enrolled in school, you were taken to a photographer, you wore your Sunday best clothes, they combed your hair and gave you this long, cone-shaped thing made of shiny paper with a bow on top like a piniata filled with all sorts of goodies and candies. This was supposed to ease you through the trauma of being left by your parents. My first elementary teacher, Frau Janotte, was a kind, gentle woman. All the kids liked her and she was very understanding of my sight problem. I went there for two years until the government built a new school on the grounds of the old exercise area of that indestructible garrison complex, a stone's throw from our apartment. The name of the new school was Die Welfenschule, Welfen being more or less the name of the great dukes of Hannover. It was a typical postwar modern shoe box style design with lots of windows — very antiseptic, German institutional postwar structure, sterile and de-humanizing looking. Unfortunately when I moved over to the new school, I didn't have motherly teachers like Frau Janotte and my problems began. My new teacher was relatively young, a woman who, as if to reinforce the sterile institutionalized image of the school, wore a long white lab coat.

With a lack of schools and teachers following the war, necessity dictated substantial class sizes, forty pupils per class and a rotation of classes each day. In order to accommodate all the children, one shift would attend classes from seven to one in the afternoon, and another would come in at two and go until seven at night. It was kind of a mass assembly line education. To make all this work there had to be a lot of discipline and the children by and large were raised to shut up and pay attention. I had no problems with that. The difficulty for me was that I couldn't see the blackboard. My mother mentioned to the teacher that it would be best for me if I sat in the front row, which she did arrange. But this still was insufficient for me to read the board effectively. So with having to constantly ask her what was on the board, it just wasn't a meshing of personalities. As kids often do when they have a disability, I tried to avoid sticking out anymore than necessary. Kids tend to tease with names like 'Four Eyes' and you can't just turn around in front of the teacher and slap someone upside the head. You have to bite your tongue and it makes you feel awkward. If you then have to raise your hand all the time and say, "I can't read that. What is it?", it's disruptive to the class, the teacher doesn't care for it, and you feel intimidated because the last thing you want to do is draw attention to yourself.

Reluctant to assert myself, I became more introverted. I did not do well. My mother noticed my grades slipping and sensed that I was not happy. I would try to avoid going to school, feigning various illnesses. Unfortunately when she attempted to broach the subject with my teacher she did not receive a lot of sympathy or cooperation. My mother has always felt, if not guilty, then responsible in some way for my eyes. That became the key to her decision to investigate some other form of education for me.

While in the employment of her wealthier clients doing alterations in their homes, she mentioned my problems in school. Some of these families sent their children to a private school, the Freie Waldorf Schule or Waldorf School established by a noted Austrian humanist educator, Rudolf Steiner. After publishing several books at the turn of the century on enlightened education techniques, the Waldorf-Astoria Tobacco Company in Germany approached Steiner to set up a school for its employees. The first Waldorf School opened in Stuttgart in 1919. Steiner's aim was to develop an educational program designed for the total student, a holistic approach based not merely on academic subjects but encompassing a thorough understanding of child development. His methods were a fresh new approach to educating children that combined both physical and psychological development in harmony with an appreciation of the aesthetic such as art, music and nature. All this was taught at a pace best suited to the natural development of the child. Several Waldorf Schools opened in Germany and Britain in the 1920s but were shut down throughout Germany during the Hitler years. Apparently they were viewed by that regime as rather too humanistic. Waldorf Schools reopened a few years after the war.

My mother was not so much concerned with the theories on which the institution was based but on finding a school where the class sizes were smaller with the opportunity for more individualized attention. There was, however, a waiting list and if accepted, an annual fee to be paid which necessitated sacrifices from a working family like ours (in the end, my orphan stipend from the government helped defray the tuition expense). She asked her clients about the Waldorf School and one of them suggested a way to possibly avoid the waiting list. There was a woman pediatrician whose husband was on the Board of Directors of the school. If I could become her patient and she saw my problem, she might put in a good word to get me into the school. That's all my mother needed to hear. No sooner said than done.

After a few visits, my mother raised the subject of my schooling with the doctor who offered to speak with her husband on my behalf. Soon afterward, I was admitted to the Waldorf School. My mother had no idea at the time just how influential that school would be to my later development.

I encountered a completely different attitude and atmosphere at the Waldorf School: smaller classes, not the rote drilling of facts and figures as with traditional forms of education. They were open minded and viewed education as a long term process. I entered at the fourth grade but ideally they preferred to have students from kindergarten through to grade twelve. They took an integrated approach to education rather than simply grade by grade, subject by subject in isolation of one another. For example, students learned English over a longer period of time, from grades one through twelve which was a much more effective method than public schools which crammed English into four years. The Waldorf approach gave students a chance to absorb the language and come to terms with it through reading at an appropriate age and grade level. It was a completely co-ed environment. Boys and girls did everything together: gym, swimming, crafts classes, and planting rhubarb. The extensive school grounds had fruit trees, flowers, and rows of vegetables, all grown and tended by the students. We spent a considerable amount of time in the garden or swimming in the outdoor pool. Academically, the program stressed the humanities with an overview of all major religions in order to understand the similarities. They also had their version of a kind of Tai Chi consisting of slow, controlled, almost dance-like movements. We learned how to sew, crotchet, and make useful things. There were music classes where we learned to play the recorder. Everybody got a taste of what makes life whole and complete, a well-rounded education.

My attitude toward school totally changed once I enrolled in the Waldorf School. I was more relaxed, and I liked my teacher, Herr Doctor Riehn. One had the same teacher from grades one to eight for the first two hours of every day. He or she saw you develop and knew your strengths and weaknesses. The other teachers you saw one hour at a time for French or whatever. In Herr Doctor Riehn's room the desks were bolted to the floor but he saw that I needed to be closer to the board so he simply brought in another desk and put it where I needed it and he would read to me directly off his paper at times. I was a happy kid in that school. The kids there accepted me, bad eyes and all.

I didn't have any clearly defined career ambitions at the time. I loved animals, so I thought about perhaps becoming a veterinarian. I also enjoyed building things, so I might have pursued architecture. The Waldorf School graduated many students into the university stream, but at that time in Germany university was still the preserve of the wealthy and privileged. It seemed an unlikely destination for me. If you did not show sufficient promise in school or if your parents lacked the means to send you to the upper schools, then after age fourteen you were doomed to attend trade school or become an apprentice. Letting the individual find his or her own way in the world was not in the picture in postwar Germany. It's difficult to say what I might have become had I stayed in West Germany. Certainly being a musician and traveling the world wasn't a destination the education system or society encouraged.

During these years I would spend as much time as possible attending the circuses and traveling carnivals at the Welfenplatz. Germany has a long tradition of carnivals with elaborate and ornate rides. These would pass through at least three times a year and stay a week or two near our apartment. Another yearly event in Hannover was the Schuetzenfest, a gigantic festival. I would spend my time and money at these carnivals, enjoying the rides and observing other kids. It was a fascinating collection of sights, sounds, and smells. A sign of the times was the grand prize draw: a bucket of food. For one mark people bought little pieces of paper that said win or lose, more often lose. The lucky winner received an enamel bucket with a huge salami sticking out of it, a dozen eggs, two pounds of butter, a can of sardines and that sort of thing.

When the circuses came to town, I would go to the evening performance with my mother or stepfather. We usually had the cheap seats where your head almost touched the canvas of the big top. With my eyesight, the only thing I could make out were the damn elephants. Years later, my wife and I discovered we shared many childhood experiences. When we were in Germany on a holiday after Steppenwolf was already successful, we rented a car and were driving around Hamburg when we came upon a big top circus like the ones we used to go to as kids. "We gotta do this!" I said to her. We drove right up to the box office, looked at each other and said, "We always had the cheap seats. We gotta do this right this time." The circus had a single ring surrounded by box loges with upholstered seats and red velvet ropes, six or eight seats in each. We didn't want anyone to spoil our fun so we bought a whole box. That night we were like two kids in a candy store. The elephants were so close I could count their teeth. Sure enough, someone tried to sneak into our box and I told him that we had all eight seats. It was the best money we ever spent.

On two occasions we made trips into East Germany to visit my stepfather's family who lived near Pommern. His parents, sister, and brother-in-law lived on the family farm, of which they had been allowed to keep a portion, including the barn, the stable, and the yard with a vegetable garden and some fruit trees. They could keep that for personal use but had to work in the communal fields. His sister and brother-in-law had two boys, both of whom were later drafted into the *Volksarmee*. The older boy, Reinhart, rode an ancient looking bicycle with an auxiliary motor added to it that looked as if it had been ripped from a refrigerator and stuck on the frame. It made such a god awful racket that they nicknamed it "Huener Schreck," which means chicken fright, because every time he fired it up all the chickens would head for the hills. I never saw these people again until 1992 when I performed in Berlin and Reinhart and his wife came to see me.

The first trip took place when I was nine, my mother, stepfather, his two daughters and I went together, traveling by bus across the border. The three of us kids hung out in the barn or went out into the fields to pick the potato beetles off the plants which the East German government told people the Americans dropped from airplanes. I took a liking to Fritz, an old Belgian draught horse and would spend hours in the barn grooming him. They let me ride him a few times, my little legs sticking out from the sides of his broad back.

The family spoke of certain subjects only in private. They listened to Radio Free Europe surreptitiously, though it was often jammed, and sat by the dial so they could quickly change it if someone walked in unexpectedly. They were suspicious of strangers and even of people they knew whose motives were suspect. While we were visiting the movies came to town. They put up a portable screen in a large, roughly hewn building and a government fellow came out with a projector in his car to show Russian movies with German subtitles, all propaganda films. There was a festival in the village with a band, lots of beer and sausages, and a variety of activities. After everyone had gotten into the spirit of things and the beer had loosened their tongues, I remember overhearing somebody advising a friend to watch his mouth because he saw a couple of people in the crowd who might be from the Party. The older generation were careful about what they said around younger ones. I was told a couple of times that I was only a guest and to watch what I said. That left an impression with me as a boy. It made me keenly aware of the differences between the two countries.

The second time we visited was to say good bye before emigrating to Canada. I was about twelve. At the border where you enter on the way to Berlin, there was a jukebox. I was leaning against it having a Coke and checking out the tunes when an East German fellow came up to me and said, "Whatever you pick, make sure it's not American!"

Around that time, I decided that I wanted to be a rock 'n' roll star. Though not yet thirteen, I looked like a sixteen year old and started to hang out with the older rock 'n' roll crowd. I was fairly tall for my age and dressed the way they did. These guys were from my street, out of school and in a trade. The first thing they did once they started working was to buy a Moped motor bike. This gave them mobility to go to rock 'n' roll bars. I identified with them and tried to fit in. I was the baby of the group but they tolerated me as long as I didn't give them any trouble. I spent the year or so before our departure to Canada hanging out with the boys wherever rock 'n' roll was to be had. I was determined that I wanted to be a rock 'n' roll performer. It seems funny to think about that now. There I was on the wrong side of the Atlantic, legally blind and speaking the wrong language. It's still amazing to me that the dream came true.

From as far back as I can remember I always liked music. Although classical and church music weren't my cup of tea, I liked a variety of folk music. Anytime I heard the radio, no matter what kind of music it was, I would listen intently. The Don Cossack choir used to perform Russian folk music in Germany. Their singing got you deep inside your gut and stirred your emotions whether you understood the lyrics or not. The incredibly heavy sadness of hundreds of years of suffering that led to some of the songs was apparent in the sound of the voices which were almost mantra-like. You couldn't help but be moved by it. I also remember my Aunt Ida singing a terribly sentimental song, an old German story about a false nun and two star-crossed lovers. It brought tears to my eyes every time I heard it when I was six or seven years old.

The people living across the hall from us, the Luensers, were a younger couple and often hosted parties that we would attend. The woman's father played guitar and sang German folk songs, particularly funny songs, to which everyone knew the refrain and sang along. I loved those evenings. That was my first close up experience with someone playing a musical instrument.

A classmate of mine at school had an interest in electronics and built a cigar box radio. It was fairly easy to do: basically he took a cigar box, removed the lid, drilled some holes in it, installed some electrodes or whatever, and got a little rotary pot to sweep the frequencies. Since it had no speaker, in order to listen to this thing he used a single ear cup headphone from an old German tank radio. He brought his homemade radio to school; I was absolutely fascinated with it. We had a radio at home but this thing was more portable. I asked him what he would trade for it. We worked out some kind of deal and I brought the radio home. I found a place for my new acquisition under the mattress in the box spring so that I could lie on my pillow and reach the dial. I lay the ear cup alongside the pillow in case someone walked in so they would think I was sleeping.

A couple of nights later I was sweeping the dial and stumbled upon Armed Forces Radio. I didn't know what it was at the time but the first thing I heard was Little Richard. It was just goosebumps time for me. I had never heard anything like that before —the intensity, the gospel fervor, all the rest. They played *Tutti Frutti* and *Long Tall Sally*. He wasn't singing about much as I learned later when I could understand English better, but the intensity, the rhythm, the ferocity with which he attacked both the song vocally and the piano instrumentally was incredible. Little Richard was the first person to really make a strong impact on me, no question about it. From that moment on I was on the hunt for that kind of music.

Rock 'n' roll music on West German radio was extremely limited then. Besides American Forces Radio, the government controlled German stations started to play one hour of rock 'n' roll per week. It was the American and English hit parades hosted by a legendary British DJ, Chris Howland, who spoke German with a broad British accent. Radio Luxembourg was another radio station I could pick up reasonably clearly at night without too much static. They played the pop charts.

The other important source of rock 'n' roll music for German teens were the carnivals. The carnies realized that rock 'n' roll drew kids like a magnet. American records were becoming available in Germany in the form of singles, and the carnival rides played them nonstop. Each ride had its own PA system and its own disc jockey who would play the latest rock 'n' roll records — Little Richard, Fats Domino, Elvis. The DJ would be shouting in German, "Ain't this fun! Ain't this great!" and pulling whistles, flashing lights, and ringing bells. Girls would be screaming going round on the rides. When I was twelve or thirteen, around 1956 and 1957, my friends and I would come home from school, quickly eat supper, and head out to the carnival to dig the music until we had to be home. I didn't have the money to take in the rides, so I would just hang out and listen to the music. Kids from ages sixteen to their early twenties, girls and boys, danced in and around the rides and behind the utility vehicles. It was tremendously exciting. The ride that had the best music was the Caterpillar. It was legendary throughout Germany.

We never had a television set but my mother later purchased a record player and a collection of old 78 rpm shellac recordings which contained an English language course. She bought it all from a pawn shop and it had this old heavy stylus and wind up crank. The thing was in poor condition so I made a strong case for buying a new portable record player. The moment we had that machine, I started buying my own records, exclusively rock 'n' roll. Almost all of my money went towards 45's. My first acquisition was the Everly Brothers' *Bye Bye Love* because the store was out of Little Richard records. By the time we left Germany, I owned several Little Richard records, some Presley and Everly Brothers, and a few other things. I didn't understand a word they sang, but that never mattered. I'd mouth the words phonetically. My favorite remained Little Richard. Other popular American hits in Germany at the time included Guy Mitchell's *Singing The Blues*, Fats Domino's *Blueberry Hill*, and Johnny Ray's *Yes Tonight Josephine*. Elvis was really big. *Hound Dog, All Shook Up, Teddy Bear*, and *Don't Be Cruel* were all hits.

I also saw rock 'n' roll movies: *The Girl Can't Help It*; *Don't Knock The Rock*, with Bill Haley and Little Richard; and Elvis in *Love Me Tender*. I was just knocked out by these movies. Once I saw a photograph of Elvis with a Gibson guitar and was so taken by it that I talked my stepfather into making me one like it. He did a beautiful job on the body, and although made of laminated cardboard and not wood, it looked sensational.

My mother had a long full length tailoring mirror in the living room because her alteration customers came to our apartment to try things on. It was perfect for me to perform in front of, miming to my records. I'd crank that little record player up, stand in front of the mirror, and sing along. It was nonsensical stuff because I had no idea what the hell was being said. Phonetically I mimicked them as closely as I could manage and the rest I made up as I went along.

Postwar German teens embraced American rock 'n' roll with wild abandon. Concerts by Bill Haley and Jerry Lee Lewis caused pandemonium in Hamburg as crazed kids, pumped up on rock 'n' roll, trashed the theaters where they performed. Most wanted the real thing and rejected German language versions of American songs, regardless of whether they understood the language. At the time there were a few artists who covered American rock 'n' roll records, one being Peter Krauss who did German language versions of Elvis Presley songs. But for most German kids like me, these sounded atrocious. I never thought rock 'n' roll and German went together in the first place and I could not conceive of achieving my dream of being a rock 'n' roll performer in Germany.

The stereotypical image of Germans, that rigid stiffness, was loosening up in postwar teens. Rock 'n' roll became the voice of the new, young German youth born during or after the war. It was our own form of rebellion against not only our parents but our parents' past, the war and the collective national guilt over it and how the world perceived us. Rock 'n' roll was not merely a form of rebellion for me but my salvation. It was my release from the confinement of the spirit that came with conformity.

In the wake of the Marshall Plan, German teens became willing tools in American Cold War propaganda by learning to love all things American in order to counter what was happening behind the Iron Curtain. We were being Americanized in a big way. What did we want to wear? Blue jeans. What did we want to listen to? Rock 'n' roll. How did we comb our hair? Like Elvis Presley. What did we want to see? James Dean and John Wayne movies. I remember going regularly to a place called the America House, a kind of American cultural embassy where you could read and see and learn about America. I loved it. To me, North America was adventure, the land of opportunity. All the stuff I was in love with came from there — the music, the look, the lifestyle.

There was a movie theater in the central train station in Hannover called Aki which stood for *Actuelles Kino*. They had a program that was repeated every fifty-five minutes for people who were in transit and had time to kill, newsreel upon newsreel, then a Laurel and Hardy short. I would stay all day watching newsreels that offered glimpses of the States. America was constantly in my consciousness.

Everything American was exotic, exciting and different for me. I read American books, saw American movies, listened to American music, and dreamed of someday visiting the USA. But being able to live those dreams remained extremely remote to me until my parents began thinking about emigrating.

By the mid 1950s, the West German economy had recovered sufficiently so that people were now more status conscious and preferred purchasing their clothes from brand-name stores. Consumer goods were now more readily available and in demand. My mother could see that there was less demand for alterations. A few years earlier in 1951, my uncle Willy, his wife Leni, and their two children Rita and Detlef (or Ted as he became known later) had emigrated to Canada. By 1956 we were receiving good reports from them. Tuta and Robert had also emigrated, as well as a younger sister of my mother's named Meta and her husband Ernst. So there were three families in Canada, all in Toronto. They sent us care packages of things they thought were still being rationed like coffee and Cadbury's chocolate. Along with these came photos of their homes, cars, furnishings. They were obviously doing better than we were. A light went on in my head when my parents started talking openly about moving to Canada. Both my parents were in their forties, a somewhat late point in life to make a decision like that, so they weren't sure what to do. I already had the bug for rock 'n' roll, and seeing my opportunity, began promoting the idea of following the relatives. Every time those letters would arrive, I dropped hints like, "My, they're certainly doing well," to get the ball rolling.

Emigrating to the United States was out of the question. They weren't taking many Germans. Besides, we had relatives already established in Canada who could help us get settled. For me, Canada was fine. After all, it was still North America and as close as any country could get to my rock 'n' roll mecca, the USA. The decision to emigrate was made in 1957 and we left in March of 1958. It was not easy for two people their age. For me, the thought of completely uprooting myself at age forty and moving to an entirely new country, learning a new language and a whole new way of life, is phenomenal. I'm not sure that I could do it, yet that's what they did. I admire them both for their spirit.

Once the decision was made, preparations began in earnest. We had to travel to the Canadian consulate in Hamburg to fill out the necessary papers for visas and undergo a health inspection. My stepfather negotiated the lease take-over for our apartment. Decent housing was still at a premium so you could choose who you wanted to take over the apartment and receive a little money in return. We had to decide what furnishings to take and pack them. The shipping people came by and built a crate for the things we were sending over. Initially our plan was to travel by ship because my stepfather assumed it was the most inexpensive means of travel. However, around the time we were preparing to go, Sabina Belgian

World Airlines managed to beat even the economy class fare on the boat. For me, the anticipation of flying added even more excitement to the adventure.

I had a few odds and ends of my own to tie up before leaving. I said good bye to my friends in the neighborhood and to my classmates at the Waldorf School. They took a class photo and gave it to me to remember them by. Once we decided to emigrate, my mother approached the pastor who instructed my confirmation classes at the local Lutheran Church and asked whether I could be allowed to complete my confirmation in an accelerated fashion. He agreed to move it up to six Sundays from then. There I was in a new suit at the altar with all my family on hand to witness my confirmation into the Lutheran Church. As was the custom, I received several gifts, one being a small automatic camera. A week later, a month shy of my fourteenth birthday, I used the camera to record my great adventure as we left Hannover for a new life once again, this time in Canada.

*My mother and "new" father,
Gerhard, on their wedding day, 8
August 1950, in Hannover.*

My first day of school, 1950.

*Aunt Ida, me, Elsbeth, and Gerhard
celebrating Christmas, 1954.*

*My 16-year-old cousin and me at age 13
in front of our home at "Kronenstrabe 34."*

*Friends and relatives bid us farewell at the Hannover airport
as we leave for our new home in Canada, March 1958.*

THREE

FOR ROCK 'N' ROLL

Now everybody in the school yard
Was rockin' for their life the whole week through
Come Friday afternoon when school was over
We'd plan our secret rendezvous
And late at night when all were sleeping
I would steal away to find my crew

FOR ROCK 'N' ROLL, 1981

For most Europeans in the 1950s, Canada conjured up images of cowboys, Indians, Mounties, and snow. I had grown up on the American dream — Elvis, James Dean, and John Wayne. So had most Canadians. Canadians of my generation grew up on American movies, television, and music. There was little left that was British other than place names like Prince Albert or Victoria and the presence of the Queen on coins. For that matter, there wasn't much Canadian popular culture to call its own, swamped as it was by all things American. For me Canada was exciting because it was as close to American culture as I could get.

After a twenty-four hour series of flights from Hannover to Dusseldorf then to Brussels, Ireland, and Montreal, we arrived in Toronto where we were greeted by Uncle Willy and Aunt Leni, Meta and her husband Ernst, and their three-year-old daughter Carmen. After assorted hugs all round, off we went to Meta and Ernst's house on Durie Street in the west end High Park area of Toronto. Arrangements had been made for us to rent the upstairs flat. Meta, Ernst, and little Carmen lived on the main floor. It felt good to be among family in our new home.

The first thing that impressed me about Canada in general, and Toronto in particular, was its size. I've since traveled from one end of the country to the other and know its vast natural beauty, but at the time the distance from the airport to my Aunt Meta's house took forty minutes. In Hannover, in forty minutes you could be on the outskirts of the city, from one side to the other. Peering out the car window I was struck by the tremendous similarity in the neighborhood houses. They all had a front porch with two pillars, one tree in front, a little lawn, driveway on the side to the backyard, back porch, two to three floors, little dormer on the attic, half basement. Two doors down you'd see the same house except maybe a different color. Germans tend to appreciate nice, neat neighborhoods, clean streets, lawns nicely kept, beautiful trees, houses very orderly, so my parents and relatives liked Toronto. But I found the city big and sleepy. Downtown was dreary, dark, sooty, not much of a sign of life.

Originally settled by British Empire Loyalists who had fled the United States during the Revolution, Toronto had grown to become Canada's industrial and business center. With a population of a million people by then, it was Canada's second largest city, eclipsed only by Montreal. The city's focal point was and remains Yonge Street. There, Toronto's night life could be found. But in 1958 you had to look pretty hard to find it. Now a huge multicultural center, Toronto in the fifties was as WASPish as they come, and proud of it. It was a big city with a small town attitude. There was almost a Victorian air about the place — stuffy, prim, and proper. Everything was closed on Sunday, even movie theaters. Drinking laws were archaic: twenty-one to drink, government run liquor outlets that required a signature, no standing with a drink in your hand in a bar. This was 'Toronto the Good'. To me it was like Mars. In Germany, at sixteen you could drink legally, and in Hannover there were already rock 'n' roll clubs.

The rock 'n' roll scene in Toronto was virtually non-existent in 1958. There was the odd teen dance that might feature a local band, matching suits, saxophone and Fender guitars, playing the latest American hit parade, but other than that, you relied almost exclusively on the radio for rock 'n' roll. There was no bar scene to speak of. Toronto was still a year away from Ronnie Hawkins' Arkansas invasion and violation of its innocence. When I arrived full of Little Richard and Elvis Presley, Gordon Lightfoot was singing in a barbershop quartet and Neil Young was plunking away at an Arthur Godfrey ukulele in rural Ontario. Canadian pop artists like the Diamonds, Crewcuts, Four Lads, and Paul Anka had all fled south of the border earlier, affirming the fact that there was no Canadian recording industry. Even Toronto's annual hoopla, the Canadian National Exhibition or CNE, a sort of hybrid country fair *cum* Coney Island amusement park, was tame by comparison to the carnivals in Hannover.

Within a few days of our arrival my aunt, Meta took me down to Humberside Collegiate to enroll me in grade nine. I spoke very little English but felt confident that I could learn. It was late March 1958. To help me ease in to the school, I was assigned to a German-Canadian boy who spoke both languages. He sat next to me in my classes and translated as much as possible. I was only in that grade with those kids until the end of the school year in late June. I knew I could eventually learn the language, though those first few months were difficult. What was insurmountable, however, was again the eyesight problem. Even though I sat in the front row, I now had to decipher the hand scrawling of someone writing in an unusual handwriting style, in a language I didn't understand, all from a distance I still couldn't see from. So it didn't really work. The school administration called in a vision consultant who advised my mother that it would be beneficial for me to attend the special sight saving classes at Deer Park Elementary School sponsored by the CNIB (Canadian National Institute for the Blind) and the Toronto Board of Education beginning in the fall term. All in all, it was a frustrating introduction to Canadian education after the uplifting Waldorf experience. It was too short a time and I was too new a kid on the block to be able to make friends in that particular class. Further complicating my feelings of isolation, there were no kids on the street my age to hang out with. As school ended in June, I envisioned a long, lonely summer.

One thing came out of that brief experience at school, my new name. Not long after starting at Humberside, the gym teacher, a crusty old guy who had considerable difficulty pronouncing Joachim announced: "Krauledat, from now on you're name is John."

Gerhard found a job as a bricklayer's assistant, working long, hard hours doing tough construction work. It wasn't what he wanted and for a man in his mid forties, found the manual labor difficult. But he accepted what he could get because he needed a job. My mother found work almost immediately in one of the immigrant-dominated sweatshops in the garment district along Spadina Avenue. It was nothing like the work she had in Hannover where she was her own boss doing alterations and tailoring for a regular clientele of middle and upper class patrons. Here, she worked eight hours a day bent over a sewing machine, alongside forty other immigrant women, under the vigilant gaze of a shop foreman. She was a piece worker, which meant she was paid for each completed piece. She was good so she made decent money. She would come home with stories to tell about the other immigrant workers. It wasn't with a song in her heart but work never scared her. She did miss not working out of her home, though. After two or three years there she moved onto a better place where she returned to doing alterations.

I think she regretted leaving Germany, at least in the first few months. Not because we went without anything, she and Gerhard had a little nest egg to help us get settled. But I do know that there were some tears in the first year or two. My stepfather had a terrible time with English, never mastering it, limiting the kinds of jobs available to him. Initially, the combined amount of money they made was fine, allowing them early on to buy a second-hand 1955 Chevy. But the amount of work that was required to get a step above where they were was difficult. There was definitely stress and frustrations. After my stepfather would unload his frustrations on her, my mother would then, together with her own difficulties, break down to me. There would be a few tears and I would try to console her. Then I'd leave the room and a half hour later, she was her old self again. "Life goes on. Let's get on with it."

I, too, was going through certain changes. I missed my friends back home. I couldn't speak the language, so I couldn't really make any new friends. I was lonely. There I was by myself in a strange land unable to communicate with anyone beyond my house. I didn't have any real close friends until I started hanging out with a German youth group a couple of years later when Klaus Schultz and I became regular friends. Until then, the only social activities I had were family events. They were my salvation socially. The radio and my records were my real friends for that entire period. The Canadian experience made me even more of a loner than I had been before. To a certain extent my lack of eyesight and my lack of friends drove me more into music and made me pursue it with more diligence and determination than I probably otherwise would have. The solitude that was a necessary byproduct of learning and doing things by myself also made me learn early on that, in the final analysis, it's up to you as an individual to achieve your goals. You can piss a lot of time away just being a social gadfly and while that can be gratifying in its own way, it can distract you from your goals. From those first six months or so I learned that being by yourself is not necessarily something to be feared. You can draw strength from it and learn about yourself.

Much to my delight I discovered a far greater number of radio stations playing rock 'n' roll in Toronto than in Germany. In addition, I could pull in rock stations from Buffalo, New York. It was a feast to my ears. Rock 'n' roll was still happening that summer — *Sweet Little Sixteen, The Book of Love, Good Golly Miss Molly* — but from 1959 on, the music changed. In the wake of a number of scandals, tragedies, and Elvis's draft notice, the cleancut pop idols were thrust into the limelight to fill the void and to win parental approval. What was to dislike about Fabian, Frankie Avalon, or Bobby Rydell when compared to Elvis Presley's lewd stage antics or Jerry Lee Lewis' marriage to his thirteen-year-old cousin? For me, this brief glitch in rock 'n' roll's history offered no appeal. I did however discover during this time another form of popular music. One day, while sweeping the dial, I stumbled across country music when I accidentally tuned in a Saturday afternoon country radio show. I said, "What is this? This is quite different, not as rhythmic or intense as rock 'n' roll but it has interesting sounds." Country music was quite popular in Canada. Being for the most part a largely rural nation, there were radio stations formatted exclusively for country music, both the real thing from the States, including the Grand Ole Opry, and Canada's own version of country music, combining what was termed 'Down East' music, an almost Celtic-like fiddling style from the Atlantic region, with the prairie cowboy laments of singers like Wilf Carter and Stu Phillips. Nova Scotian Hank Snow was Canada's country music pride and joy at the time. Country music was also popular on Canadian television with shows like *Country Hoedown*, a forerunner of the American *Hee Haw*, and *Don Messer's Jubilee*. Soon after my country music revelation, I discovered a Sunday morning gospel broadcast from Buffalo that I also found exciting, hearing for the first time the roots of Little Richard's music.

In hindsight, the summer of 1958 was really an important one for me, though it didn't seem like it at the time. My aunt, uncle, and both of my parents were working so my cousin Carmen was home all day. I babysat her and my aunt would slip me a couple of bucks a week. I had the house to myself and the radio along with my records that I brought with me. I often accompanied my mother to the local Loblaws supermarket to help her carry the bags home, and while she shopped, I would check out the record rack in the store which stocked the kinds of music I was into — Elvis, Little Richard, and the Everly Brothers. I never bought record albums in Germany because they were too expensive and the market there was for singles. Albums were a big part of the North American music market, and by the end of that first summer, I had half a dozen albums. Playing my records and listening intently to the radio, I picked up more and more English, getting the hang of the language from the speed rapping deejays on the rock stations. Obviously my comprehension preceded my ability to speak, but by the time I went back to school that fall I could at least say the basic conversational stuff to get by.

That summer, I accompanied my mother one day on a shopping trip downtown to Yonge Street. At the Simpson-Sears department store (the same store, incidentally, that Joni Mitchell would work at a few years later to support her budding music career), in the musical instrument department, I spotted an inexpensive sunburst acoustic flat top Kay brand guitar priced at $55. I knew nothing about guitars, but it looked killer to me. I embarked on a long campaign of softening up my mother to convince her to buy that guitar, even promising to forgo allowances indefinitely. Eventually I wore her down and acquired my first guitar. When we brought it home I was absolutely elated. Now I figured I looked the part, but I knew diddlysqwat about playing it. I had enough of an ear to hunt and peck single notes and play simple melodies, but what eluded me was the ability to get a fuller sound. What I lacked was the knowledge of strumming chords. With no one to help me I continued to pick around for the remainder of the summer until school resumed in September.

Deer Park School where the sight saving classes were held was on St. Clair just a few blocks east of Yonge Street in the Mount Pleasant district of Toronto. I had to get there on my own, but the CNIB provided me with a free bus pass. I took the street car to Yonge Street and the subway to St. Clair, then walked the two or three blocks east to the school. The program was a special class to bridge the gap between those who could see adequately enough to function within a regular school situation versus the totally blind who had their own special schools. It was one very large single classroom with four separate grade areas of seating, run by an English woman, Miss Simpson, who taught every subject. She was a wonderful woman, very dedicated and hardworking, who had a hell of a time handling all these kids in one room. The grades were seven to ten and I was put into grade nine again, recognizing that my time at Humberside was a waste. I attended two years at sight-saving classes, grades nine and ten, whereupon I returned to Humberside, enrolling in grade ten again. The wisdom behind that was that the sight-saving classes were all well and good but not sufficient enough academically. I lost a year of schooling in Canada.

Everybody in the sight-saving class lived scattered throughout Toronto so the local friendships I longed for were still missing. But I met Stan King soon after the start of the school year and we got along well. He was a little older and had an acerbic sense of humor. His eyesight had been damaged in an accident and was deteriorating. Stan lived in Scarborough at the eastern end of Toronto and to my amazement rode a motorcycle. I asked him how he did it and he replied dryly, "I just stick out my white cane and tap, tap, feel for the curbs." When I told him I had a guitar, he asked me if I could play any chords yet. I replied, "No, what are they?" Sometime thereafter, he brought to school a Hank Williams songbook and said, "Take this with you. See those diagrams? That's where you put your fingers to make chords." After a few days of slow, tedious practice arranging and rearranging my fingers and becoming fairly proficient at changing from one to another, I mastered half a dozen chords. I then discovered that there was a whole lot of music out there that I could now play with just a few chords. So, besides being a good friend, Stan put me on the right path in music by giving me that Hank Williams songbook.

Stan King: *The teacher asked me to give John a hand, to show him around and get him acquainted with people; sort of show him the ropes because he was new to the school and didn't speak much English. With the reputation I had back then, I can't imagine why the teacher would have asked me to look after John, but we got on well and found we shared similar interests. When I first met him, he had no friends in Toronto. John was not very comfortable in a gang of people. He preferred things one to one rather than being with a large group. He and I started hanging out almost immediately. I was running with a bit of a wild crowd and John was a kindred spirit. We all thought we were pretty tough, kind of like James Dean.*

By Christmas, his English was incredible, totally fluent. He still had a bit of an accent but he picked up the language incredibly fast. It was amazing. John was a fairly good student. Certainly, he had no problems with grades and scholastically could handle anything that was there but it wasn't high on his list of priorities. It wasn't cool to be a good student, and if you got higher than 51% you figured you worked too hard at it.

John and I both had similar tastes in music, a lot of the black rock 'n' roll and rhythm and blues that was coming out of the States rather than the hit parade stuff at that time. It was interesting getting his impressions of the rock 'n' roll scene in Germany in those days. Of course, it was just American rock 'n' roll, the stars were all out of the US because Europe and the UK had nothing. And it was all driven by the American rock 'n' roll movies that were being produced at that time. All those Don't Knock The Rock *and* The Girl Can't Help It *type movies that had no plot, just an excuse to fire a bunch of rock performers up there on the screen to sell more records. It was also fun introducing him to the Toronto scene because he had no friends and found it so different here from Germany.*

John had this burning drive, even back in those days, to play music. I was just doing the 'hum along, strum along kind of stuff' on guitar but he was much more serious. The first time I ever heard him perform, he got up with his Kay guitar and did one of the Everly Brothers songs, Bye Bye Love, *at a talent night at the school. I remember being quite impressed. I was amazed he had the nerve to get up and do it at all. He wasn't half bad, but I wouldn't have bet his future on it.*

Stan left the sight saving classes a year before me to attend the School for the Blind in Brantford, Ontario where he finished high school. We lost touch with one another over the years but when Steppenwolf played in Toronto in the mid 1980s, out of the blue, Stan called me at my hotel. We had a ball for hours reminiscing over the phone. That night he came to the concert and tried to get to see me afterwards but we had pretty tight security backstage. I was back there yakking to people when I heard someone loudly making his way through a phalanx of security, then I heard Stan's distinctive voice shout out, "Jesus Christ Kay, getting to see you is tougher than getting a bloody audience with the Pope!"

The CNIB assigned me a social service counselor to help me deal with my sight problems and provide services to overcome my disability. Not long after we met she asked if I might be interested in talking books recorded on reel-to-reel tapes. I replied, "Not really. I have nothing to play them on." She then told me that the CNIB would provide me with a Wollensach reel-to-reel tape recorder to listen to these tapes. Seeing my window of opportunity I immediately jumped at the offer, not for the taped books but for the tape machine itself. It allowed me (may the RIAA forgive me) to tape songs from the radio and borrow records to tape as well. Once I had that recorder I also started taping my first attempts at singing in English. I didn't feel comfortable with my voice at first but gradually I gained more confidence and started singing and playing for friends informally — rock 'n' roll, country and western, anything that I could accompany myself on.

After a few months living in Meta's house, my mother had begun to feel cramped. There was too much family in one house. We moved to 140 Quebec Avenue a block or so from Humberside Collegiate. The area was your typical Toronto middle-class urban community: tree-lined residential streets, older, wood-framed two and three-story homes with a veranda or porch, a driveway separating one house from the next. My mother felt more at ease in our own place.

Initially, we resided in two large adjacent attics connected by a hallway between them. One had kitchen facilities and a dining area and the other was a living and bedroom area. The bathroom, a floor below, was shared with the occupants of the second floor apartment. My stepfather had in the meantime taken a position with a Ukrainian or Latvian bakery in Toronto. When the couple in the second floor flat moved out, we took their place. Now in my own room, I covered one wall with publicity photographs and album covers of my favorite rock 'n' roll stars. I enrolled in the Everly Brothers' fan club and received an autographed 8 x 10 photo of Don and Phil to post on that wall. There must have been something about their songs of teenage angst that appealed to me, but I also liked their harmonies and rhythm guitar work.

My infatuation with music was becoming an obsession. I channeled all my energy into my one reliable constant companion, music. I had been a sociable teen in Hannover and wanted to be the same in Canada, but it took a year or so before that came about, before I had a group of friends who shared common interests —

music and girls. I was still the new kid on the block who didn't speak the language all that well, a bit of a loner, excluded from some activities by my eyesight.

At the sight saving classes all the kids would be outside in the school yard during recess, their ears glued to transistor radios for their favorite rock 'n' roll songs. For teenagers then, music was almost everything. We had a radio in the classroom, and in February 1959 we all heard of the death of Buddy Holly. I had by that time become a big Buddy Holly fan and I was stunned by the news.

I started taking the streetcar down to Maple Leaf Gardens on my own whenever Dick Clark's Caravan of Stars came to town. The first one I saw featured Duane Eddy, Paul Anka, the Coasters, the Skyliners, and three or four other acts. It was so exciting for me to experience live rock 'n' roll. Between the radio, my records, some of these concerts, photographs, and programs, I was surrounded by rock 'n' roll.

My mother joined a German Lutheran church not long after our move to Quebec Avenue, and in the summer of 1959, my parents sent me to the Lutheran Church youth camp, where I gave my first public performance. The camp counselors organized a talent night where everybody dressed up like they were at a masquerade ball. I was drafted into performing. With my Kay guitar I played and sang an Everly Brothers song.

A couple of years later I joined the youth group which held meetings on Sunday evenings in the basement of the church. These meetings were not strong on religion, just young people talking and doing activities together. I met a young woman there named Jutta (not the Jutta I later married) who went under the name Judy for convenience sake. She and I began seeing each other and going on the occasional church group outing to the cottage country northwest of Toronto. I performed a few times for the youth group that fall and winter. A group member named Freddie played clarinet and asked me to accompany him on Acker Bilk's *Stranger On The Shore* at one of our little get-togethers. Slowly, I was beginning to feel more at ease performing in front of others.

I returned to Humberside Collegiate in the fall of 1960 more confident with my English. The socio-economic background of the students there was largely middle to lower middle class, so at least in that way I fit in. But I found most of them too brown-noseish for my liking. Most of the students were first generation Canadians born of immigrant parents who strove to be one hundred percent Canadian, to fit in and not stand out. The parents encouraged this so that their kids were not stigmatized as foreigners or 'DPs' (Displaced People). Being perceived as Canadian was very important to them.

These were your typical well-mannered, well-groomed kids with crewcuts and desert boots. The girls tried out for the cheerleading squad, while the boys went out for the sports teams. Good grades were paramount. It was all very vanilla, very Pat Boone, Loretta Young, and Father Knows Best — it made me puke. I was already showing a streak of non-conformity in my adolescence, a teenage rebelliousness that started in Germany when I hung out with the rock 'n' roll crowd. To be fair, once I got to know many of these students in a social setting away from school, I found more to them than met the eye, another side of them that they rarely exhibited in school. They were merely conforming to the pressures and conditions outlined for them by their parents who had worked hard to achieve more for their children than they had in the old country. They weren't all geeks or nerds and I didn't detest them — their scene just bored me.

There was another school two or three blocks away, a technical-vocational school, Western Technical High School, which was more of a working-class school with shops and mechanics. I identified more with the crowd at Western. They rode around in cars or on motorcycles, had duck tail haircuts and black leather jackets. To my mind, they were what I had imagined America teenagers to be. Because the campuses were close, I often went over to Western Tech at noon hours to hang out with that crowd.

Still, I met Jim Oskirko at Humberside Collegiate. He lived on Birchview Crescent just up the street from me. Jim wasn't in my class but we knew each other from working at Maple Leaf Gardens. Somehow we discovered that we had music in common. He played rock 'n' roll piano and was quite good. Jim was the first person I ever met who actually played in a rock 'n' roll band — Jay Smith and the Majestics. I was just a kid with a guitar playing at home but he was kind enough to invite me along to listen to the band play. They were good, very popular, and featured Bobby Starr on guitar. Bobby was a fine guitarist. He used to play *Memphis* by Lonnie Mack; he had that thing nailed down note for note. I'd close my eyes and I'd swear I was listening to the record. The Majestics used to play at the Club Trocadero regularly and I often tagged along with them.

Black people were relatively rare in Toronto. There were blacks who had moved up from Detroit and Buffalo or who had immigrated from Britain but they were still few in number. This preceded Canada's Points System immigration policy in the late sixties that opened up the doors to massive numbers of non-white immigrants. Before that, Toronto, and Canada as a whole, was still very white. In the flood that followed the change in policy, large numbers of black immigrants settled in Toronto giving the city a distinct Afro-American community that remains strong and active to this day. But despite the lack of blacks, Toronto teens dug black rhythm and blues in a big way. At the root of what in the mid to later sixties became known as the Toronto Sound was a heavy rhythm and blues influence that emanated from the many R n B clubs in the city. One such place was the Club Trocadero. It was just an open banquet hall that you imagined holding Polish weddings or Bar Mitzvuhs in but on Friday and Saturday evenings they hosted dances. The patrons who went there were young people from all over the city and the music they played was stone R 'n' B — James Brown, Etta James. You rarely heard a white artist being played. No Presley or Everly Brothers. It wasn't rock 'n' roll; you were hard pressed to hear even Chuck Berry.

Jim Oskirko: *I knew John from before Humberside Collegiate because we both worked at Maple Leaf Gardens hustling peanuts, chips, crackerjacks, and cold drinks. When John and I worked at Maple Leaf Gardens together, we'd go shoot pool afterwards and with his eyesight, he was pretty bad. We used to take advantage of him. 'Gee, John, you scratched again, you hit the brown ball.' Besides the hockey games at Maple Leaf Gardens, John and I worked the rock 'n' roll shows. It was a younger clientele and a lot more girls than the hockey crowd, so we would try to be cool selling popcorn to these girls. I remember us being there for Duane Eddy, Clarence 'Frogman' Henry, Fabian, and others. Gabriel Metzfeld was the guy who got us the jobs at Maple Leaf Gardens and he'd teach all of us how to really hustle. One time, before anyone had thought of it, Gabe went*

*out and bought a hundred and forty-four of these birds on a stick.
You'd swing 'em and they'd make a squeaking noise like a real bird
on a string. We sold those things at the Grey Cup parade and made
pretty good money with that. Gabe was a real hustler, an
entrepreneur, and he influenced all of us.*

*After school I would drop in at John's house on the way home
and he'd show me what he was into. I knew he was playing guitar
but he wasn't playing with any other musicians. I remember him
playing me Everly Brothers records and picking up his guitar and
playing and singing one of their tunes. He would mention country
and western stuff and Hank Williams things that he was listening to
but I didn't relate to that music. I was more into rhythm and blues.
When I started playing with the Majestics at the Club Trocadero,
John would hang out with us. We were almost the house band there.*

*The club acts in the early 60s were bands like Robbie Lane and
the Lincolnaires, the Majestics, Little Caesar and the Consuls,
Ritchie Knight and the Midnights, the Silhouettes. But the big guy in
Toronto in those days was Ronnie Hawkins with the Hawks.
Everybody was into going to see them. They'd have a dry side at the
Concord Tavern, and for 85 cents on Saturdays, you could have a
Coke and fries and watch this incredible band playing. They were
the nucleus of what became The Band. Everybody raved about them.*

Oskirko took me to the Concord Tavern one Saturday afternoon to
see Ronnie Hawkins and the Hawks. Ronnie, a genuine Arkansas
redneck with rock 'n' roll oozing from every pore, had come north
in 1959 along with his band to tap the market in the Great White
North. Upon his arrival he became an immediate phenomenon,
turning staid Toronto on its ear. By the mid 1960s, Ronnie was the
king of Yonge Street. As each of Hawkins' Southern boys grew tired
of the cold winters and headed back home, he replaced them with
young Canadian kids hot to learn at the heels of the master. By the
time I saw them, the only remaining American was drummer
Levon Helm. That lineup eventually graduated from Toronto bars
to back Bob Dylan on his controversial electric world tour, transforming themselves a few years later into The Band. They had so
much talent and drive that even Hawkins, the grandaddy of Canadian rock 'n' roll, couldn't hold them back.

Before he took over the Le Coq D'Or Tavern on Yonge Street as his headquarters, Ronnie held court upstairs at the Concord Tavern on Bloor Street. Every Saturday afternoon the management allowed under age teens in to watch the Hawks perform. They had a specially roped off area on the left side of the room where they served Cokes for the under twenty-one crowd. Every young musician in Toronto idolized the Hawks. Even the guys in the Majestics would go down to the Saturday afternoon matinees to witness the searing rock 'n' roll they dished out. For aspiring guitar players, Robbie Robertson was God. His disciples dressed like him, played blond Fender Telecasters like him, and emulated his stinging staccato lead guitar style. Bobby Starr was one of those disciples. Still just a teenager himself, Robbie Robertson was incendiary on guitar, infusing every lick with the intensity of a young man possessed. He used a banjo string for his high E string in order to bend it. There was all sorts of speculation concerning how Robbie achieved that raunchy, distorted sound. It was rumored that he slit his speakers with a razor blade. My eyesight prevented me from being able to cop Robbie's, licks but I wasn't interested in being a lead guitarist. I saw the guitar as an instrument to accompany my singing.

The Hawks would play two sets for the matinee and we would all sit there nickel-nursing our Cokes. Hawkins would defer to the band because he knew the room was full of young musicians there just to hear the Hawks. He would do his *Bo Diddley, Forty Days,* and *Who Do You Love.* The rest of the time it was the Hawks doing their thing: Richard 'Beak' Manuel doing *Georgia, Sticks and Stones,* and all the other Ray Charles stuff; Garth Hudson wrenching the eeriest sounds from a Lowery organ; Levon's rock solid rhythm; Robbie ripping the paint off the ceiling. They had a tenor sax player then, Jerry Penfound, who did a killer version of *Twelfth Of Never.* Garth would pick up a baritone sax and the two of them would form a two piece horn section. I couldn't believe what Robbie and Garth were doing. They had so much raw energy it was frightening.

The thing that impressed me was that these guys sounded so incredibly authentic. I had heard stories that Ronnie was from Arkansas and a cousin of Dale Hawkins (of *Susie Q* fame) and that Levon might be from there. We knew that Robbie was a Canadian and Garth might be too, but we weren't sure about Richard or Rick

Danko. There was an incredible amount of talent in this group. They sounded raw sometimes, sophisticated at other times, always so intense. When they hit the stage it was snappy, tight, loud, and ballsy. They showed a degree of musicianship that no one could hold a candle to. They wore the matching mohair suits and slicked back hair that was typical of bands at the time, but there was nothing typical about the way these guys played.

When I went to the States, I was appalled to think that this incredible band back in Toronto was scratching around playing in Ontario bars when American surf groups with big gigs were so mediocre. The Hawks were so far ahead of anything that was happening in the States. In the early 1960s the white kids in the States, especially the ones I saw in California, were generally into white music, surf music, the watered down Philadelphia pop thing, very sanitized. The music in Toronto was much more authentic sounding to me than what I heard in the States, supposedly the birth place of rock 'n' roll.

After the Hawks left Ronnie to go on their own and play with Bob Dylan, the Hawk managed to recruit the best players in Toronto, guys like Dom Troiano, and the Majestics' Bobby Starr and Jay Smith. Some of these guys considered it the height of their career to be in Hawkins' band. In Toronto it was the top of the heap.

Back at Humberside, I became what I referred to as a high-school drop *in*; I dropped in for classes when I wasn't sleeping. I was working evenings at Maple Leaf Gardens, walking up and down the steps with these baskets, ten bags of potato chips, ten crackerjacks, ten cups of Coke hollering, "Cokes here! Peanuts here! Chips!" The regular weekly Gardens fare was wrestling on Thursdays (heavily supported by the large Italian community), Maple Leafs' hockey on Saturday nights, and junior hockey Sunday afternoons. Occasionally we'd have Dick Clark's Caravan of Stars, Ice Capades, the Moscow Circus, even a ballet once. Ringling Brothers Circus would come for a week and have two shows a day. They'd bring in kids by the bus load. I'd skip school for that and make a killing. At one of these shows I was actually propositioned by a couple of promiscuous girls who couldn't have been more than seventeen years old. But I thought the better of it because I did value my job. It gave me a degree of financial independence; I was a free man, I could come and go as I pleased. I've always enjoyed that kind of freedom. My stepfather never exercised any authority over me and my mother always treated me like an adult, so whatever discipline I have, I acquired on my own.

I started to hang out with the guys I worked with and we would go out to shoot pool after work, staying out until all hours and getting home at two in the morning. I soon discovered in relatively short time that snooker was not my cup of tea unless they invented some sort of braille cue with a scope mounted on it. If I was tired the next morning, I'd sleep for the first two classes. I opted for German class at school and the 97% I got with no effort whatsoever pulled my overall average up to allow me to squeak through each year. I was terrible in algebra, barely adequate in geometry, okay in history and in literature but not grammar. Because my eyesight prevented me from participating in team sports, the gym teacher suggested I work on the weights. I even sent away for a course on isometric exercises. These things kept me in pretty good shape.

If I was bored with school I would cut classes, get on the subway, and go downtown to these seedy theaters like the Rio, the Broadway, and the Downtown. For fifty cents I could see a double feature, then go from there to Maple Leaf Gardens. Between getting by in high school, playing guitar, checking out the music scene with the Majestics or at the Concord, working at Maple Leaf Gardens, and hanging out with my friends, I kept busy and had enough money to buy records and pay my own way.

With my earnings I purchased a Harmony electric guitar and a little Harmony amplifier with a twelve-inch Jensen speaker. With this gear, I would practice every chance I had. I still had my acoustic guitar, though I'd moved up from the Kay to a Framus which I took with me on outings with the German youth group. I was constantly adding to my record collection, buying a great variety of things, like Hank Williams' *Luke The Drifter* and started going to see live shows like Hank Snow and Johnny Cash at Massey Hall. I developed an enthusiasm for country music; in fact, my first truly public performance was in country music.

There was a radio station in the Rainbow Bridge at Niagara Falls, Canada about a hundred miles away that I could pick up at night. On Wednesday evenings, they had a live amateur country show. The DJ would say, "If you think you can do a good song, come on down and let's hear it." So off I went on the Greyhound bus, guitar in hand, and introduced myself to them. "What are you going to do for us, son?" I did Hank Williams' *I'm So Lonesome I Could Cry*, learned from Stan's Hank Williams songbook. They sent me back the first time suggesting I might consider returning when I had developed a stronger voice. But a few weeks later, they let me perform that song on the show. Perhaps they felt sorry for me coming all the way from Toronto. Just being there and seeing this funky little studio with real microphones was exciting.

In addition to my regular gig at Maple Leaf Gardens, I worked a few times at the CNE, the big fair which takes place every August in Toronto. I sold punchy balloons and souvenirs and worked at midway games, all of which had some gimmick to them. The seasoned pros taught me the tricks and cons. I worked the fish pond and I had to screw these little six-year-old kids out of their money. I felt bad. I didn't last more than one day. I later worked the grandstand shows at the CNE, and even helped out with the elephants, hosing them down and cleaning their compound as well as feeding them.

On the recommendation of my mother, I entered the workaday world, albeit for a brief two weeks. It was at a factory that made kitchen furniture. I hired on for $1.25 an hour, twelve hours a day, Monday through Saturday. The job required me to clean arborite kitchen counters by rubbing acetone on them and buffing them. After two weeks of that I was happy to be out of there. Renting my body to somebody else six days a week was never going to be for me. I took my pay and ran off with Shirley, my Chinese-Canadian girlfriend (whose real name was Ling Me), and spent a long, hot weekend camping out at Long Point Beach on Lake Erie.

Another memorable summer, I traveled out west to work the biggest rodeo event in Canada, the Calgary Stampede. The guy I worked for at the CNE promised us that there would be work for us if we could make our way to Calgary. In July 1961, Gabe Metzfield and I started to hitchhike the two thousand miles or so from Toronto across the rugged Canadian Shield and flat Prairies to Calgary, Alberta. We made it as far as Sudbury on the first day, but it was so cold in the evening we decided to stay at a Salvation

Army hostel. The next morning we went to Loblaws and bought breakfast. Behind the store, Gabe saw a freight train and figured it must be going west. The combination of arriving in Calgary earlier by train and the glamor of riding the rails was inducement enough for us to hop the train. As it slowed down through town we jumped onto the ladder of a box car and slung our bags up onto the roof of the car, then climbed up. To avoid detection, we lay down flat on the walkway that ran down the center of the car. Just outside of town it started to rain, and combined with the soot from the engine, the walkway and the car roof turned slippery. Gabe stood up to look ahead for better shelter and spied two British army trucks on a flatbed two cars ahead. He called out, "Follow me. I think we can get inside the truck." The walkways on the railroad cars jutted out at the end toward the next car but they didn't quite meet. There was a gap that had to be jumped. With my bad eyesight, I had difficulty seeing where I was going. I made the mistake of looking down and saw all these railroad ties flying by and froze. Meantime, the train was turning, rocking from side to side, and my bag was throwing me off balance. I took a leap, making it to the next car, passed by some huge concrete pipes wrapped in sheets of cardboard and made it to the army trucks.

We got inside the forward facing truck and discovered it had no windows, just a windshield and half doors, like a carnival ride, with two seats. We settled in and pulled out a coffee cake from our pockets. Looking out, I could see we were getting further and further into the thick woods. It was starting to get dark and we were moving fifty miles an hour with the wind blowing in and no windows. Man, it was getting cold, too cold to sleep. Gabe decided to go get some of the cardboard from the other flatcar and managed to block the brunt of the wind but it was still bloody cold. We took out every bit of clothing we had and put it on, two pairs of socks, two sweaters. Meanwhile the freight train rumbled its way through the dense forests and worn down mountains rounding the north shore of Lake Superior.

The next thing I knew, we weren't moving; the sun was out and I could hear voices coming towards us. All of a sudden my door opened, the cardboard fell out, and there were two railroad cops staring at us. The train had stopped in Port Arthur and these cops figured they'd caught a couple of fugitives from jail or something. They told us to get out, and I as opened the door of the truck I forgot that I wasn't on the ground but on a flatbed and I fell off the car, twisting my ankle. As was the rule for stowaways, the cops took Gabe and I back to their office, took out a rate schedule. "Where'd you boys board this train?" Before I could blurt out Sudbury, Gabe interjected, "We hopped on at the last stop." That was likely Nipigon or Marathon, a much shorter distance than from Sudbury. Consulting the rate sheet, the cops then charged us the price of two tickets from that point. Money received, we were promptly escorted from the railroad yard with a few sharp words of advise regarding any further attempts at rail transportation.

There we were in Port Arthur, Ontario eight hundred miles from Toronto, a few dollars less in our pockets, with the Stampede beginning in a couple of days. Sitting on the highway on the outskirts of town, we looked up to see the same freight train pulling out of the yard. We looked at each other and said, "Why not," and off we went once again. Gabe and I eventually made it to Calgary after changing trains somewhere along the way. We tried unsuccessfully to get into a refrigeration car, only to end up spending the night in a livestock car. Arriving in Calgary a lot worse for wear on the afternoon of opening day, we managed to find jobs for the ten-day event. With money in our pockets and no desire to hop freight trains again, Gabe and I hitched all the way back to Sudbury. Dead tired, Gabe hit on the idea of walking into the police station and informing the officer in charge that we had no money, no place to stay and could we sleep in a cell for the night. "You want to sleep in a cell? Help yourself." The beds were six-foot-long metal slabs bolted to the walls. The local police wanted to make sure that nobody, winos included, ever wanted to make this their regular place to hang out. When I woke up there wasn't a single bone in my body that wasn't sore.

The next morning, standing on the outskirts of Sudbury heading south east, we again stuck out our thumbs. We must have stood out there for the better part of a day before realizing the reason we failed to snag a ride. We were standing near a sign announcing the presence of a federal prison. We eventually flagged down a ride, straggling into Toronto a little bit wiser, quite a bit of wear on us, and a couple of hundred bucks in our pockets to show for our adventure.

During my last year in Toronto I started hanging out with a guy from the German youth group named Klaus Schultz. Klaus was already out of school and working, was a ham radio operator, had a cool little Triumph TR-3 sportscar, and was a hell of a nice guy. He in turn liked the fact that I played guitar and sang a variety of songs. I hung out a lot with Klaus and his set of friends, mostly German kids. They all had cars and would head out of Toronto for weekend adventures. We had a good time together just being young and having fun. But despite my friendships, I never felt that I wanted to stay in Toronto for the rest of my life, drop roots, settle down and raise a family. I was restless to get out, see the world, live my life. I even joined the German theater group and wound up playing a minor role in their performance of *Our Town* as a grave digger, with a total of six lines in the play. It was presented in German at the German Social Club, marking my one and only foray into acting.

My first sexual experience took place one summer while I was living with my parents on Quebec Avenue. There was a young woman on the street who's marriage wasn't working. She took a liking to me. I certainly enjoyed it but I also didn't feel right about this clandestine relationship so fairly soon after I started to distance myself from her. Although I didn't know her husband, there was something in my upbringing that made me uncomfortable with the fact that she was married.

Eventually I started seeing a girl from Humberside Collegiate who was more sexually adventurous but there was at that time a degree of paranoia about teenage pregnancy. After being with that older woman I was sufficiently knowledgeable about birth control and I didn't want to get stuck. There were stories from Western Tech, where the kids were somewhat wilder, about so and so being knocked up and the father going after the boy. I didn't want any part of that. And I very definitely did not want to bring any more grief to my mother who had suffered enough in her life. I always kept in the back of my mind my mother's trust in being able to rely on my conduct.

Like most teenagers, I had my under-age drinking adventures.

The one thing, though, that could have landed me in serious trouble was the bootlegging I did while at Humberside Collegiate. Because of my eyesight, the principal allowed me to wear my prescription sunglasses in school, the only kid to do so in the whole student body. This, coupled with my black leather jacket and boots, fostered my rebel image. I definitely stuck out. Oskirko and I, along with a few other misfits including a guy named Boris Paladichuk who was by then a daily drinker, formed a kind of pocket of resistance in the school and congregated together. Another member of our group owned a beat-up old 1952 Ford. I was tall and looked older than my years (in fact, I was older than the other kids because I had been set back once), so I put on a dark trench coat I had brought from Germany, a nice shirt and tie, and with my dark glasses and hair slicked back I walked into a Liquor Control Board. Calmly, I forged a phony name and signature on the order and bought a bottle of Smirnoff's Vodka. I figured, "This is too easy." Ever quick to seize on an obvious enterprise, the guy with the car and I decided to supply liquor to Humberside seniors who were eager for a little illegal fun on the weekends when their parents were away. I sized up the market and determined there was a need. Every Friday I took orders. The deal was: "Whatever the retail price, double it and we'll deliver." We'd drive around to a number of government run liquor outlets in the vicinity, buying limited quantities to avoid suspicion, then make our deliveries.

During the winter of 1962 to the spring of 1963, my stepfather began making noises about moving across the border to Buffalo, New York. He had a route delivering ethnic baked goods all the way to Buffalo, and he noticed that there was a large demand for these goods among the ethnic communities there. He figured if he could live in Buffalo he'd have that whole territory to himself. We had been in Canada long enough to apply for Canadian citizenship but put it off while my parents considered a move to the States. For me, it was a dream come true. But I still had to complete high school. All the other adventures were merely a pleasant diversion from that reality.

My parents ended up moving to Buffalo in April of my last year at Humberside. In order to graduate, I stayed in an apartment with two guys from the German youth group. With no parental presence, I set school as a low priority and really let things slide. But I did graduate from Humberside Collegiate in June 1963 and joined my parents in Buffalo. I was now determined to pursue my musical goals seriously, but there were few options open to me because of my poor eyesight.

Performing with my first guitar for a "costume ball" at a church camp north of Toronto, 1959.

Partying with Klaus (far right) and friends, with my first guitar amp, a Harmony, shown on the left, in 1962.

Performing with my first "real" guitar, a Gibson J-45.

Brian, Tanis, and me at the Boar's Head Coffeehouse and Folk Music Club, Buffalo, 1964.

*Heading for California along Route 66 in
Klaus' trusty TR3, 1964.*

FOUR

GOIN' TO CALIFORNIA

Wake up mama, grab your walkin' shoes
Your daddy's got 'em
Those goin' to California blues
Mama's got 'em, papa's got 'em
Sister's got 'em, everybody's got 'em
We're going to California
Mama, do you want to go
Well, if I can't take you
I believe I'll take the girl next door
Goin' to Chicago, goin' to St. Lou
Goin' to Kansas City and Frisco too
I'm leaving here tomorrow
I'm headed for the Golden Shore
I'm goin' back where the climate suits my clothes

GOIN' TO CALIFORNIA, 1965

By the time I joined my parents in Buffalo, they were renting a luxurious main floor flat in a stately old house on Woodward Street out towards Williamsville. The flat was large, much bigger than we could use, with nice old wood and big Christmas trees in the yard. My mother had found work in the alterations department at Berger's, a department store downtown, while my stepfather had started his own import-export business, distributing ethnic foods.

Our five years in Canada proved us worthy of acceptance into the United States, but not without a price. Soon after arriving, Uncle Sam came calling for me. Like all healthy young American boys, the United States Army requested my presence to register for the draft. With typical military efficiency, they put me through an extensive physical checkup. As the guy filled in the form I started to tell him about my eyes, "By the way, I. . . ." but he interrupted with "We'll get to everything son, just continue." So I performed all the physical tests, meantime, he's going, "Blood pressure's good, feet, no deformities . . ." Then he asked, as though he knew the answer already and was tossing it off as a mere formality, "Any disabling functions that would prevent you from serving your country?" "Well, I'm legally blind." He looked up from his clipboard and replied sardonically, "Couldn't you have said something earlier? Read the chart on the wall," to which I responded, "What wall?" Consequently, Uncle Sam declared me 4F. My father died in a war, and if my eyes had been fine, I could very well have been on my way to Vietnam. For the first time in my life my poor eyesight proved beneficial. I'm a very lucky man.

Now that I was out of school, I figured that I needed a job to support my evening activities in the folk clubs and coffeehouses. On my mother's recommendation, I applied for work as a stock boy at Berger's, but upon learning of my sight disability, they passed me over because of the worker's compensation liability. I encountered the same response elsewhere and was quite discouraged. I contacted the Buffalo Association for the Blind which offered me a job upstairs in their building on Main Street making candles for churches. The pay was 75¢ an hour. Minimum wage was about $1.25 but this was a non profit organization not bound by that law. A job's a job, so I swallowed my pride and accepted. It was humbling but at least it allowed me the opportunity to pay my share at home and pursue my career. I took home $32 each week, gave some to my mother for room and board and saved the rest. I worked the night shift at first with a Polish guy whose advise to me on the first night was, "Take it slow and easy, kid. At 75¢ an hour, nobody's gonna kill themselves."

I was working at the candle factory the day President Kennedy was assassinated. We heard the news over the radio and we both cried; we weren't embarrassed about our tears, nobody was that day. It was a turbulent time in the United States. Political events were far more prominent there than in Canada where Canadians weren't directly involved with issues like civil rights, the Cold War, the arms race, or Vietnam. The folk music scene saw itself as an integral part of various movements revolving around these issues. Protests songs, although not yet referred to as such, were part and parcel of the folk revival. Through a growing interest in folk music, I found myself becoming quickly educated in the political realities of life in America. Coming from Europe and Canada, I had no context for the civil rights movement or the Vietnam War. I had lived through the Cold War but missed the political rhetoric and propaganda from this side of the Iron Curtain. Kennedy had already been to the Berlin Wall and declared to the world, "Ich bin ein Berliner." When I arrived in Buffalo in 1963, the Vietnam War was still somewhat distant, and although Americans were involved, their commitment was not as solid as it would be a year later with the Gulf of Tonkin Resolutions, a virtual declaration of war by LBJ. These events were my introduction to the Buffalo folk music scene. The voice of concern for young Americans came not from rock 'n' roll but from the political side of folk music. Bob Dylan was at the forefront, followed by Phil Ochs and Joan Baez. Listen to Woody Guthrie, The Weavers or Pete Seeger. The union movement, civil rights, anti-war, it was all there. The Kennedy assassination brought it all home to me.

The civil rights issue really touched me. Having arrived as an immigrant and lived in Canada, a nation that encouraged its cultural diversity, I had developed a greater tolerance of ethnicity and race. That attitude characterized the Canadian perception of the civil rights issue in the USA. In Buffalo one night a friend of mine, Jackson Frank, told me Josh White Jr., a black blues singer, was playing at another club in town. He and I went to catch the show, met Josh, and hung out with him at an all night eatery. The next night we went with Josh and his conga player to an all black club to see Ahmad Jamal play; Jackson and I were the only two white faces in the place. Another time I saw Muddy Waters in a similar club. I never felt uncomfortable because I had no preconceived notions of blacks and whites. There was an undercurrent of racism among many whites. It was difficult to argue with them because they'd say, "You're from Canada so you don't know about this." I tried to get my bearings on the matter but it took awhile.

During my last few months in Toronto, I had often met my friend Judy in the Yorkville area. It's roughly a two block section of downtown Toronto not far from Yonge Street's noisy bar scene that, at the time, was home to the more avant garde, bohemian artistic community of the city — artists, poets, jazz and folk musicians. Bordered by Avenue Road and Yonge Street on one side and Davenport and Bloor Streets on the other, this little enclave was dotted with boutiques and coffeehouses. The latter were nothing more than century old two and three story homes whose front room or basement had been converted into a club. Patrons would cram into these coffeehouses like sardines in a tin to sip jasmine tea and dig local folk entertainers like Ian and Sylvia or jazz singer Don Francks with guitarist Lenny Breau. It was a cool scene, almost a well-kept secret in Toronto, and I was attracted to it because of the mystique, the atmosphere, and the music. Yorkville was the antithesis of the slick, raucous Yonge Street bars. Coffeehouses like the Mousehole, the Half Beat, and the Penny Farthing offered a friendly place for local folk artists to perform. The folk music revival that was going strong in the United States, especially on the east coast, had taken root in Canada as well.

Aside from the commercial stuff that was all over the radio like the Kingston Trio and Peter, Paul and Mary, I started to get into traditional folk music. There was an obvious connection for me through my interest in Hank Williams and country music. However, by then country music had taken on the Nashville sound, a homogenized, slickly produced, and formulaic approach which had no appeal to me. I preferred the simpler, rootsier acoustic country folk sound. The teen idol rock 'n' roll scene turned me off completely so I found myself gravitating towards the folk revival. I was introduced to the recordings of blues artist John Hammond Jr. around then and liked that raw, stripped down sound. Through

Klaus I met a Canadian folk singer named Doug Brown who seemed hip and sophisticated. His notoriety among the Yorkville community was derived from having set the poem The Highwayman to music. Doug lived the bohemian, free-spirit lifestyle — hanging out in coffeehouses, taking amphetamines, and staying up all night. Klaus and I started going to the Village Corner, the Gate of Cleve, and the Bohemian Embassy to have coffee, meet friends, talk, or hang out with Doug.

When I came to Buffalo I searched out the folk clubs. There were only two of any note, the Boar's Head on Pearl Street and the Limelight Cafe on Edwards Street, a stone's throw from one another. I hung out at both places, gradually earning acceptance among the local folk habitués. But I still hadn't abandoned rock 'n' roll completely and listened to George Lorenz, the Houndog, on Buffalo radio as well as R 'n' B like Ray Charles. Buffalo had a strong black rhythm and blues scene.

My little Harmony amplifier couldn't cut it any more so I saved up enough to buy a bigger Ampeg with two twelve inch speakers and a built in reverb unit. I still had my Harmony electric guitar and was practicing and practicing. A boy from the neighborhood who heard me playing came over one afternoon and introduce himself. He played bass and had a friend who was a drummer; the three of us formed a rock 'n' roll group. Kennedy was still President and, coincidentally, my initials are JFK so we called the band JFK and the Congressmen. We rehearsed in a nearby church basement, got a few tunes together and played a bowling alley, a high school dance, and two or three other places. We did cover tunes, I sang a bit and played a little lead guitar. We lasted until one of the guys defected to a rival group. I felt myself leaning more towards folk music by then anyway so the split forced me into pursuing it seriously.

In the folk clubs downtown I noticed everybody played professional instruments like Gibsons, Martins, and Guilds. As I was drawn further into the folk milieu, the less I needed my electric instruments and the more I realized I had to have a decent acoustic guitar. In a hasty decision I traded in my Harmony guitar and Ampeg amp; with a few bucks thrown in, I acquired a Gibson J-45 acoustic guitar. I loved that guitar. It was my first real axe, my first serious instrument, a real quality acoustic instrument which I owned until it was stolen three years later in Los Angeles while with The Sparrow.

The majority of the performers in Buffalo were young white guys who played a variety of different American folk styles. The blues was not predominant, but there was one fellow named Eddie Taublieb, a blues purist who had to learn every note the way the masters had done it, right down to the out-of-tune D string. It had to be authentic or it wasn't worth shit to him. He didn't like anything electric. Despite his apparent eccentricity, Eddie was respected among the folkies.

Ed Taublieb: *The folk scene in Buffalo was probably at its peak of activity when John arrived. There were several folk clubs or coffeehouses in operation. I don't know if any of then made much money but they had a lot of people on weekends. The scene was primarily a weekend thing though they would be open during the week. The one that John and I went to a lot was the Limelight run by Gerry Revzin of the duo Hackett and Raven. Sunday night the Limelight had an open mike or hootenanny where anyone could perform. The other place was the Boar's Head a few blocks away. Both were downtown, a couple of streets off Main Street. Neither of these places was large. The Limelight had maybe fifteen tables squeezed in, eight on the lower level and maybe seven or eight on the upper level. It had been an old restaurant before it was converted into a coffeehouse.*

I had completed school and was working a day job, hanging out in the coffeehouses in the evenings when I met John. I was doing acoustic blues stuff and that attracted him to me. We'd meet each other at the coffeehouses on a regular basis along with a few other folkies, but most of us never saw one another outside of the scene. The folk crowd was pretty small, and there was a sense of elitism because the big music scene in Buffalo was rock 'n' roll. Most of the college kids were folk fans so the campuses supported the scene. Duos and trios were popular then and it was tougher for a solo act to click with the audience. In Buffalo, the popular trio at the time were the Grosvenor Singers.

John told me he was interested in country blues and asked me whom he should listen to. I knew we had a good selection of blues recordings at our local library downtown, so I recommended he try

there and in particular I mentioned that he should listen to
Leadbelly. I don't know if he had heard of him before. He went
down to the library and took out a few things including Leadbelly.
It was a real shock to me that somebody did what I said. John
learned his blues song Go Down Old Hannah, *an old black field*
song and did it for me a few days later. I was knocked out. He
really captured the essence of the song. It was not an easy tune, it
didn't have a lilting melody or anything; it's the feeling that's the
whole song and he picked up that feeling. Most people wouldn't
listen to the authentic stuff because they wanted it sanitized and
modernized. They didn't want to hear the originals because the
artists were generally not great singers. But John listened to that
stuff a lot. He listened to it very carefully and absorbed it. He paid
particular attention to Leadbelly's last sessions, a four record set. I
really liked the stuff John was learning.

You have to understand: the blues is not something you choose
to do because you think the public wants to hear it or because you
think it will give you a good future. It's something you do because
you know it's what you gotta do. When John first got exposed to
the blues, it just seemed right for him.

Eddie was very helpful in pointing me in certain directions where I
could learn something. He told me to go down to the Buffalo and
Erie County Library at Lafayette Square and take out their blues
albums. So I went to their music department and was amazed to find
shelves full of this music, mainly Library of Congress field recordings. I brought home things like TEXAS SUGARLAND PRISON WORK
SONGS AND FIELD HOLLERS, Leadbelly, McKinley Morganfield, and
dozens of others. Listening to those prisoner's work songs and
gospel music, I was able to trace rhythm and blues all the way back
to its roots. I made a project out of it and fell more and more in love
with the music. I gradually shifted my emphasis from performing a
variety of folk music and concentrated on country blues. But I listened to the entire spectrum — from old-time fiddle champions and
bluegrass banjo pickers to Delta and Texas blues and almost everything in between. I loved it all.

I could see the connections. "So that's where it comes from:
blues, country, rockabilly, Elvis, New Orleans." I understood how

the proximity of black and white in the South, interacting with one another musically, created a hybrid music that was uniquely American. I kept going down to the library regularly. I went back to the very early days of metal cylinder recordings and studied everything I could find on records and in books, not only Afro-American music starting with field songs and live recordings at prison farms, but also Saxon-Elizabethan ballads mutated through Appalachian mountain music to hillbilly and country and western. Since leaving Germany I had progressed musically from rock 'n' roll to country & western, then to folk and into blues. I found myself developing a keen interest in musicology and later considered studying it at university, perhaps at UCLA studying American folklore and folk music history with the idea of teaching it as a performer. But rather than having to take other academic courses they stick you with in college, I decided on a more hands on way of learning — traveling, playing, and listening to others. I also bought a few new things. Dylan had come on the scene, so I bought THE FREEWHEELIN' BOB DYLAN and liked it. I could hear where he was coming from, though it took a couple of listenings to get used to his voice. I picked up the harmonica and a bit of slide guitar in Buffalo from listening to records from the library. But I really got into slide guitar when I moved to California a year later and started listening to Robert Johnson.

Once in awhile, I'd play at the open mike hootenanny nights at the Limelight or the Boar's Head. Sometimes I'd play for the gate, but it was really more of a learning ground for me. I'd work at the candle factory and hang out as much as possible at these clubs. There I met a young singer/songwriter passing through town named Paul Siebel who taught me the chord changes for *Corinna Corinna*. He said he learned them from Peter Yarrow of Peter, Paul and Mary. The song became a staple in my solo folk repertoire and made the transition to electric blues through both The Sparrow and Steppenwolf. Paul Siebel later made his way to Greenwich Village, becoming a mainstay on the folk circuit there for a number of years and recording two fine albums that not enough people took note of. A number of his songs were covered by several artists, including one of my favorites, Bonnie Raitt.

Another fellow folkie from that period who I met was Monte

Dunn, a multi-talented string player who went on to become accompanist for Ian and Sylvia. He was from New York and attended college in Buffalo but spent far more time hanging out in the folk clubs. He and I jammed a few times at The Bell, Book and Candle in Crystal Beach, Ontario on the Canadian side of Buffalo. The club operated more in the summer because of an amusement park there. The first Buffalonian to leave and garner national attention was Eric Andersen. He was the local folk kingpin and everyone was in awe of him. Hackett and Raven, a kind of Bud and Travis act, were fixtures on the Buffalo scene with their own folk music show on local radio. Compared to guys like Eddie Taublieb and myself, they were slick, with the whole folkie repertoire and presentation down pat. I met a lot of nice people in the folk circles, including Jackson Frank, a quiet, soft-spoken guy who had been seriously burned in a school fire as a kid. When he turned twenty-one he came into a hefty insurance settlement and went on a wild spending spree. Besides the coffeehouses, we also hung out at the Parkway Tavern where everyone went for a beer and a slice of pizza.

One thing Buffalo gave me was my first taste of earning money as a performer. I was hired along with two other players for a folk concert at a local college, one half hour set for fifty dollars, more than I cleared in a week and a half at the candle factory. Afterward I thought, "Heh, this is for me. This could work." In the folk clubs I had started using the name Kay. My mother remarked once that everyone at Berger's referred to her as Mrs. K because it was easier than trying to pronounce Kyczinski. So I just added the "ay" to it and became John Kay. It was a simple thing. Years later I legally changed my name from Krauledat to Kay.

I remained in contact with Klaus and would occasionally cross the Peace Bridge to the Queen Elizabeth Highway, stick out my thumb, and hitch a ride to Toronto. I must have done it a dozen times in the year I was in Buffalo. I'd crash at friends' houses and hang out in Yorkville. While I was visiting Klaus in the summer of 1964, he told me he was planning a trip to California for his holidays. Friends of his family owned a motel in Lake Tahoe where he could stay. He planned to see San Francisco and Los Angeles, returning via Route 66. It sounded like a terrific idea to me. There had been a television show called *Route 66* about two young guys cruising around the US in their red Corvette Stingray looking for adventure, and I imagined Klaus and I in his TR-3 doing the same.

A few weeks later Klaus swung through Buffalo to pick me up and off we went on our American odyssey. We traveled cheap, eating at McDonald's and sleeping by the side of the road in a pup tent to save on accommodations. Neither one of us shaved throughout the trip and had straggly beards when we returned home. I brought a knapsack and a beatup guitar because I didn't want to have my Gibson messed up. I remember driving through St. Louis heading for Route 66 listening to Chuck Berry's *Nadine* on the radio and thinking that was great because Chuck is from St. Louis. Somewhere in Kansas we were stopped by a highway cop who gave us a hard time because of our beards, accusing us of looking like Fidel Castro. We made it to Lake Tahoe and stayed with Klaus's friends for a couple of days. Then it was off to San Francisco. We next headed south along the magnificent coastline to Santa Monica. It was there that I fell in love with southern California. The girls looked good, the sunshine, the palm trees. I said to myself, "This is the place for me."

When we made it back home, I announced to my mother that I intended to move to California. I had no money but I was so enamored with the place that I was determined to make it my home. My mother absolutely floored me with her response: "Funny you should say that. While you were gone we spoke to your Aunt Meta and Uncle Ernst who sold their house in Toronto and moved to Santa Monica. They're doing really well and like it there a lot. Your stepfather's not that thrilled with the business he started here so we've been thinking of doing the same thing. Why don't we go out there together." A month or so after my return we sold everything worth parting with, loaded up a U-Haul trailer, got into our white 1962 Chevy, and headed west. Once again the family was on the move, no simple task for two people now in their fifties. For me, barely twenty years old, I was heading for my sixth home.

Shortly before our departure for California, a folk singing friend Chuck Furoy and I hitchhiked to Newport, Rhode Island for the Newport Folk Festival. We brought our guitars with us which, strangely enough, helped us get rides. Being dedicated folkies, our hair was still fairly short despite the burgeoning long hair scene. We looked fairly clean cut and with our guitars I guess people

figured anyone who played an instrument couldn't be a mass mur-
derer. Folk singers were still considered fairly safe. We stayed in
Newport for three days; the experience was an absolute revelation.
In Buffalo there were maybe three dozen people who regularly
shared folk music together, a secret society dedicated to preserving
this music. In Newport, however, there were thousands of people
from all over the country into the same thing we were. I felt a
degree of solidarity that had not existed before, a reassuring feeling
that there were more like me out there. Here were hundreds of people with guitars, banjoes, mandolins, whatever, playing all over the
periphery of the actual performance grounds — on the beach, on
the lawns, everywhere. The music was great, the camaraderie wonderful. We played our own music and were joined by many others.

In the midst of one of these impromptu jam sessions, a black
dude popped up playing Mississippi John Hurt stuff really well. I was
fingerpicking a syncopated blues riff and he said, "That's that West
Coast stuff. Can you keep that up?" I said, "Sure, I can play it all
day." Then he really took off; he had a truly authentic sound. His
name was Taj Mahal, and I was to see him again months later in
California. Chuck and I went to see a variety of performances and
workshops. One was all blues, another a topical or 'protest' songs
session. We saw Phil Ochs, Len Chandler, and I believe Tom Paxton.

At the festival we met a couple of New York girls who invited
us to stay with them in the Bronx and see Greenwich Village. We
checked it out but didn't hang around long.

When my family moved to Santa Monica, we found a typical
California-style apartment on Sixth Street. My reaction to living
within five blocks walking distance from the beach was like achieving Nirvana. I was living the ideal vacation, each and every day —
water, beach, sunshine, relaxation, girls! It was like something out of
a Beach Boys' song. Armed with a letter of recommendation from
Berger's, my mother marched into Bullock's, a high quality department store in Westwood near UCLA. Leaving my stepfather in the
car to have a cigarette, she went right up to the alterations department; when she returned forty minutes later, she announced, "I start
Monday." A few years later she became manager of that department.
Gerhard found the job of his life, working for the German consulate
in Los Angeles as the Consul General's chauffeur. He worked there

from 1964 until his retirement in 1978.

Looking back over our many moves, I never felt rootless. Restless yes, but not rootless, because I was never uprooted from anywhere that was truly home. I feel perfectly at home anywhere in western Europe or on the North American continent. I've gone through all fifty states, eight of ten Canadian provinces, and most western European countries several times over. There isn't anything so strange to me that I feel out of place or threatened. As long as my mother and I were together, that was the extent of my roots. It's quite possible that my lack of roots enabled me to focus on my goals. I never worried, "What am I giving up and leaving behind?"

I was determined to find work in LA but I wanted to find something music related this time. Looking through a newspaper one morning, I came upon an ad for a place called the New Balladeer on West Sawtelle in West LA, on the border of Westwood, not all that far from Santa Monica. I took the bus up there and walked into the place. Inside was obviously what had once been a store of some kind — large windows, a door on the corner, large checked linoleum, miscellaneous chairs and tables, and a little area sectioned off to be a kitchen with an espresso machine and a stove. The owner, Angelo DiFrenza, was originally from New York. Angie and a singer named Judy Fine from a folk group called The Womenfolk were an item. The group had scored a folk-pop crossover hit with *Little Boxes (Made of Ticky Tacky)*, and she fronted him the money to open the club.

The New Balladeer was your typical coffeehouse — folksingers, once in awhile a comedian, old movies on odd nights, hoot nights where anyone could take the stage. The clientele was fairly regular and the entertainment generally amateur with semi-pro folk singers drifting through. I hit it off immediately with the manager, Morgan Cavett. We became good friends and remain so to this day.

Morgan Cavett: *John showed up one night not long after the New Balladeer opened and started hanging out. The folk scene was still going in LA in places like the Ash Grove and the Troubadour. It was a slow night as it often was during the week, and he had his guitar with him and was basically looking for a gig. After I gave him a ride back to his parents' place down Wiltshire, we became fast friends. Then he started sleeping on the floor at my place* *behind Ciro's on Sunset Boulevard.*

Our lives revolved around the New Balladeer. We'd be out late at the coffeehouse then go grab a bite to eat and by then it would be too late for him to take a bus home so he'd crash at my place. He later got an old Schwinn bicycle and would ride that back and forth. For somebody who couldn't drive he was always very mobile. He always seemed to somehow make it to this side of town on his own and didn't depend on anybody. In those days John and I had very little money, maybe a dollar a day each for food, so we'd go to the Sunset Grill and have a hot dog. Back then, there was always something to do, somewhere to hang out. You didn't need a hundred bucks and a gold card in your pocket to impress somebody or have fun. It was a very simple, innocent time.

What attracted me to John was the unique selection of songs he was performing. He was doing stuff I had never heard before. He turned me on to Lightnin' Hopkins, swamp songs, and things like that. And he was believable when he sang that stuff. His guitar style and the slide playing and harmonica, it all fit together. His voice was strong, like the real thing.

Morgan's background was impressive. His father Frank Cavett had been a very successful screenwriter with two Academy Awards for *Going My Way* and *The Greatest Show On Earth*. Born in Hollywood, Morgan grew up around musicians like Johnny Mercer and Artie Shaw and movie stars like Henry Fonda, who would drop by his home, a large house behind the Chateau Marmont in Hollywood. He attended Hollywood High before his father's drinking problems forced his mother to leave. When I met him, Morgan had been living on his own since age eighteen, working first as a stage manager and light man in a little theater on Santa Monica Boulevard. While delivering for a liquor store he met Angie and came to work at the New Balladeer. He was living in the basement of a house directly behind Ciro's.

Angelo let me perform whenever there was an open slot at the New Balladeer. I'd play for whomever came through the door just to get some experience, and he'd slip me a free pizza. It was a 'hang around and do what you can' relationship at the New Balladeer. Morgan and I really ran that place; Angie was too busy being an impresario. As Morgan describes it, "Angie hired the talent and screwed the girls; we made the pizza and dumped the trash." At one point, Angie asked me if I wanted to be the manager. Morgan had quit for some reason. I asked, "What does being a manager entail?" He said, "Well, you sweep the floors, make the pizzas, work the door, fix the coffee and drinks, whatever needs doing." The pay wasn't tremendous but I could still play whenever I wanted. The job did have one distinct advantage however. Up to this point I wasn't making it home every night. I would crash at Morgan's pad or Angie's place or with musicians I met on a particular night. As manager, Angie told me I could stay the night if I had no way back to my parents' place. There was an electric blanket and a pillow stored in the back room if I needed it. The stage was carpeted and about eighteen inches high with a dimmer on a red spotlight that hit center stage. There was a whole gaggle of Westwood girls who frequented the club, all in their teens and bored with their suburban scene. They thought it was kind of exciting to hang around folksingers. A couple of them spent the night with me on that stage with the red light dimly glowing.

A number of people came through the doors of the New Balladeer who later went on to bigger things but who at the time were still scuffling like me. Taj Mahal, for example. He and Jesse Lee Kincaid wandered in one night, took the stage and proceeded to blow everyone away. Tim Hardin showed up out of the blue. He was already a fixture on the east coast but I didn't know who he was. Tim informed Angie that he was popular in Greenwich Village and said, "Just put me on that stage and let me do my thing a few times and I'll have this place full in no time." That rubbed Angie the wrong way. Still, we all know now just how talented he really was.

Another group of people that came by fairly regularly were some of the guys who were to become The Byrds. They were already talking about dropping the acoustic folk sound for electric instruments. They had seen the Beatles' movie *A Hard Day's Night* and realized the potential a pop group had. David Crosby played at the New Balladeer, and we took turns playing sets a couple of times. He had a reputation already in the folk scene after hanging around on both coasts for a few years. One of the first times we met we almost came to blows. I was in the kitchen running a noisy espresso machine while he was on stage. There were maybe ten people in the club, but he turned to Angie and demanded loud enough for me to hear, "If he turns that thing on again, I'll kick him!" So Angie replied, "Don't say that. He's put people in the hospital. He's a killer." Needless to say, I was not pleased, my young male ego somewhat bruised. I considered discussing the matter further with him out back but I thought better of it. David was a strong-willed Leo and I'm a strong-willed Aries. We were not attracted to each other, though we acknowledged each other's presence and talent.

Jim McGuinn would come in frequently, as did Michael Clarke who'd play congas or bongos for anyone who let him. McGuinn's folk pedigree was impressive by any standard, having backed up the Chad Mitchell Trio and supported Bobby Darin when he donned a jean jacket for a brief folk music fling. Smitten by the Beatles, McGuinn began performing their material on acoustic twelve-string guitar at the Troubadour hoots where he met Crosby and ex-New Christy Minstrel Gene Clark. The three of them became the nucleus of the Byrds a few months later, with Michael Clarke and Chris Hillman joining them. There was a young kid, Bryan Maclean, kind of cocky but nevertheless a nice kid, who hung around Crosby and McGuinn. He wasn't their close friend but idolized them from a distance. Bryan later became a roadie for the Byrds before joining Arthur Lee in the LA band Love. Another young man who frequented the club was John Locke, a jazzer and piano player who became a founding member of Spirit. For a lot of these people, the New Balladeer was a comfortable place to hang out and hear different music, not the usual commercial fare.

Two of the nicest people I met there were a couple of gentle souls named Bob Kimmel and Kenny Edwards. They performed as a duo, Bob played guitar, Kenny played bass and both sang really well. Some time later they teamed up with Linda Ronstadt in the Stone Poneys. One of the few comedians who used to come to the club to try out material was an unknown named Pat Paulson. He would bomb every time but kept coming back every few weeks. He went on to become a television star on the *Smothers Brothers Show*.

Various people had been telling me that the real happening place was the Troubadour. I had also heard of the Ash Grove and a place down in Huntington Beach called The Golden Bear. I took the bus into Hollywood to the Troubadour to check it out on Hootenanny night and couldn't believe how big it was compared to the coffeehouses in Buffalo and even to the New Balladeer. I didn't perform that night, although some time later I did get up at the Monday night hoot and played a couple of Lightnin' Hopkins songs. Being the new kid on the block, they gave me the last spot, the house-clearing act.

I started hanging out in both places during the fall and winter of 1964. By then the British Invasion was happening everywhere, but I was pretty oblivious to it all, at least until early 1965. I watched TV shows like *Hullabaloo* and *Shindig* but much of the music had no appeal to me, nor did the image. I did not like *I Wanna Hold Your Hand*, thinking it was silly, light-weight fluff. Beatlemania had broken out while I was still in Buffalo and some of the folkies were fairly open minded about it. After their appearance on the *Ed Sullivan Show*, Monte Dunn walked in to one of the clubs raving about the Beatles. "Listen to these changes, these cool minor chords." I must confess I didn't become a Beatles fan until RUBBER SOUL. Then I thought, "Man, this is really different and fresh." I could relate to The Rolling Stones right away because they were listening to Howlin' Wolf, Bo Diddley, and the like. Until the Byrds came along and Dylan went electric, the two worlds, folk and rock, were separate. There was the Beatles and all those British Invasion groups on the radio, a few pop records still coming out of the States, R 'n' B such as Stax and Motown records, and folk music. The whole thing didn't really mesh until later when the barriers broke down. At the Monterey Pop Festival it didn't matter whether you were Otis Redding, The Mamas and The Papas, Jimi Hendrix, or Ravi Shankar. To a certain extent, the folk scene had become elitist, the preserve of the 'serious' musician and the educated mostly male college crowd, while the British Invasion appealed mainly to white female teenagers. I was still into the jeans, boots, fleece-lined roughout jacket, guitar-slung-over-your-shoulder look.

The folk revival of the early sixties never really took hold in LA like it did in San Francisco or on the East Coast. Folk music's bastion remained Greenwich Village and a string of coffeehouses and university campuses from Boston to Washington D.C. All the biggies sprang from there — Dylan, Baez, Ochs, Peter, Paul and

Mary. To the pseudo-hip LA music intelligencia, Trini Lopez's *If I Had A Hammer* was folk music. The real aficionados were a dedicated minority on the periphery of the LA music scene who supported the Troubadour, the Ash Grove, the New Balladeer, and a few other clubs. It remained that way until the emergence of folk rock. Then LA found its feet.

Hanging out as much as I did at the Troubadour, someone finally offered me a job as a dishwasher. It wasn't exactly what I was looking for but it paid minimum wage and I got to hear the music. I only worked three nights a week there, the other nights were spent at the New Balladeer. I washed dishes at the Troubadour for awhile, but with my eyesight I had to use the Braille system. When the owner of the Troubadour, Doug Weston, hired a woman to be the club manager, she recognized that I was useless in the kitchen and moved me out front as an usher. Since I was the only usher, I figured I could call myself floor manager. It had a nicer ring to it.

At that time, the Troubadour arranged its seating the length of the room. As you walked in you saw the stage at the far end. At the front of the stage were tables behind which were rows of theater seats with a balcony off to the side. I realized very quickly that as floor manager I had power. I was like the maitre d'. People were thrusting twenty dollar bills into my hand saying, "I'm sure you can find better seats." Suddenly a table for four up front became a table for eight.

The performers who came through the Troubadour were a notch above those at the New Balladeer. The venue was a major stop on the folk circuit. Artists like Odetta, Joe and Eddie, the Dillards, Buffy Sainte-Marie, the Stoneman Family, Bud and Travis, and all the ubiquitous, generic folk ensembles like the Ramblin' Four and Rovin' Five graced the Troubadour stage while I was there. But the man I saw most often was Hoyt Axton. He really made an impression on me. I listened to his songs and fooled around with a few things I saw him doing. He had certain tunes that were really powerful. One was called *Red, White and Blue (Was His Shroud)*, an anti-blind-patriotism number. I performed it on my own when I went back East. *The Pusher* was another standout. That song always received a tremendously intense reaction from the crowd. I stored it away, performing it in my solo days and later with The Sparrow and

Steppenwolf. That song had a life of its own.

> *You know the dealer, the dealer is the man,*
> *With the love grass in his hand.*
> *Oh but the pusher is a monster,*
> *Good, god, he's not a natural man.*
> *The dealer for a nickel,*
> *Lord, he'll sell you lots of sweet dreams.*
> *But the pusher'll ruin your body,*
> *And leave your mind to scream.*
> *God damn the pusher.*

The Pusher, 1964

Hoyt was in his prime then. A husky guy, he had been a football player in his youth. He could fill the Troubadour for a week, two shows a night. He'd be there every three months, a real fixture in the folk community. He'd stand with one foot on a chair when he performed, playing a bluesy guitar style and singing in a powerful, expressive voice, to my mind one of the greatest voices around. I don't know whether it was just anger or flashes of insecurity but sometimes he would have these moments of sheer intensity that could really take you aback. I remember one night he was playing longer than the usual set would run. It was late on a Sunday night and people had to go to work the next morning. A couple of patrons got up to leave. Without making any noise, they walked toward the door. Here was Hoyt on stage with a lone spotlight on him, with the rest of the room in pitch blackness, and they opened the door. A stream of light shone through the opening, Hoyt was distracted by it and lost his concentration. The moment, the intensity, was lost. Realizing that some people were leaving, he stopped in mid-song and said, "What's the matter? Is it not good? Is it not happening? Okay, I'll tell you what. . . ." He put his guitar down, ran into the kitchen, opened the cash register, took out all the money, ran back into the room and went from table to table throwing five dollar bills or whatever he had in his hand at people. There must have been sixty people or so in the club. Then he grabbed his guitar, went upstairs and smashed it on the side of the steps on his way to the dressing room. He was intense!

On a couple of occasions I journeyed to the Ash Grove where the traditional ethnic folk performers played. Ry Cooder was there, and although I never met him then, years later I bought every album he released. He, as much as anyone, has kept America's roots music alive and is a helluva slide player. There was a contingent within the folk music revival that felt that to be authentic, you had to mimic every aspect of the original recording by a Blind Willie McTell or whomever. They'd learn even the mistakes from these old recordings and faithfully performed them that way. Perhaps they felt they had no right to desecrate the original work. These were the Ash Grove school of music people. At the other end were the Troubadour performers like Hoyt Axton who drew on the influences of the blues masters but put their own stamp on it. It was not their experience, not their cultural background. They liked the music but felt the lyrics had to be more personalized in order to be something more than a retread. When I started messing around with blues forms, I also felt that the rather personal blues of a Lightnin' Hopkins or John Lee Hooker for the most part didn't fit me lyrically.

Around this time I started noodling around with my own songs. In Buffalo, I had stuck to interpreting other people's material but now I was ready to try my hand at writing and came up with my first song, just some ditty, more of an experiment than anything else. Afterwards, I was surprised that I could do it and it gave me the confidence to write more material. At that point I was laboring under the misconception that songs came strictly from inspiration. It didn't occur to me to sit down and work at it. At first I wrote songs based on blues patterns that I liked and continued to do this up until joining The Sparrow. *Goin' To California* was based on Blind Willie McTell's *Statesboro Blues*. I simply adapted the melody and the feel. *Twisted* was another early song I wrote based on Muddy Water's *I'm Troubled*. I didn't see anything wrong with that approach since many blues greats freely borrowed from one another.

I hung out from time to time with a guy named Butch from the Valley. One night he asked me if I had ever gotten high. Obviously the drug scene was already happening in LA and was certainly around at the Troubadour and New Balladeer. Up to that point I had either managed to avoid it or it had avoided me. Angie first turned

Morgan on to grass after he started at the New Balladeer. Grass was well-known to the folkies and jazzers as well as other drugs. Psychedelics were just starting to creep into the LA scene by 1964. Once the whole Ciro's thing with the Byrds and the Sunset Strip freak scene appeared a year or so later, psychedelics — acid, mescaline, whatever — became the high of choice for many. Up until Butch mentioned it, I was a stranger to the drug world. I'd been heavily indoctrinated in Canada and Buffalo by the 'Reefer Madness' scare and was convinced that marijuana was addictive and to be avoided altogether. When I balked at his question, Butch responded, "Come on man, that's nothing but propaganda." Not convinced, I asked, "Are you sure, man?" "Yeh. I've been smoking grass for awhile now. You've got to try it," he replied. So one evening, Butch, his friend, and I were invited to another friend's house for dinner. They were a young married couple and the wife made a big spaghetti dinner. Afterward someone said, "Let's get high." They passed around a pipe but I was so uptight, so paranoid, that I didn't get high. I just sat there saying, "What's supposed to happen? What am I supposed to feel?"

A week or two later we were all back at the house, only this time Butch took me into the bathroom and said, "You're not getting out of here until you're good and high." He closed the door, out came the pipe, and fifteen minutes later I came out a babbling idiot. They were playing a Koerner, Rae and Glover blues album and I remarked, "Gee, I never heard those guitar parts quite that way before." I kept giggling as if absolutely everything was outrageously funny. The sound was tremendous, the food tasted great, and I was having the time of my life. The next day, to my surprise and relief, I discovered that I didn't wake up raving, "I gotta have some!" No monkey, no addiction. All those films had lied to me. After that I started chipping in to buy grass. The stuff mostly came from Mexico and was fairly low grade so you had to smoke quite a bit to get really high. Smoking grass put a completely different perspective on the world, particularly on music and making love. If you and your girl got a little high together, it was wonderful.

I started mingling with the crowd that came through the Troubadour and met Van Dyke Parks, a member of the Greenwood County Singers. Among many other achievements, he went on to become lyricist for Brian Wilson's most esoteric works with the

Beach Boys. Van Dyke had parties where everybody got high and not just on grass. Once someone handed me what they called Romolar which gave me a strange, weird high bordering on LSD but even more intense. I got sick to my stomach.

A fellow who often performed at the Troubadour as an opening act was a comedian from Britain named Jonathan Moore. He was a pretty funny guy and we got to know one another. He had been approached by the producer of a *Shindig* TV show derivative called *Shivaree* who thought that, because Jonathan had a British accent, he could knock off a novelty record to cash in on the British Invasion. Jon was adept at making frog sounds, so he said, "Let's make a record about a dance we'll make up called The Frog." He found some musicians, had a couple of rehearsals, and asked me to play harmonica. The producers agreed to pay me scale, about fifty or sixty bucks, and set a date to record this thing out in the Valley at Whitney Studios. The problem was, the night before the session, I had been at Van Dyke's and had taken some of this Romolar shit and I was really flying. I was there until three a.m. when I suddenly remembered the morning session. This was pressure time, my first recording session, albeit for a novelty song called *The Frog*. Somebody drove me home to my mother's but I couldn't sleep worth a damn. I was vibrating off the bed on this stuff. So I got up, showered, poured some coffee in me, and waited for Jon to pick me up. I was still buzzing at the studio but I did manage to play while Jon was yelling, "Yeah baby, do the Frog, nee-deep wop wop, nee-deep, wop, wop." Every time we did a take, I was praying it was the last one. That was my dubious recording debut.

My first acid trip occurred around that same time. I had spent the night with a girl I knew and the next morning had planned to head up to San Francisco with some friends from Huntington Beach who were picking me up in their Volkswagon van. At breakfast the girl mentioned, "I've had these blotters of acid for weeks. They're probably decomposed by now but you can have them if you want them." I took one of them from her, put it under my tongue, and waited for the guys where Santa Monica Boulevard meets the San Diego Freeway. I was standing there for a while when all of a sudden things started to change. I started hallucinating in vivid black and white (you have to understand, I've never seen color in my life). It felt sensational! But then I started feeling a little paranoid. A cop car came cruising by slowly, "Shit, can he tell I'm high?" Pretty soon a motorcycle cop passed by, followed soon after by a sheriff's bus full of prisoners. "Christ, what the fuck's going on?" I turned around to discover that I had been standing in front of a damn police station. Finally, the van arrived and, very much relieved, I got in. We never made it to San Francisco, though; the van broke down.

A group (called The Men) rehearsed at the Troubadour during the day, ten guys, an all male folk revue. Doug Weston was involved in putting them together and they performed at the Music Box Theater in Hollywood for awhile. One of the guys in the group was an artist named Tony Mafia, part Sicilian and part Cherokee. Following a difference of opinion with the others, Tony was thrown out of the group. The remaining members went on to become the pop group The Association, whose first hit, *Along Comes Mary*, was written by Tandyn Alma who lived upstairs at the Troubadour in a little room next to Doug Weston's office. He was reclusive but friendly, a truly talented piano player and songwriter.

Tony and Doug Weston figured that if they could do it once with The Men, they could do it again with another folk ensemble. The two held auditions at the Troubadour for young, male folk singers. I went down to the audition along with my friend Butch and out of ten or so people we got picked along with an easy-going guy named Jim, whose last name, along with Butch's, escapes me. Together, the four of us become Mafia's Men.

We were an unlikely crew thrown together in a folk quartet. Tony figured that if we were going to pursue this thing seriously, we had to be together all the time, so he rented a small apartment down on West Adams and Curson, bordering on the black community of Watts. Except for us, the only non-blacks in the neighborhood were an Oriental couple who ran a little grocery store. The rent was cheap enough, we slept on air mattresses, had a television, not much else. Our staple diet consisted of peanut butter sandwiches and spaghetti dinners. We spent our time rehearsing, hanging out at the Troubadour, and getting high. The Adams West Theater was down the way from us, and on Saturday nights at midnight they would feature live jazz, big bands, Lou Rawls, and so on. Morgan was a big band jazz fanatic, so he and I ventured down there a few times. We'd walk in and there'd be everyone slouched down in their seats, shades on, cool, higher than kites. The entire place was filled with black people but nobody hassled us.

Tony wanted the group to be a macho, chest out, virile troop singing traditional work songs, the "Whoa Black Buck Gee By The Lamb" stuff. We bought black jeans, black cowboy boots, black western style shirts with the mother of pearl diamond shaped buttons, and white kerchiefs for our necks. I was playing my steel string Gibson J-45 guitar, Tony had a nylon string guitar, and the other two guys just sang. We rehearsed constantly but we needed a gig to gain some experience, and Doug Weston came up with a few freebies to get our feet wet. The first was in a folk club down in Santa Anna for a hootenanny night. We bombed at the club. The next gig was playing at a Jewish Synagogue for some social get-together. Again, stone silence followed our performance.

Then Doug came up with the most unlikely gig anyone could dredge up: a rally for President Lyndon Johnson entitled, and this is the honest truth, "Jews For Johnson." It was held down on Fairfax Avenue in the heart of the Jewish District, across from Cantor's Restaurant in front of a hole in the wall place that served as the headquarters for the Johnson-Humphrey campaign. A flatbed truck had been parked in front of this office decked out with flags and banners to serve as a stage. Tony looked at it and wondered out loud: "So what's next, Goys For Goldwater?" We got up on the flatbed and proceeded to do our three or four tunes. The entire audience consisted of middle-aged Jewish people. What do they know about Mississippi field songs? Here were four guys dressed in black with white scarves. All we needed were helmets and a couple of lightning bolts on our sleeves and we'd have look like the Nazi SS. We received a smattering of polite applause so we took the hint and promptly left the stage to stand in the wings. Right then who should walk on but Eddie Fisher. He had come as a surprise to address the crowd about the merits of the Johnson-Humphrey ticket, but before he could get two sentences out, women began shouting, "Sing *Oh My Papa*, Eddie!" He tried ignoring them but it just kept building in the crowd. "Sing *Oh My Papa!*" He turned to me, I was the only guy around with a guitar, and said, "*Oh My Papa* in B flat." I strummed a B flat chord, 'Brrriiiiing', to give him his pitch. Now I wouldn't know the chords to that song from the Tasmanian National Anthem. By the third chord I was in never, never land and Eddie and I were heading toward opposite polls. His pitch was going down the toilet and my strumming trailed off into total silence. He finished it acappela and I beat it off the stage. No sooner had Eddie and I completed our duet when Hubert Humphrey arrived with the Secret Service guys in tow, dark suits and shades forming a wedge through the crowd and pushing us off the truck.

With yet another bomb under our belts I was fairly obvious that this thing wasn't working. I said to myself, "This isn't really going anywhere, we have yet to make a dime, we're living off peanut butter sandwiches and canned spaghetti in the poorest area of the city, and we're rehearsing ourselves to death doing the same goddamn songs for nothing." Butch really dug my blues stuff and kept telling me that acoustic blues was the way I should go. Tony was desperately trying to hold it together but the whole folk ensemble thing was dying anyway. So we split.

I had been living more or less off and on with my parents whenever there was no place else to crash. After the Mafia's Men folded I started staying more often with Morgan in his little apartment behind Ciro's. Now I'm a creature of routine, I like things done a certain way. Quite simply, I like order. Morgan's life was more chaotic. He's one of those guys who gets up in the morning and is an absolute bear. It takes him hours to get himself together. He would scrounge around muttering, "I must have a shirt here somewhere that's reasonably clean." We were not exactly The Odd Couple but sometimes when he wasn't looking I'd straighten a few things out.

Morgan Cavett: *John is a tidiness freak, terribly fastidious. He has to know exactly where everything is. If you switched the toothpaste, you'd hear him crashing around the bathroom trying to find it. This was partially due to his eye sight; everything had to be in its place for him to find it. His mother was like that. John's Mom even came over once with a vacuum cleaner and tidied up.*

Another apartment I had off Hollywood Boulevard in Laurel Canyon had this really large walking-in closet, so when John stayed over, he slept in this closet. It was just a one room apartment with

*a bathroom, no kitchen, just an ice box. He put a mattress in the
closet and that was his room, nice and tidy. He had a little table
and lamp in there so when we'd pick up girls, he'd go into his closet
with them and close the door. It was his little hideaway.*

I admit I hate clutter. With my eyesight, it's an absolute source of
frustration for me. I cannot pick out my own clothes by color since
I'm color blind as well, so I have to know where everything I own
is, literally. I can be on the road and phone my wife and tell her
exactly where a particular file is in the fireproof safe because I know
I put it there. I'm the one who organized it. Everything in my
sphere is organized the way I need it — records, tapes, books, files,
clothes. I sometimes make snide comments about stereotypical
German characteristics but some of them have always appealed to
me — structure, order, everything in its place. I also tend to take
care of my possessions because it wasn't that long ago that I didn't
have many things.

There was a black woman I knew who owned a little hole-in-
the-wall fashion store around the corner from the Troubadour. This
was in early 1965. Her name was Rita and we used to go dancing
together at Ciro's on Sunset Boulevard. There we'd see Vito, the
madcap artist of Hollywood, with his band of freaks in sandals, long
beards, earrings and beads mingling with the Alpaca sweater and
pipe crowd that used to hang out at PJ's where Trini Lopez and
Johnny Rivers played. The kids trying to emulate the new British
Invasion look were there, letting their hair grow, wearing velvet
coats and the like. It was a real melting pot of L.A. lifestyles. There
was no cover charge, you just had to buy a couple of drinks, and the
people danced constantly. They were dancing to the Byrds.

Jim McGuinn, David Crosby, and Gene Clark, together with
conga player Mike Clarke and bluegrass picker Chris Hillman, had
traded in their acoustic instruments for electric ones to create a
unique musical hybrid combining their traditional folk roots with
the rock 'n' roll beat of the British Invasion. They had created folk
rock. The whole city was abuzz about what the Byrds were doing
down at Ciro's. Even the radio stations got involved. In very short
order, Ciro's became the place to be and the Byrds became the
hippest group in LA. They created a fresh new sound with an electric

twelve-string guitar and folk harmonies. Unlike the British Invasion, I loved it immediately. I saw them several times and felt a real sense of excitement to be at the beginning of something new. It was inspiring to see these guys who I had known a few months earlier as folkies up there on stage making this marvelous new music.

The Byrds had signed with Columbia and had been in the studio to cut *Mr. Tambourine Man* but it had yet to be released. The fact that they didn't have a record out didn't matter. We were all convinced that they had something big. They had the look (the long hair, Beatle boots, and McGuinns' granny glasses), the right material, consisting mainly of Dylan's catalog, and their timing was right, coming as an American response to the chart-dominating British Invasion. What's more, they had the blessing of Dylan himself who was also taking tentative steps toward electric arrangements. Dylan even came down and sat in with them at Ciro's one night when Morgan and I were there, playing harmonica and trading verses with McGuinn on *Tambourine Man*. Folk rock definitely had an impact on me and the direction I would later take as a musician.

Morgan Cavett: *In early 1965, John met this young girl from the Valley named Marsha, a really sweet girl who had recently split up with her boyfriend. The two of them hung out together, kind of a regular steady thing. I had this old 1950 Cadillac and one night John and I drove out to the Valley to see Marsha. The car broke down in Laurel Canyon so we left it and hitchhiked to her apartment. There we were spending a nice evening, her parents were gone, when there was this banging on the door. Marsha looked out and shouted, "Oh my God, it's Bob, my old boyfriend, and fourteen of his friends!" While she staved them off at the door, John and I escaped out the back way and down an alley. We were both big guys but there were a lot of people looking for us. Once we were a safe distance away, John pulled out this big pocket knife, menacing, "If they'd have come after us, I'd have taken care of them!" And I thought, "Christ, now you say this. Why have we been running all this way if you were going to take them all on? You weren't saying that as we were running down the stairs!" It was sort of a delayed macho on his part.*

As my relationship with Marsha grew, she became pregnant. All my fears back in Toronto as a teenager immediately surfaced. "What about our lives? We're too young to look after a baby." We both knew that we weren't planning to get married. I was, in her own words, her "ramblin' boy," more prone to moving on than putting down roots. I had waited too long for the kind of freedom I now enjoyed and I was not about to give it all up. The only solution I could think of was to arrange for an abortion in Tijuana, Mexico. That, unfortunately, was fairly common in those days.

When I called the abortionist place in Tijuana, they said to come down and bring three hundred dollars. Along with another girl and a guy who worked at the Troubadour, I set out to pick up Marsha at home before heading to Mexico. We were on the Cuhuenga Pass going to the Valley when the LAPD pulled us over. I had a couple of bennies on me because I wanted to stay awake for the all night drive. I tucked them between the cushions in the back seat of the car. The guy in the front seat stuffed a joint or two into the glove compartment. The cops approached our car and went through the routine of asking for a driver's license, where we were going, who we all were. It turned out that there was a warrant out for the arrest of the guy in the front seat. The cops proceeded to tear the car apart and the poor girl who owned it freaked out. Unknown to us, her Dad was with the West Hollywood sheriff's department. In their search the cops discovered the grass and the bennies. They impounded the car and took us down to Parker Center, the LAPD station, where we were put in separate rooms and interrogated.

"Jesus Christ", I thought, "Here I am getting busted. I'm supposed to be going to Mexico to score an abortion for this poor girl and everything in my life is falling apart." They questioned me about the bennies and the grass but I played dumb. I told them that as far as I knew the bennies could have been there before I got in; I was in the back seat so I didn't have anything to do with the grass. Meanwhile, the other guy started feeling guilty about the girl and her car so he fessed up to the grass. But the cops were still trying to settle the pills issue, and after more questioning, said to him, "Look, why don't you just say the pills are yours too. It's a one count thing anyway and let's get this over with." So he copped to the bennies too. I managed to squeak out of that mess because of his cooperation. In the end, the girl got her car back once her Dad stepped in.

Upon my release I immediately phoned Marsha. In the intervening hours she had reconsidered, and for reasons of her own, decided against the abortion. Added to that, her old boyfriend got wind of her pregnancy and was looking for me. So I paused to assess the situation: "I just got arrested yesterday, Marsha's decided to keep the baby, some guy from the Valley is out to do me serious harm. This is not the way I want to live my life." Marsha assured me that she definitely wanted to have the baby but planned to put it up for adoption. That was her decision to make and I accepted it. She knew I did not want to be a father at this point in my life and I did not want to feel obligated for us to be together because of the child. Adoption seemed like the best choice for the child and for us both. She later sent me a photograph of the baby, a boy. She was assured that he was given to good home. Although that murky chapter in my life has long been closed, it's one about which I shall always feel unsettled.

Things had soured almost overnight for me. The promised land had turned into a bad B movie. Morgan had split for San Francisco to live with his sister. My mother and stepfather were still in LA but we didn't see each other that often. I was living my own life and not doing a very good job of it. I needed a change of scene so I made plans to head back east to look up my old folkie friends and maybe catch the Newport Folk Festival again. I packed my duffel bag with a couple of changes of jeans and t-shirts, took a sleeping bag, my rancher jacket and cowboy boots, grabbed my guitar, bid farewell to my parents and set off. Although my mother was concerned about what I was doing with my life, she didn't try talking me out of it. Besides, I figured I would go back east for the summer, play a few of my old haunts, bum around a bit, and return to California. I viewed California as my home now.

I hitchhiked back to Buffalo, riding most of the way with a blue collar kind of a guy in an old Ford who dropped me off at the bus station in Gary, Indiana, where I caught a ride to my old hometown. I had only been away from Buffalo a year but I figured things would still be the same, the coffeehouses, my folkie friends. I was in for a surprise. The rock 'n' roll scene had taken its toll on the little folk community there. I couldn't locate any of my old friends. Monte Dunn had gone off with Ian and Sylvia and everyone else had scattered. Many years later I learned that Jackson Frank had left for England where in 1965 he recorded an influential folk album (produced by a then unknown Paul Simon) before drifting into obscurity. I met a young woman who put me up for a few days during which time I played a couple of guest spots at the Limelight, but it had been sold to new owners and the place just wasn't the same.

> *I fried in the sun just outside San Bernardino,*
> *Flagged me a ride in a rattletrap Ford.*
> *Rollin' back east to the northern border,*
> *I'm back in town to find my favorite folk.*
> *But nobody knows, and nobody cares,*
> *'Cause nobody plays here, nobody stays here,*
> *Nobody lives here anymore.*
> *I drift by winos near the Greyhound station,*
> *Searching for shelter like a castaway.*
> *But there are lookers and lechers in a pagan bookstore,*
> *That once held a home where I could sing and play.*

NOBODY LIVES HERE ANYMORE, 1973

In short order, I crossed the border, stuck out my thumb, and hitched a ride up to Toronto. I figured I still had some friends there who would put me up while I sought out a paying gig. I had done enough woodshedding by now, learning tunes, honing my craft, getting my own style together. I was ready to take a shot at something serious. And I thought the best place to do so was Toronto's Yorkville.

Learning to love the blues, California, 1964.

FIVE

MY SPORTIN' LIFE

I sang 'em a glad song, played 'em a sad song
Sang 'em the whole night long
Just for a dollar or what they could offer
To somebody's ramblin' boy
When the fun was done
I would pack my bags and I was gone
Though the women were kind
There was nothing to bind me to one
'Til somebody changed my rough and rowdy ways
Somebody changed my old carousing days
Oh when I was a young boy, I learned to survive
'Til somebody came and stayed my sportin' life

My Sportin' Life, 1973

The Buffalo folk music scene may have died during my absence but Yorkville was flourishing. Yorkville had developed into a breeding ground for folk talent. The level of expertise was astounding compared to what I had seen in Buffalo a year earlier and even in LA. Ian and Sylvia, the real god parents of the Yorkville folk movement, had since moved on to the States, but in their place was a whole crop of fresh new talent, like Gordon Lightfoot, Elyse Weinberg, David Rae, and Joni Mitchell who had drifted in from Saskatoon. Neil Young, recently arrived from Winnipeg, had dropped his rock 'n' roll band to become a Yorkville folk singer.

There were at least a half dozen more coffeehouses going strong and several boutiques. The Village had become a magnet drawing not only the bohemian artistic crowd but also kids from the suburbs who came down to check out the music, the dope, and the vibes. The whole scene had spilled over onto Cumberland and was moving into Hazelton Avenue going all the way up to Bay Street. The New Gate of Cleve, one of the original coffeehouses in Toronto, had moved from Davenport down to the Village next to the Purple Onion and the Half Beat Club on Avenue Road.

There was the Night Owl on the west side of Avenue Road, the Cellar which still featured mostly jazz but occasionally folk, the Penny Farthing, Chez Monique, the Village Corner at Davenport and Avenue Road, the El Patio, and *the* folk club, the Riverboat. On the east side of Avenue Road was Webster's, a real greasy spoon close to the Cellar that everyone went to because it stayed open all night. Further down was the Devil's Den downstairs beneath the Avenue Road Club which attracted the R 'n' B dance crowd with bands like the Five Rogues and Jon, Lee and the Checkmates playing there. By 1965, rock music was starting to infiltrate the Village. A few clubs were experimenting with it while others tried resisting it as long as possible. The Yonge Street bar scene was still going strong featuring bands with mohair suits and short hair, whereas Yorkville was the long hair crowd. The Mont Blanc was the other coffee shop everybody in the Village hung out at. If you wanted to see anybody from the Village community all you had to do was kill time at the Mont Blanc and sooner or later they'd show up.

The Purple Onion had been transformed from a folk to a rock 'n' roll club while I was away. I had seen Buffy Sainte-Marie there in

1963; now it was Luke and the Apostles playing rock 'n' roll. Around the corner was the Grab Bag, originally a pipe shop that had evolved into a hip version of a 7-11 store for all those people who were high and had the munchies. Further along the north side of Yorkville Avenue past the Riverboat, the Mousehole, and the Penny Farthing was the Mynah Bird Club run by Colin Kerr, a true entrepreneur. He originally opened the club as a vehicle to sell mynah birds. Later he organized a band of the same name which featured Raja, a real talking mynah bird he attempted to teach to say "Hello Ed Sullivan" as a gimmick to get the band booked on Sullivan's television show. It never worked, though. He even tried topless dancers and body painting to draw patrons to the club. Typical of the time, there was a go-go girl in a glass case upstairs above the club to attract passersby. Past the Mynah Bird was the Chez Monique, the last club on that side of Yorkville. It was just a regular house that had been gutted on the ground floor with some walls removed. It had bay windows at the front and tucked beneath was a tiny stage protruding into what had once been the living room with a fireplace on the right side.

On the other side of the street was the Club 77, a couple of boutiques, then Old York Lane, which was an alleyway that connected Yorkville to Cumberland where the El Patio was located. The Kiki Rouge, a discotheque after-hours club that didn't have live entertainment, was on Old York Lane. After that a few brownstone apartments, then the Inn On The Parking Lot club on Cumberland, cleverly named as a play on words after the elegant 'Inn On The Park' Hotel in the Don Mills area of Toronto.

During the day business people who worked nearby came and sat outside at the Penny Farthing or the Half Beat for coffee and sandwiches. The local residents, many of them musicians or artists, would be going about their business, meeting friends, getting a bite to eat. In the evening, the Village took on a whole different flavor. People came to enjoy the warm evenings outside, stroll around, or go to coffeehouses. On a Friday or Saturday evening in summer the streets were wall-to-wall people. Everything was geared toward the young. There was a youthful vibrancy about the place, a look, smell, and taste that made it unique. Yorkville was at its peak in 1965 when I hit town.

Within a day or two of my arrival I met Bill Klotzhoff, manager of the Half Beat Club, which was owned by John and Marilyn McHugh who also operated the Penny Farthing. I offered Bill my services as a folk singer, and he invited me to come down that evening to audition. I wound up playing there for several weeks. The club was an old house with a long, narrow front room stretching to the back yard. Small tables lined the room along the walls. At the back, steps led down into a beautiful back yard with a few trees and a fence that separated it from the Purple Onion. Patrons in the front section along Avenue Road had very little room and it was noisy and cramped so Bill had me alternate a set inside and a set outside in the back area. The pay was ten dollars a night for three sets, Wednesday through Sunday, hardly overwhelming but adequate enough for an upstart entertainer. I'd play maybe forty minutes, put my guitar away, roam around Yorkville, make some contacts, check out other places to play, then come back and do the next set. I was billed as "John Kay from California." My sets consisted mainly of the country blues material I had been perfecting over the last year or so. I was doing *The Pusher* and *Red, White and Blue* by Hoyt Axton, *C.C. Rider*, some Lightnin' Hopkins things, my own *Goin' To California, Corinna Corinna, Girl From The North Country, Ramblin' Boy, He Was A Friend Of Mine*, and a few other things, mostly blues.

Bill offered me the basement at the Half Beat to sleep in until I found a place of my own. My needs were simple: a place to stay, enough money for food, cigarettes, a little grass, some change for the laundromat, and bus fare around town. They fed me fairly regularly at the club. It wasn't where I intended to spend the rest of my life but for the moment I had somewhere to go each night.

One day I ran into a kid I knew on the street who invited me to play harmonica at a jam session over at Vicki Taylor's place above the Night Owl. Vicki was a folk singer who played at the Mousehole a few times but, more importantly, she was a strong supporter of young talent. Although she herself never became famous, she can be credited with helping several others on the road to success. As the night wore on joints were passed around and things got relaxed. People started drifting off home, so Vicki turned to me and offered, "If you want to crash here that's fine." So I slept on her living room floor. The next morning we had breakfast together and really hit it off. She invited me to stay at her place and I accepted.

I severed a few old ties during this period. Judy, my German girlfriend from the German youth group, had planned a weekend with me when I broke it off to go do a gig at a coffeehouse in Hamilton with Vicki. Jim Oskirko came by the Half Beat one night and we talked a bit but found our musical interests had diverged. By then I was completely absorbed by the Yorkville scene and a whole new cast of characters. One tie I maintained, albeit rather sporadically, was with my parents in Los Angeles. I was terrible at writing letters but I did let them know I was safe and sound.

I was at a party at Bill Klotzhoff's place above the Half Beat when I met Johnny Sea, a country singer from Nashville who recorded on the Phillips label. At the time, Johnny's manager was nudging him toward playing more folk music. He was gigging at the Edison Hotel on Yonge Street and he invited me down to do a couple of tunes. I did *Red, White And Blue* as well as *He Was A Friend Of Mine*. The crowd liked it. Johnny and I talked afterwards and he invited me to come see him at the Bitter End in New York. It was August, so I figured I would follow through with my original plan when I left LA and hitchhike to the Newport Festival. On the way back I could hit New York and look up Johnny.

Once again Newport was a re-affirmation for me. There was so much great music being made everywhere. One of the more memorable acts I saw was Jose Feliciano flatpicking *Flight Of The Bumble Bee* on nylon string guitar. It was totally unorthodox but he blew even the purists away with his speed. I remember thinking, "This guy's playing faster than I can listen." Electric music was starting to creep in, causing some controversy. The Butterfield Blues Band debuted there and I thought their electric Chicago blues was great. The Byrds' *Mr. Tambourine Man* was already a runaway hit. Dylan took his cue and strapped on a Fender electric guitar for a short electric set backed up by Butterfield's band. It was a disaster, a chorus of boos forcing him to flee the stage. The purists were stunned. Their anointed one had forsaken them.

I met a girl from Brooklyn there who invited me to stay with her in New York. I used the opportunity to check out Greenwich Village much closer. The first place I went to was McDougall Street which was *the* street in the Village. I found some club that Dylan had allegedly played at in his early days. It was hoot night so I signed up to perform. The manager said kind of stand-offishly to me, "Am I supposed to know you?" Apparently you had to have a bit of a name or have someone recommend you in order to perform so I didn't get to play there. The next place I stumbled into was the less than reputable Café Why Not, not to be confused (or possibly to be confused) with the legendary Café Wha across the street where at that same time a young Jimi Hendrix was performing under the name Jimmy James. The Café Why Not was the width of a beach towel, so skinny it only had tables along one side of the wall. There was a stage slapped together from orange crates with a stool, one lamp, one microphone, and little dinky speakers. Outside, the guy was hawking like you would witness the second coming inside.

They put my 8 x 10 outside and I did my half hour set. Five sets a night, same damn songs. The scam was that the joint had three performers who would each do a half hour set, one after the other. Within an hour and a half, all three were done. Then the first act had to go back on and play the exact same set as he had done before. The reasoning was that if Maynard and Mabel from Ohio were still sitting there saying, "I'm gonna get my five bucks worth, by gum," eventually Mabel would say, "Maynard, we heard that boy. He's singing the same songs again. Come on, let's go." When you were done with your set, you took your basket and walked by all the patrons waiting for them to drop some coin in. Some of the more seasoned hustlers would not pass a customer until they coughed it up. These guys would get really blatant about it because often tourists could be easily intimidated. "We're on vacation, Maynard. For God's sake, give the boy some money and let's get out of here." The whole thing was based on the lemming condition: shoe horn enough people into this dinky little joint and if they see other people putting money in, they'll do the same. Some nights I went away with twenty-five bucks.

I went to see Johnny Sea at the Bitter End a couple of times while in New York. Once while I was back stage visiting him before he went on, I noticed this little guy talking to himself. It made me uneasy just watching him because he was so nervous. Everybody shared the same dressing room so he was off in a corner trying to memorize his act before he went on. I remember thinking to myself,

"Why does he put himself through all this grief?" It turned out to be Woody Allen doing a guest set, working out some new material. Years later I played the Bitter End with the John Kay Band and found myself in that same dressing room.

Because I never had a steady paying gig in Greenwich Village, the experience in the basket joints colored my view with a slightly negative tint. Greenwich didn't seem to have the positive community spirit that pervaded Yorkville. The two had different flavors: Greenwich was more aggressive, more New York hustle, while Yorkville was more innocent, more relaxed, friendly, fresher. Following my fling in Greenwich Village, I was back in Toronto for my regular gig at the Half Beat.

At another of Bill's get togethers above the Half Beat, I met Art Ayre, a piano player in a rock band called The Sparrows. We were taking turns trading songs and harmonizing when Art leaned over to me and said, "Why don't you come over to the Devil's Den sometime and play harmonica with my band?" I didn't know at the time that The Sparrows had scored a number one record in Toronto a year or so earlier as Jack London and the Sparrows.

Jerry Edmonton: *My brother, Dennis McCrohan, and a friend Dave Marden, or Jack London as he called himself, had started the band in Oshawa, east of Toronto. They took the name Sparrows from the Hawks, though sparrows didn't sound quite as menacing. Their drummer couldn't make a commitment, so Dennis knew that I played a bit of drums and suggested me. We were all still teenagers. When the British Invasion thing took off we jumped on the bandwagon, especially Dave Marden. Whenever I'd go over to his house, he'd be talking with this English accent. Then I'd hear him talking to his Mom in a normal accent. When people were around he went into this thing about how he was from Liverpool. Strange guy. Then we all had to put on these fake British accents. Once when we went to Niagara Falls and were eating roast beef in this restaurant, a very British place, the waiter came up and asked us what we would like for dessert. So Dave, or Jack London, in his best fake British accent says, "Yorkshire pudding." The waiter just stared at him in amazement. Then Jack caught on and went, "Ha ha, just joking."*

Dennis and I never legally changed our name to Edmonton, (I'm still McCrohan). We used Edmonton for a couple of reasons. We wanted it to sound English and also because our Dad had the Jubilee Auditorium in Oshawa, a big dance hall, and he was in competition with places we'd be playing. So I felt that if they found out we were that guy's kids they wouldn't book us. Thinking about it now, McCrohan sounds more British than Edmonton. At the time though, we just figured it was the thing to do. If you wanted to be a star you had to have this star name.

Bruce Palmer ended up in the band after we moved to Toronto to do gigs around there. Art Ayre joined us on keyboards. Art was a jazz musician and the first guy to introduce me to grass. Not long after, we traded Bruce to the Mynah Birds for their bass player, Nick St. Nicholas. Neil Young joined the Mynah Birds before he and Bruce headed for California to form the Buffalo Springfield. We signed with Capitol Records of Canada and recorded an album and some singles, one of them reaching number one in Toronto. We thought we were famous.

Jack had signed the Capitol Records deal so he would go in and collect the royalties and we'd see him the next day with a new fur coat, going out to the restaurants. We just thought, "Someday we'll get our royalties." Later we found out he got all the royalties. I don't ever remember getting a penny. And he became a jerk, basically. There was a 'hate Jack' feeling starting amongst the rest of us in the band. One night at the Avenue Road Club, Nick looked over at me like, "Watch this." He knew Jack was going to swing around and do this big move he always did so Nick moved the head of his bass right up where Jack was going and when he swung around he hit his head on Nick's bass. It was, "Oh, sorry Jack." We just reached a point where we figured we didn't need him. Dennis was doing most of the writing and all of us were singing so we went our separate ways. That's when we started gigging at the Devil's Den.

A few nights later, I wandered over to see The Sparrows and sat in with them. The Devil's Den was in a basement with a concrete floor, a stage, low ceiling, and kids in groovy clothes doing the Watusi. The hippie thing hadn't happened yet; it was more the Mod, go-go fashion. I sat at the edge of the stage and we did a couple of blues tunes like *Bright Lights, Big City* and *C.C. Rider,* singing and playing mouth harp. People liked it well enough, and the guys in The Sparrows did as well. We did this once or twice more over the course of the next few weeks, me dropping in after my gig at the Half Beat. I got to know the guys in the band and found them fairly compatible. They were in the process of jettisoning the British pop-rock image for a bluesier style — Jimmy Reed, Paul Butterfield, that kind of approach — so they liked what I added to their sound. But as far as I was concerned they were a group of nice guys who just wanted to jam.

An English fellow hanging out in the Village named Bill Benson, who had seen me at the Half Beat and witnessed one of my jam sessions with The Sparrows, approached them first then spoke to me regarding the notion of my joining the band permanently. With that combination, he thought he could get us work in England. For my part, I liked the fuller sound that a band offered. There was an intensity and excitement that was absent from performing solo on acoustic guitar. I couldn't match the sheer balls of a full band — bass, drums, electric guitars. Being a part of a band increased the possibility of success, perhaps making records. So I was definitely interested in the proposal. There were changes going down in The Sparrows at that time anyway; Art Ayre was leaving to pursue jazz full time. Before anything was discussed between us, The Sparrows had to decide whether they wanted me. Jerry wrestled with the idea of whether it would be good for the band. Dennis, ever analytical, thought it might be worthwhile, and Nick loved the idea. Nick and I shared much in common. He was born Klaus Karl Kassbaum in 1943 in Plön, near Kiel in the Schleswig-Holstein region of Germany. His father had run a stationery store there before the family emigrated to Canada in 1951.

Nick St. Nicholas: *When we started playing at the Devil's Den there was no rock 'n' roll in Yorkville Village, it was all folk music. I went over to the Devil's Den, the old Avenue Road club, and with some friends we cleaned it up, built a little stage and made that into a rock club. We became one of the first bands to play in the Village. The Penny Farthing tried out rock 'n' roll on off-nights and we played there once. I remember because one of our speakers fell* *off the back of a booth and hit some lady in the head while we were playing there.*

Initially, what attracted me to John was his vocal quality and the kind of songs he was singing. He had a real casual presence yet there was a lot of depth to what he was singing about. He made the songs sound real and put himself into them. He was playing Goin' To California, Corinna Corinna, Hootchie Kootchie Man, *and* The Pusher. *It kind of registered that this guy could possibly be a singer in a band. We would have two guitars and a lead singer. So I proposed the idea of him being a part of what we were doing. His whole image then — the acoustic guitar, the wandering minstrel — made him more worldly than we were and I was intrigued by his presence. He was always 'Rope' to me. That's what I called him. He was his own man. He liked to do things his own way on his own time. So I was very fond of him. He was the first guy I ever met who used the word 'clap'; when I first met him he asked me to find him a doctor because he had the clap.*

John and I got along all right from the start but my fondness for him grew even more so the day we were up in Scarborough where my Dad ran a speed skating rink. We came back from a gig out of town and were in the parking lot. These two older guys who were drunk from a wedding reception started calling us long-haired freaks. I was first out of the car and asked them what they were doing there. They immediately attacked me, pounding on me and dragging me down on the ground. John got out of the car and protected me, fought them off and helped me overcome this attack. John rescued me and I've never forgotten that.

Jerry Edmonton: *My first impression of John was, "His hair doesn't look right." It was all slicked back. He looked more like James Dean, black hair, greasy and combed back. He was an interesting person from the first time I met him. He was a bit pudgy and he was wearing white Levis which I thought was odd. He called himself "John Kay from California" but actually I thought he was more Spanish from down near Mexico because of his dark complexion and dark hair. But he was playing blues and that's what I liked about him. After John joined, I took him down to Cy Mann's for some decent clothes and we washed his hair. Bill*

Benson, this guy from England who Nick's girlfriend Solveigh knew, suggested that John join us. He went back to England to line up gigs for us but we never heard from him again. I remember telling girls in Yorkville that we were going to leave for England and they were crying, "Oh, you can't leave us."

Because he was from California, or so we thought, meeting John was kind of exciting. I was just a kid from Oshawa so just talking to him about California, him being on the road, and the style of music he was playing — Jimmy Reed, John Lee Hooker, Muddy Waters — was kind of exciting. What John played with Dennis on guitar was a real interesting sound that made The Sparrows' sound unique. He always gave us the feeling that there was something more down the road. He had been out there and he had an experience that we didn't have, so he kind of instilled a sense of adventure in us as well as a sense of security, even though we never knew sometimes what might be around the corner. With John, we always felt it would all work out.

In The Sparrows, Jerry sang the Rolling Stones, Manfred Mann, Jimmy Reed stuff, Nick did *Walkin' The Dog* and some of the R 'n' B rockers, and Dennis sang the ballads. He also had an electric twelve string for the Byrdsy things. Art did a bit of singing too. They had their own tunes that Dennis wrote but were beginning to listen to the real funky blues. Bill Benson wanted to propose his merger idea so he invited me to come out to the Commodore Hotel in Kingston, a couple of hundred miles or so east of Toronto, to see The Sparrows' last night there. We arrived in time to catch the end of their second set. It was a typical lounge with the stage on the short side of the room directly facing the bar which had mirrors on the wall behind it. They finished up, came over and proceeded to tell Bill and I what a nightmare the gig had been. All their Fender amps were turned towards the curtains to reduce the volume. The manager complained constantly about the noise. Jerry pointed to him at the bar and vowed, "That fat toad's been on us all week. 'Turn it down! Turn it down!' I've had it. We've been paid, we're packed and ready to go. This is the last set ever in this place, but just wait until we get to *Stormy Monday*. We've got a surprise for that guy." They went up and proceeded to play their final set, very subdued. When they came to the guitar solo in *Stormy Monday* — it's a quiet, slow blues tune, Dennis took his little finger, cranked the volume on his Telecaster full blast, and hit an E chord BLAAANG! as loud as he could. Glasses started dancing around on the shelves in front of the mirrors behind the bar. Up to this point the manager had been sitting on a stool at the bar smiling because the boys were finally playing at a decent level. When he heard that chord his jaw dropped and the cigar fell from his lips. As the band packed up their equipment, he told them never to come back. No problem. That night in mid-September of 65 I joined The Sparrows.

The guys shared an apartment on St. George Avenue near the Village and they asked me to move in with them so that Dennis could show me a lot of the guitar parts I had to learn. My playing rhythm guitar freed him up to do more lead playing. I informed Vicki that I was moving out. It wasn't a very traumatic parting because we always knew that our relationship was temporary. A week later I returned to pick up a few odds and ends and met another fellow there. Vicki introduced him: "This is a singer/songwriter from Winnipeg named Neil Young." He had just dropped his band after working their way from Winnipeg to Toronto. We said hello and talked briefly. He had a guitar, I played him something, and we talked about music. I got the impression that he was a singer primarily who used his guitar to back up his vocals. I didn't know he was a lead guitarist. He went off into the bedroom, I finished my business with Vicki, and we said our goodbyes. That was the last time I ever saw her. I ran into Neil a year and a half later in LA when he was with the Buffalo Springfield.

When I joined The Sparrows, Art Ayre was replaced by the ex-keyboard player from the Mynah Birds. The Mynah Birds were fronted by Rick James (Rickey James Matthews as he was known then), a self-styled black Mick Jagger. Rick James was becoming a bit of a legend on the Toronto scene. He lived in an apartment beneath my future wife in Yorkville but was such a party animal that he was thrown out in short order. Bruce Palmer, who had originally been in Jack London and The Sparrows, was now the bass player in the Mynah Birds. Bruce was one of the nicest guys I met in the Village, always getting people together to make music. The Mynah Birds played in Yorkville regularly and were getting a lot of attention, especially after millionaire retailer John Craig Eaton threw his financial clout behind them. Neil Young joined them for a brief spell when they signed with Motown Records. John Goadsby, or Goldy McJohn as he soon became known, had already left the Mynah Birds by then. Goldy came on board the same weekend I did and we went off to Oshawa to rehearse in the McCrohan's garage for our first gig two nights later at Waterloo Lutheran University.

Jerry Edmonton: *We auditioned Goldy then he went home and we contemplated whether we liked him or not. All of a sudden Goldy showed up at our door with his suitcases. He had left his family, he had a wife and kid, quit his job selling shoes and was ready to go on the road. So we thought, "Oh shit, what are we going to do now? I guess he's in the band." We felt bad for him so we let him join but we really weren't sure we wanted him.*

Goldy was a funny guy, kind of a class clown who would do just about anything for a laugh. He was very entertaining on stage. The five of us learned thirty songs that weekend to prepare for our first gig. Goldy had a Lowery organ, the kind people had in their living rooms, with a little Leslie speaker, and I had my J-45 acoustic with a D'Armand pick-up slapped in the sound hole. I plugged into one of their Fender Bassman amps and it sounded okay. I did the growly stuff, the 'in-your-face' tunes, because I had that gritty kind of voice (you should have heard my version of Barry McGuire's *Eve of Destruction*!) that gave the band the heaviness they had been lacking. The Sparrows' fans seemed to like the changes. We went down well at that first gig and received the phenomenal fee of one thousand dollars. I thought to myself, "These guys are doing okay!" It was the biggest crowd I had ever played for, the most money I'd ever received.

As the weeks went by, we worked some of my solo material into the act, blues tunes like *Hootchie Kootchie Man* and *Goin' To California*, and began to develop our own musical identity. I brought *The Pusher* out from the West Coast, and when we performed it in Toronto, people thought we wrote it. Hoyt Axton's popularity was predominantly in the Western States, only marginal on the East Coast and almost non existent in Toronto. The band arrangement had a lot more balls than the acoustic version, the electric lead guitar giving it more punch.

Because we all lived together we could spend more time working songs out. Everybody seemed to have a role in the band. Jerry was the treasurer, looking after all the bills, and he also cooked breakfast. He was a real practical kind of guy. Dennis was practicing a lot, developing his guitar chops and songwriting. Nick was the hustler, dealing with the agents and getting the gigs. I did a lot of playing with Dennis initially and started to write more. Goldy was still living with his father in North Toronto. These guys were well-organized. They had a record deal with Capitol, money in their pockets and a few bucks in the bank, a charge account at Long and McQuade musical instruments store, a leased 1965 Chevy station wagon and a U-Haul trailer, plus the band apartment. They paid for all this and still had enough money left per person that was rather respectable for the times.

Jerry took me down to a tailor shop on Yonge Street to acquire some pop clothes. I had some corduroy pants made, got a pair of Beatle boots, a suede black sports coat with black leather lapels, and an ugly green shirt. I'm color blind, so what did I know? My wife later made me throw it out. It was the first time I had come out of the jeans-and-Levi's jacket folk musician uniform.

We lived the life of typical Yorkville denizens: sleep late, get up, go to the Mont Blanc for breakfast, regain consciousness, go over to the Chez Monique or El Patio for an afternoon rehearsal, break for dinner, return to the club by nine, play two or three sets and finish at midnight or so depending on the crowd. Then we'd go hang out with other musicians until all hours. There was a lot of networking between players going on in Yorkville. Our usual routine consisted of playing Yorkville during the week, then one nighters on weekends — dances, high schools, out of town gigs in places like St. Catherine's, Hamilton, Galt and as far away as Ottawa. By late 1965 there was a feeling that something was definitely happening in Yorkville. Gordon Lightfoot was already flying high after his songs *Early Morning Rain* and *For Lovin' Me* were recorded first by Ian and Sylvia then by Peter, Paul and Mary. Joni Mitchell caught a lot of attention but had already moved on to greener pastures.

Gradually, the Yonge Street tavern crowd and the Yorkville coffeehouse scene began to merge in a cross-pollination of musical approaches. People like David Clayton Thomas, The Paupers, and Roy Kenner and the Associates started playing in both places. We often hung out with The Paupers after hours. The Ugly Ducklings were playing regularly at Charlie Brown's on Cumberland Street behind the El Patio. J.B. and the Playboys from Montreal played at the Night Owl. Some coffeehouses like the Penny Farthing, Mousehole, and Riverboat stuck to folk music as long as they could. I saw Jesse Colin Young at the Riverboat as well as David Blue. Lonnie Johnson, one of the founding fathers of the blues, had moved up to Yorkville from the States because he was so well received there. I hung out with him a few times. He was truly a gentleman. The Purple Onion kept its feet in both camps — folk music one week, rock the next.

Because The Sparrows had a record contract, we recorded some demos for Capitol Records with Marshall Shapiro producing. The first session included *He Was A Friend Of Mine, Hootchie Kootchie Man,* and *C.C. Rider.* However, nothing was released. We later cut some of my tunes, including my first foray into social commentary, *Square Headed People,* basically about the square contingent of society giving me a hard time. Marshall suggested that it might not be appropriate because "square heads" was a derogatory term some people applied to Germans. Capitol passed and eventually the contract lapsed. We weren't into being a pop band. *The Pusher* and *Hootchie Kootchie Man* were hardly top forty material.

A month or so after I joined The Sparrows, Nick came up with a week's engagement at the Belton Hotel in Sudbury, a tough mining town about 250 miles north of Toronto. We were given two rooms and a rollaway bed and we played four sets a night in the beverage room. Nick thought it was a good idea because, besides paying decent money, we could rehearse during the day. He was kind of the disciplinarian, always wanting us to keep improving. The hotel had seen better days but at least the rooms were clean. As we were setting up our gear, some guy arrived with two go-go girls, maybe eighteen years old, straight out of high school. They had never done this kind of thing before. They were wearing sparkly tops, mini skirts with tassels, and white go-go boots. They were booked to dance for the last fifteen minutes of each set as sort of a kicker. We weren't too keen on this but no one we knew was going to be in Sudbury to see us humiliate ourselves.

The audience consisted of miners, lumberjacks, soldiers, construction workers on the Trans-Canada Highway, and maybe two women, probably working girls. All they wanted was to get drunk, hear the music they wanted to hear, see some tits and ass. Here we were, a long-haired band in Mod clothes, straight from Yorkville's hip scene, used to playing to stoned crowds at Chez Monique. Something told us these guys didn't want to hear *The Pusher*, so we sprinkled our sets with things like *Wooly Bully* and *Mohair Sam*, both of which Goldy sang. We finished the first set and got a bit of a hassle from a couple of guys who kept yelling to hear this song and that song and making wisecracks about our hair. There were two hefty lads at the front table, one of whom was a big black dude, a miner. Early in the first set he hollered out, "You guys know *Walkin' The Dog*?" It was Nick's big number. We played it and he loved it. From that moment on he was our buddy. If anyone gave us a hard time, he just glared at them and they'd shut right up. He was there at least every other night and we played *Walkin' The Dog* every set.

With our long hair we couldn't really go anywhere in Sudbury and it wasn't safe for the girls to be out alone, so we hung around in our rooms all week. One night I awoke to find this bizarre vision before me: the four remaining members of The Sparrows nude except for neck ties, and the two girls completely nude standing over me giggling. All I could muster was, "Nice ties." We made it through the week to the last set on the final night when Goldy disappeared. He was nowhere to be found, so we limped along without him. About three tunes into the set, Goldy popped up out of nowhere. Apparently he had been in his room with some girl and just when he was getting ready to come play some guy started pounding on the door yelling, "Emily, are you in there?" So Goldy waited until the guy was gone then climbed through the window, down the fire escape, and into the beverage room.

Back in Toronto, there was a definite buzz starting to build around us. We did a photo session for *Maclean's* magazine (Canada's version of *Newsweek*) wearing the latest pop fashion outfits in some trendy nightclub. We opened for Gary Lewis and the Playboys at

Massey Hall. That was the first time I had ever experienced scream-ing kids. It didn't matter who you were, if you had long hair and were on stage, they screamed. By now the media was starting to take note of the Yorkville music scene. We were featured in a cou-ple of newspaper articles and did some television shows — *After Four* and *Au Go Go 66*. Throughout all this, Yorkville remained our base of operations.

In October 1965, Nick secured an unusual engagement for us, a week at the Sapphire Lounge and Restaurant in downtown Toronto. It was a traditional dinner and nightclub establishment with lob-sters in the tank and an over-forty dance crowd. The place had come to the realization that their clientele was dying out, literally, and they needed a new approach to bring in younger patrons. Their plan was to hire some hip entertainment. They had booked the Mynah Birds who had gone down well. Nick saw this kind of high class gig as a way to attract wealthy backers. He had been hustling John Craig Eaton who, at the time, was looking to dabble in rock bands, but much to Nick's dismay, he chose to back the Mynah Birds instead of us.

At the Lounge one night, Nick said to me, "I've brought my girlfriend Solveigh and her friend Jutta. Why don't you come over to the table and meet them." I had met Solveigh Schattmann already. She was German, born in German-occupied Czechoslovakia during the war but raised in Dusseldorf and Munich. She had come to Canada in 1963 as an *au pair* before quitting to head for Yorkville to work as a waitress in the coffeehouses. Sitting next to Solveigh was a girl with very short dark hair, dark eye make-up as was the fashion then, high cheek bones, a tight white sweater and short skirt. Nick introduced her to me as Jutta Maue. I was immediately taken by her. She had an easy-going demeanor that I responded to instantly. She was not brash, yet confident and very natural in the way she han-dled herself. I found myself perfectly at ease and chatting with her within a few minutes.

After the gig, the four of us ended up at Solveigh's apartment above the Harlequin House in Yorkville. Jutta lived on her own in a room at 17 Lowther Avenue, the same direction as The Sparrows' apartment on St. George. After awhile, Jutta said good night and left. Seizing the opportunity, I bid a hasty farewell and tried to catch up with her to walk her home. At first she wasn't sure who was following her and tried to outwalk me. When I finally caught up with her she was relieved to find it was me. We talked until reaching her door, then she invited me up. I came in and stayed. Twenty-nine years later, we're still together.

Jutta Maue-Kay: *John and I had very similar backgrounds. I was born in Hamburg, Germany in February 1944. My father had been a house painter until he was drafted into the infantry. He was home when I was born but returned to the Russian Front soon after and was killed two months later, May 1944, just outside of Leningrad. My mother was on her own with two girls; my sister was six years older. Like so many other war widows in Germany, she remarried in 1947 but unfortunately there were slim pickins' in the men department after the war and my stepfather was not much of a prize. He had served in the German Marine (U-Boat Service) and apparently deserted while in the US. How he made it back to Germany, I don't know. Like John's mother, my mother told me that my father was the love of her life and that she had married my stepfather more out of convenience to give my sister and me a father.*

Hamburg was bombed badly by the Allies in 1945 because it was the most important harbor in Germany. You can still see areas in ruins. As children, we would play among them.

My stepfather was very authoritarian, and he and my mother were always fighting, so I would go out all the time to get away. I started going to the clubs. I was sort of a rebel. In Hamburg there were some great clubs back then. I was into jazz and skiffle at first, the existentialism movement and the beatnik thing. Then I discovered rock 'n' roll. The St. Pauli district near the harbor front was a very loose and sleazy district where the sailors went. All the strip clubs were there and the prostitutes sat in open windows. That's where the best rock 'n' roll clubs were like the Top Ten with Tony Sheridan, Lonnie Donegan, and the early Beatles. Then the Star Club opened later on with the Beatles and I would see them every night. They would start at eleven and play every hour until early morning. Among others I saw Bill Haley, Gene Vincent, Ray Charles, and Little Richard.

I left home at age eighteen. I always wanted to go to art school but I completed high school and started working because I wasn't allowed to pursue any higher education. I had to go out to work to pay my mother and stepfather back so I went to work at a newspaper in the ad department taking ads. Then a girlfriend of mine from school showed me an ad for an au pair job in Toronto, Canada. The agency supplied the working visa for one year and paid for the flight over. She chickened out so I went instead.

I knew very little about Canada before I arrived. I thought it was all polar bears and igloos. But I was never a worrier. I had one suitcase, a little raincoat, a hundred dollars, and my high-school English which was very limited. I arrived in Toronto about 2 o'clock in the morning and all that was there was this little wooden shack in the middle of nowhere. They were about to build the new airport. My first reaction was, "Oh my god, what have I done." I arrived in Canada the day of the Cuban Missile Crisis, October 22, 1962.

The next day I went to work for a family in the well-heeled, upper crust Forest Hills area of Toronto. I received room and board and a hundred dollars a month from which they deducted sixty for the flight until I had it paid off. I had some hassles with the woman so I worked until it was paid off and then I left.

The first people I met were some Germans on New Year's Eve, 1962 who invited me up to Parry Sound just north of Toronto for a party. That's where I met Solveigh. She had come as an au pair and was ready to leave her employer, too. We had come over the same time, were the same age, almost the same height, both German kids in a strange country so we hit it off right away. We're the best of friends still.

Not long after that I started going out with an Austrian fellow who had in apartment in Yorkville. That was in April, 1963 and Yorkville was just starting to happen. I hung out at the Club 77, a real bohemian place run by Werner Ehrhart who gave me a job waiting tables. Solveigh moved there soon after I did and the two of us became very popular waitresses in the Village. There was an article in the Toronto Telegram *on Solveigh, myself, and a few other waitresses that referred to us as "the Belles of Yorkville." Later I went over to the Half Beat and worked there. I also worked at the Penny Farthing, managing the place for a time and living upstairs. When Bernie Fiedler opened The Riverboat and all the big*

*names in folk music came there to perform, Solveigh and I worked
for him. Bernie used to be a coffee salesman to all the coffeehouses
in the Village and he learned well before he opened his own place.
Later I worked in a club on Avenue Road called The Trip. That was
a happening place for a while run by a friend of mine named
Woody. I was the model in all their advertisements.*

   *I had the best time back then in Toronto. I was underage, under
twenty-one, but I had a fake ID. An artist friend changed my
birthdate on the card from 44 to a 41. I got caught a couple of times
for it but that never stopped me. It was really an artists, musicians,
bohemian scene then in the Village, before it became
commercialized with all the tourists. I hung out with a lot of
interesting people. I did some modeling and a little acting on CBC-
TV's* Nightcap *show. We ran with a pretty dangerous crowd for a
time, gamblers, older guys from Cabbagetown, and I worked at some
of their poker games. They didn't talk about what they did but they
were nice people and would take Solveigh and I out on the town,
fancy restaurants, classy nightclubs. It was just a real fun time.*

   *When Solveigh started going out with Nick, I met The Sparrows.
Nick was this cutesy guy but he was fun. He and Solveigh had a
relationship but Nick was more like one of the girls. He liked to
hang out with us and learn about make-up and clothes. It was kind
of an androgynous, show business thing. Jerry was always very
serious I thought, and Dennis was Dennis. I don't think anybody
really knew him except his family. I hung out with Art Ayre a
couple of times, then Nick introduced me to John who Nick said
was from California. There was a spark there right away. He
actually followed me home the first night claiming he was going my
way. I heard these footsteps behind me on my way to Lowther
Street where I lived at the time. He didn't say much but I thought
he was very interesting. It didn't take us long to get together.*

In short order, I moved out of the band apartment and in with Jutta.
We had similar schedules, both working nights. She had started
working at the Kiki Rouge because the money was better. If the band
was gigging in the Village, we would be within walking distance of
each other, so I'd go over to the Kiki Rouge after our gig and wait for
her to finish her shift. Then we'd go over to the Colonnade on Bloor

FIVE: **MY SPORTIN' LIFE**

Street for something to eat, go back to her place, and make wild passionate love until all hours of the morning, then sleep until two or so in the afternoon. We'd get up, watch *The Funny Company* on TV or listen to some blues records, maybe smoke a joint, then we were ready to face the day. We'd go to the Grab Bag and buy tons of cookies; our money went for grass and cookies. This routine went on for a number of months, through the winter of 1965-66. It was one of the best periods of my life — carefree, fulfilling, and exciting on every level. Jutta is the only woman I've ever loved.

It seems like a rather odd coincidence that four German immigrants, two boys and two girls all born during the war with similar postwar experiences, could come together in Yorkville. But there had been a lot of emigration from Germany after the war and many settled in Toronto and the Yorkville scene was a small enough place that we would have been bound to meet there anyway because of our interest in music. That's what brought us together. Initially, however, Jutta didn't know that I was German. As far as she was concerned, I was the guy from California who blew into town, knew the Byrds, and so on. That was Nick's idea, Nick the promoter crafting an image, looking for a gimmick to make the band different or more interesting.

Jutta Maue-Kay: *Nick introduced him to me as 'John Kay from California' and his English was flawless. I detected no accent at all. We were together a few nights later at Solveigh's — John and I had spent our first night together the night before — and there was Nick and Solveigh, John and I. John was sitting on the couch, very quiet, just listening. We had smoked a bit of grass and Solveigh and I were doing our girl talk in German, going on about, "So how was it last night . . . ?" Nick understood us cause he still knew German but he was just like one of the girls anyway so on we went jabbering away, with John just sitting there saying nothing. Then, out of the blue, Nick said, "You know, John's German don't you?" And I said, "No, he's from California." Nick replied, "He understands German and speaks it fluently." I turned to John and he had this big grin on his face, but didn't say a word. I refused to believe it and kept saying to him, "Come on, say something in German." Finally he did and it was perfect German! Oh God, I*

*think I turned beet red. He had listened to every single word we had
said and never let on. I was so embarrassed. He loved it.*

The guys in The Sparrows were pretty naive about drugs, in particular Dennis and Nick, who were straight as arrows. Nick had bought
into the whole Reefer Madness thing and didn't want to know anything about drugs of any kind. I didn't know about Goldy but I figured he was straight, too. Only Jerry had tried grass, turned onto it
by Art Ayre who hung out with the jazzers but he was cool about it
because he knew how Dennis and Nick felt. Jerry and I smoked
some but didn't tell the others.

Jerry Edmonton: *John was much more experienced in the drug world
than any of us. I mean, we were kids from Oshawa. What did we
know? We thought Nick was weird because he was from Toronto.*

Nick St. Nicholas: *John would give us drug classes. We would all sit
down and he would tell us what happened to you on grass and
LSD. He had been to California so knew all about this stuff. He
encouraged all of us to experiment, to open up.*

One night at Chez Monique, in walked this guy I knew from the
Troubadour back in LA. He was just back from a tour of Alaska with
the New Christie Minstrels and said to me, "I've got some acid here,
do you want it?" So he gave me some and I put it away. The next
day I asked Jerry if he wanted to do this acid with me and he agreed.
We went back to Solveigh's apartment and asked her if we could
drop acid at her place away from the band apartment. She was going
out so she said it was okay. It was early morning so we figured we
could trip during the day and be down by the time we had to play
that night at Chez Monique. Sure enough, within half an hour
things were beginning to change. This stuff was far more potent
than anything I had taken in California. Jutta came over, saw what
was happening (she was hip to acid) and decided to leave us alone to
our trip. Jerry and I got the munchies so we opened up Solveigh's
fridge but all she had was a jar of peanut butter. I made the mistake
of taking a finger of it and spent the next three hours licking my
lips. After awhile we noticed it was getting dark and we were still

really high. Realizing we had to play in a few hours, we figured we had better see whether we were in any shape to play our instruments. I picked up a guitar and started to strum it but my fingers seemed to go right through the neck. I knew we were in trouble but we convinced ourselves that if we didn't think about being stoned, we could pull it off.

Yeah, sure! By the time nine o'clock rolled around, we left for Chez Monique. Thank god it was only down the block and a weeknight in winter, so there were few people on the streets. As we came out of the apartment and hit the street, who should pop up in front of us but Freddie McNulty. Freddie was a mentally limited guy that everybody in the Village knew. He hung out with the Hawks and convinced himself that he was a member of the band, like their mascot. Jerry and I were higher than kites but trying to keep it cool and together. The sidewalk was only wide enough for two people side by side so we just kept on walking. Meanwhile, Freddie, however, wanted to talk. He would be walking in the gutter then bopping in front and around us and in the condition we were in, he looked like a gremlin. He was driving us crazy so finally Jerry yelled, "Freddie, for Christ sakes, stand still!" Freddie freaked out and ran off.

We arrived at the club and there were all of six people in attendance, all fans we knew, so Jerry and I still figured it was cool. We kept telling ourselves, "It's Chez Monique, it's a week night, six people, no pressure, just relax, it'll be fine." The other guys had no idea that Jerry and I were on Mars at that point. We picked up our instruments and played the first number. All of a sudden the band sounded like a giant pre-historic animal. The sound just went, "ARRRRRGH!!" like some great beast screaming. I turned my head and the sound kept changing. I looked at my hands and everything seemed okay so I sang my first number and made it through with no problems. Jerry and I kept grinning at one another. I looked over at Goldy and he was grinning back at us like, "Those guys are really having a good time tonight." Meanwhile, Nick and Dennis couldn't figure out what was so funny.

There was one solitary light shining onto the stage at such an angle that it hit the cymbal on Jerry's drum kit. The hammered pattern of indentations on the cymbal surface reflected up creating a spiral of what looked like sparks going off everytime Jerry hit it. We both got hung up staring at these sparks, grooving on the images. I was in the middle of *Hootchie Kootchie Man* and I had no idea what the hell I was singing. It sounded like another language to me.

Jerry Edmonton: *By that point, it was too much to handle. I was trying to sing Bob Dylan's* Like A Rolling Stone *and it has ten million lyrics so I was singing, "Once upon a time, you dressed so fine, what the fuck is the next line?" And I couldn't go on. John grinned at me and I just fell off my drum stool in between the cymbals and the snare, cackling hysterically. Naturally, when the drummer stops, the rest of the band stops.*

Jerry and I were laughing and falling off the stage and the six kids in the audience thought we were just having a yuk. I motioned to the DJ to play a record and we all congregated in the back kitchen where Monique was ranting, "You guys have only been on for fifteen minutes. What's going on?" Meantime, Dennis must have asked Jerry what the problem was and Jerry told him we had taken some acid. So Dennis, in his calm and rational way, told Monique that a couple of us had taken some pills and couldn't play but that we would make it up to her another night. I was going, "Pills?! Pills?! I've just hooked into the deeper meaning of the universe, for God sake!" We were still high when the sun came up the next morning.

Jutta Maue-Kay: *Solveigh and I had gotten into the whole drug scene in Yorkville, especially marijuana, and I loved it. It was much more innocent in those days. That's where all my money went. Nick was very straight back then. Solveigh and I did acid for the first time at her apartment with a few other friends and we had such a ball — lots of fun and laughter, the lights out, just candle light.*

Solveigh and I experimented with heroin and needles a couple of times while hanging out with jazz musicians. John saw my arm one time and said, "Unless you stop this right now, I'll leave." He meant it too, so I stopped. I'm so glad he did that because I was a little weak in that department. I wasn't hooked on it but who knows what might have happened. John's very much against needles and heavy drugs.

Throughout that winter, the band kept getting tighter but it became fairly clear that we were exhausting Toronto. Despite our rejection by John Craig Eaton, Nick was still hustling for a backer for us. I had been hyping the guys about California, what I had witnessed with the Byrds. By then, the Byrds were the hottest thing on the charts everywhere. By late 1965, early 66, California had begun to eclipse New York as the center of the music industry. Once the novelty of the British Invasion wore off, the American records replacing them on the charts were increasingly coming out of Los Angeles. Though I enjoyed the companionship of people in the Village and playing with The Sparrows was fun, I really felt during the winter months that I had had enough of cold weather. I still considered California my home and had every intention of returning, but I wanted to bring the band with me. Nick picked up on this vibe and the two of us started to promote the idea of going to the States. Canada was just too limited a market. The Canadian music scene was too regional and localized with no airplay for Canadian records in the US. Nick once remarked, "You could have a number one record in Canada and have enough money to buy four hub caps and that was it." Canada lost a lot of talent to the States during the sixties — Joni and Neil, David Clayton Thomas, Robbie, Levon and The Band, Zal Yanovsky of the Lovin' Spoonful, Denny Doherty in the Mamas and Papas.

There wasn't enough to keep anyone in Canada, but I think California seemed too far removed for the other guys. For them, the next logical step was New York. The Rascals and the Lovin' Spoonful had come out of New York. But we still needed a financier if we were going to make the leap to a larger market. We needed bigger equipment, a record deal, contacts, and media exposure.

Enter Stanton Freeman, an executive with Clairtone, a Canadian HiFi equipment manufacturer. Stanton was looking to dabble in the music business and Nick managed to snare him. He seemed rather erudite, worldly-wise, drove an Alpha Romeo Spider, dressed in fine suits, lived in the better part of town, and claimed to know the right people in New York. As far as we were concerned, Stan was perfect. He told us he was friends with Jerry Brant, The Rolling Stones' agent at the prestigious William Morris Agency. He knew people who in turn knew actor Richard Burton's ex-wife Sybil Burton, owner of a trendy, jet-set, semi-private New York nightclub called Arthur. Stan's US connections were largely through his brother who was sports editor at *The New York Times*.

Stan and Nick were in agreement that the band needed some kind of gimmick, something to get attention. Stan's thinking was, "What separates these guys from the rest of the bands?" Unfortunately, he didn't consider quality music and a tight presentation as sufficient enough. The Mynah Birds, at an earlier stage, had the bird as their gimmick with the band dressed up like Mynah birds in yellow jackets and black leather boots. They were going to get on the Ed Sullivan Show but every time they tried, the bird wouldn't say anything, just clam up. They took the bird to all their gigs with the poor thing flapping around their heads in the car. Every time someone raised the issue of gimmicks or hooks, I kept flashing on this damn Mynah bird. No way would I have anything to do with PR gimmicks.

Stan's angle was to get the jet set behind the band. He figured that was the way to get our foot in the door. Within a very short period, Stan arranged for us to drive down to New York to meet some important people and do a guest shot at Arthur. On April 28th, 1966 we cut some demos at Allegro Sound Studios. There was a real sense of excitement among the five of us; here we were down in the Big Apple in a real professional recording studio with four track machines unlike the limited facilities of studios in Toronto. We stayed at the Holiday Inn and discovered there were young girls hanging out in the lobby looking for bands. Seeing our long hair, they asked for our autographs. They didn't even know who we were but figured we must be some pop group. Maybe New York really was the big time.

At the first Allegro session, we cut three tracks with Bruce Botnick engineering — *Goin' To California*, *Twisted*, and *Square Headed People* — the same tunes Capitol in Canada had rejected. The plan was for Stan to use these demos to hustle a recording contract. Bob Crewe expressed interest but he heard strings and pop sounds, not what we were after. The irony was that Crewe produced Mitch Ryder and the Detroit Wheels and those records were smoking. David Kaprilik listened to the tapes, liked what he heard, and struck a deal between us and his production company to produce 'The Sparrow.' We decided to drop the 's' to give a more hip ring to our name. Kaprilik scored a contract with Columbia Records who wanted us back in the studio within a couple of months to record our first single. It seemed so easy.

Buoyed by our experiences in New York, we returned to Toronto and resumed gigging, putting in time until June when we packed our bags for an extended stay in the Big Apple, recording and gigging at Arthur. Jutta and I were aware that we had a serious thing happening between us but we hadn't determined where it fit into the band's aspirations. Here I was leaving her behind and heading off to New York. We knew we wanted to keep our relationship together and agreed that if the band thing fell through, the two of us would head to California. Whatever happened, we made vague plans to remain together.

Playing slide guitar at Chez Monique in Yorkville Village, Toronto, 1965, with The Sparrows (left to right: Jerry Edmonton, Nick St. Nicholas, Dennis Edmonton, John Kay, and Goldy McJohn).

Jutta modeling in an advertisement for The Trip nightclub in Toronto, 1966.

Jutta in Toronto, 1964, the year before we met.

The Sparrow at a beach on Long Island during our gig at The Barge, 1966.

Photo session in a freightyard along the Toronto lakeshore, 1965.

SIX

THE PUSHER

You know, I smoked a lot of grass
Oh Lord, I popped a lot of pills
But I've never touched nothing
That my spirit could kill
You know I've seen a lot of people walkin' round
With tombstones in their eyes
But the pusher don't care
If you live or if you die
God damn the pusher

THE PUSHER, 1964

While we gigged in Yorkville and southern Ontario through the spring of 1966, Stanton was hustling in New York and came through with an extended engagement at Arthur. This, along with the Columbia recording contract, necessitated a lengthy stay in New York, so Stan's brother arranged the required work permits to get us across the border. Off we went in June, accompanied by our nursemaid Julie Burns, enlisted by Stan to make sure his boys made it safely to the Big Apple. First on our agenda was finding reasonable accommodation for a lengthy stay. Via the musician's grapevine, we learned of the Hotel Albert on East 10th Street at University Place, a stone's throw from Washington Square and Greenwich Village.

The Albert had seen better days but it had a kind of funky chic. Seven or eight stories high, it served as a sort of seniors apartment complex *cum* musician's hangout. The Lovin' Spoonful had put the place on the musical map a year or so earlier when they emerged from rehearsing in the hotel basement to scale the pop charts. Their song *Summer in the City* was a hit when we arrived at the Albert. The lobby had dozens of framed 8 x 10s of everyone famous who had stayed there. During our stay a rotating cast of characters, including sundry jazz musicians, members of the Butterfield Blues Band, the Blues Magoos, John Lee Hooker, John Hammond Jr., David Crosby and Michael Clarke from the Byrds, all checked in at various times. We took a suite on the seventh floor and stayed for most of the summer, except for a few weeks when we played out on Long Island.

We each staked our claim to the living quarters. Nick and Goldy took the bedroom which had two beds, Dennis and Jerry each had a foldout couch in the living room, and I set up a roll-away bed in the kitchen. It was a wild place. There was this huge demented opera diva on our floor who would come out of her room and sing in the hallway while we were waiting for the elevator. We'd be standing there waiting, stoned, and she'd sneak up behind us and go, "AAAAAAHHH!" in this big operatic boom. She scared the shit out of me more than once.

For some peace and quiet, I would take my guitar up to the roof of the Albert and try to write songs but people kept coming up there. It turned out that all around the roof, in drain pipes, under bricks, everyone hid their dope stash. I'd be playing away and someone would come by and say, "It's cool man, just keep playing." Everyone was really paranoid about being busted. Some months earlier, the police had surrounded the Chelsea Hotel and busted everyone. Their trick was to turn off the water so nobody could flush their stash down the john. So the Albert patrons kept their's on the roof. New York was the first time we were able to buy grass that hadn't been filtered through the Canadian border so it was much better quality. We bought a brick between us, dried it in a frying pan in the kitchen, rolled joints until our fingers were sore, then smoked until we were drooling vegetables. That was our one experiment in seeing how much we could smoke before reaching our limit. I ended up carrying Nick from where he had passed out in the living room to his bed.

Stan informed us that the Arthur gig required us to be in uniforms so we went down to a place called the Brick Shed House in the West Village and picked out the latest pop gear: pin-stripped bell bottom pants, Beatle boots, blue blazers. I wasn't keen on the idea of matching outfits but went along with it because Stan claimed he knew what he was doing. Ever eager for some publicity to snare the jet-set crowd, Stan arranged for us to have our hair styled by the one and only Vidal Sassoon in a suite at the Drake Hotel with the media present.

The Arthur engagement went down well. People liked what we were doing, a hodgepodge of cover tunes and our own blues stuff. We did five sets a night, playing until three in the morning. Various celebrities floated in and out of the club but there was nothing extraordinary about the gig. We viewed it simply as a foot in the door. We couldn't rehearse at the club after hours so following the last set we'd grab some burgers from a joint across the street, head back to the Albert, chow down, smoke a joint, hang out until the sun came up and then sleep. When the engagement came to an end they rebooked us for later in the summer, only this time we persuaded the management to allow us to wear our own clothes as long as they were neat.

During the first Arthur engagement we again entered the recording studio with David Kaprilik producing. He wanted to record everything we knew, a repertoire demo, and then, choose the best of the lot to re-record for a single. To that end, Columbia requested our presence for a nine o'clock session the morning of June 6th. With only abour three hours sleep, we arrived at the studio and set up like it was a live gig with our little PA columns. An engineer plunked down a few mikes in front of us, and we proceeded to play our live show. There was no real producing or arranging, just playing it straight into the mikes. Later, some of these rough recordings found there way onto a JOHN KAY AND THE SPARROW album released by Columbia after Steppenwolf was successful. Most of it was pretty raw.

Kaprilik digested the tape and determined that Dennis's writing, the sort of ballady Byrds-flavored material, was where our commercial potential lay. In particular, he singled out the song *Tomorrow's Ship* which sounded like a Byrds' retread with jangly twelve-string guitar, a hooky little guitar line, pretty melody and soft vocal delivery from Dennis. Personally, I thought it was a dead end street because if it turned out to be a hit, we'd have been obligated to continue in that vein. I was, however, a team player and rationalized that Kaprilik and the Columbia brass were the experts. I figured, at best, the single might serve as an ice breaker allowing us to present a greater diversity of material more representative of our style on an album. With that game plan we once again returned to Columbia studios on June 25th to cut *Tomorrow's Ship*. A further session in July yielded the flip side, Dennis and Nick's *Isn't It Strange*, a trippy slice of pre-psychedelia. At that same session, as if to reinforce some kind of musical schizophrenia, we also cut my *Goin' To California* and *Twisted*, two bluesy rockers totally opposite to our debut single but more representative of what The Sparrow was.

Columbia released the single nationally that summer but didn't put a lot of promotion behind it. To no one's surprise it bombed, failing to garner any national attention. Toronto got wind of our New York achievements and one of the newspapers sent a reporter down to interview 'Canada's next big success story.' We were asked to compare the New York scene with the Yorkville scene. Goldy put his foot in his mouth by stating how he found people in New York more hip than those in Yorkville. The funny thing was, he was the one member of the band who hadn't even lived in Yorkville, choosing instead to live in suburbia with his Dad. The comment did not go down well back home. I'm sure our friends in Yorkville figured, 'Well, if that's what you guys think, then fuck you.' That article was probably the reason Steppenwolf had problems being accepted by our old mates back in Toronto after our success. Even if our future lay elsewhere, Jerry and I still believed that Yorkville was our home and always felt affection for that place and the music scene there.

On the heels of the Arthur gig, Stan came up with a couple of more jet-set type bookings. One was at a convention for Yardley's cosmetics and perfume who were attempting to cater to the teenage market. The other was a debutant ball, a coming-out party for the daughter of the socially prominent Wood family. We'd never heard of them but it was to be a big event with media coverage in *Post* magazine. The family rented the ballroom of the classy St. Regis Hotel for the affair and hired Peter Duchin and his Society Orchestra, flown in from Monte Carlo, to provide the respectable dance music for the older crowd, booking us for the younger set. We were paid the incredible sum of $1000 for two twenty minute sets, alternating between the Peter Duchin Orchestra. Nobody told us what to play, so we went on in our pop gear and did our usual set. All these rich kids in their ball gowns and tuxedos crowded around the stage and started dancing right away. During a break we went out on the back stairs for a smoke and found some of the guys from Duchin's Orchestra in their tuxedos smoking grass. These guys had been doing this shit since before we were born.

Following the first Arthur engagement, we moved on to a place called The Downtown in the West Village on Sheridan Square. It was a basement club with a totally different ambience than Arthur, a much funkier place with a big dance floor and lights in the center. The crowd also was quite different, multi-racial — black guys with white girls and vice versa. In the underground grapevine, the Downtown was the place to go if that was your scene. Their booking policy reflected that as well because we alternated that summer with the Chambers Brothers, a black act with a white drummer. The manager of the club was a dude named Buddy Fox and the hat check girl at the time was none other than Bette Midler.

I didn't know Bette then and have, in fact, only met her once very briefly but while I enjoy her work and love her outrageousness, I also admire her for altogether different reasons. She entered my life in an indirect way a few years ago when she sued the Ford Motor Company for their use of a soundalike version of her recording of *Do You Wanna Dance*. Ford had done the same with *Born To Be Wild* and we were not pleased. Our legal eagles advised us that we had little chance of winning a court case due to a previous ruling against Nancy Sinatra involving a soundalike version of *These Boots Are Made For Walking*. Undeterred, Bette took the automobile giant on and fought it all the way to the Supreme Court. Her eventual victory set a precedent for the use of soundalike voices. She didn't need the money, she did it because Ford was wrong. My hat is off to her for that.

The Downtown audience was pretty picky about what they liked to hear. If they weren't digging you, they'd motion to the DJ to play a record. They played some great records, too, a lot of R 'n' B like Sam and Dave. That's where we first heard Don Covay's *Sookie Sookie* which we added to our set when we moved to California. At the Downtown we could stretch out into extended blues jams. We did a version of John Lee Hooker's *Goin' Upstairs* which Jerry sang; it evolved into a lengthy workout for harmonica and guitar ending in a Yardbirds style rave-up. Those jams helped us keep boredom at bay. When you play that many sets for several nights in a row, it's easy to fall into a rut.

I met a young black woman at the Downtown who had been a dancer on the *Hullabaloo* TV show and had written *It's A Man's Man's World* for James Brown. She was very attractive and started making advances toward me. For the first time, I was torn between my male ego responding to these advances and Jutta back in Toronto, but I managed to keep things at arms length with this girl.

Jutta Maue-Kay: *Before he left, John and I made all sorts of promises to each other about being faithful. I wanted to go with him but I had to get my visa and that took time. I did manage to visit him a couple of times in New York, once while they were staying at the Albert. I had never seen a place like that. What a dump! One time, Solveigh and I were going to fly down to New York to be with the guys and were out at the airport when we ran into Bruce Palmer who was being hassled about getting into the States. He had been busted in LA and deported back to Canada but was trying to get into the US again. They gave him such a hard time at immigration that we missed the plane. Solveigh and I had to wait for the next flight so we went up on the roof of the terminal to smoke a joint. We got so out of it that Solveigh* *tripped over a cement block and when she got up and smiled at me, two of her front teeth were gone. Her caps had been knocked out. It wasn't really funny but we were both roaring with laughter. She had to go back home to get her teeth fixed and I went on to New York.*

We managed to get around town a bit and saw a few acts on our nights off, one of which was The Fugs who had an extended run at a downtown theater. They would lure in the tourists who, once safely inside, were appalled to hear songs like *River Of Shit* and *Coca-Cola Douche*. We befriended some of the guys in The Fugs but they were in a whole other musical territory altogether. There were a fair number of people we criss-crossed paths with but we weren't there long enough to become an integral part of the New York scene. Buddy Fox told us that one Monday night when we were off, several members of The Rolling Stones came down to the club to hear us and left disappointed. We were never able to verify that.

At the conclusion of our Downtown gig, we headed out to Long Island for an engagement at the Barge which, as it's name suggests, was an actual floating barge tied to a dock. If the water was choppy, the whole place rocked, literally. The Young Rascals were discovered there a year or so before, but by the time we arrived, the place was going under. The owner thought we could bring out the crowds and revive the place. The gig wasn't anything special. The real excitement was at the nearby Action House where The Vagrants, featuring guitarist Leslie West, were playing. One night we played during a thunderstorm and kept getting shocks from our equipment. We told the manager we weren't playing anymore that night. The next day we received a telegram informing us that our services were no longer required.

For the Barge engagement, Stanton rented us a one-bedroom white clapboard guest cottage in a semi-wooded area nearby. Through Stan, we acquired a first rate hifi system which we hauled around with a growing record collection. We started listening to electronic music, Edgar Varese, Stockhausen, and had some of those albums at the cottage. One night, we were all hanging out, Jutta was down from Toronto, and one of the guys brought up the subject of acid. Nick was still straight, Dennis wasn't interested, but Goldy decided he wanted to try it. So he and Jerry dropped acid.

Jerry can have a sardonic sense of humor at times and decided that night to play one of his practical jokes on Goldy. While they were both tripping, he put on an Edgar Varese record. That stuff is not the kind of music you relax to. It's like industrial music, noises, torture chambers. There was a solitary candle burning in the bedroom with this weird music playing and Jerry took out one of those rubber werewolves that dangle on a string, the kind of novelty you'd buy at a North Carolina truck stop. He dangled this rubber thing in front of the candle and it cast a gigantic moving shadow on the wall. Goldy looked up, saw this monster coming at him and freaked out screaming, "What is it? What is it?" Jerry was entertained by Goldy's first trip and thought this was a riot. Goldy went screaming off into the woods and later Jerry came to tell me that Goldy was outside stark naked doing his impression of a banana egret.

Goldy and I weren't very close; we had little in common except music. He was a fine pianist, a very inventive organ player, and anything we threw at him, whether it was Otis Spann barrelhouse blues piano or whatever, he could handle. He was a very funny guy, a clever wit, but he was also very insecure. When he left his family to go on the road with us, we became his new family, his security. What happened that night on Long Island, I believe, caused a change in his personality. That first acid trip was a pivotal moment and he was never the same again. Once we got him back inside he broke down and wept for a long time. He opened up for the first time and what came out was a degree of guilt for having abandoned his wife and kids back in Toronto. He had a lot of demons buried deep in his psyche that had always been covered up by his class clown act but the acid had unlocked a Pandora's Box and now the demons were loose. Later on, when we were on the West Coast where acid was more prevalent, Goldy repeatedly took trips which only succeeded in driving him deeper and deeper into the dark side of his psyche and he became morose and troubled. It was as if he was taking acid and other drugs in order to find where he had gotten lost inside his own mental labyrinth in order to find his way out again.

That same night, despite Goldy's troubles, Jutta and I solidified our relationship. Spalding Gray, an actor and humorist, has this thing that Jutta and I relate to called 'perfect moments' where nothing could be better in a situation at that moment. My first Christmas in Hannover was the first perfect moment in my life. Another was in that little crackerjack-box cottage on Long Island when Jutta told me she loved me. Not only that but I had the freedom to pursue my goals with her love and support. I have never been happier than I was that night.

Following the Barge debacle we returned to the Hotel Albert and resumed gigging at Arthur and the Downtown through the remainder of the summer and into the fall of 1966, but we were merely spinning our wheels in New York. The jet-set plan had gone as far as it could go with little to show for it. Our debut single had stiffed. In retrospect, we were a year too late for New York. The music scene had already shifted to the West Coast by 1966. With winter imminent, I desperately wanted to get back to California. Through Stan's connections at the William Morris Agency, Peter Golden came up with some dates in LA — It's Boss and the Whisky Au Go Go. It's Boss was formerly Ciro's where I had first seen the Byrds. The thought of playing there was very exciting to me. The Whisky had been the Johnny Rivers discotheque scene when I left LA but had since changed. We had few options left, either return to Toronto, tails between our legs, or head west. Stan was beginning to lose interest in us and our US visas were limited to the end of the year. We had to give the West Coast a try.

Before we left New York, Columbia tried one more time to pull a single from us. David Kaprilik brought us back into the studio in late October to cut another one of Dennis's tunes, *Green Bottle Lover*. This one rocked more than our first single with Jerry singing lead. Dennis wrote the song using what I considered the erector set principle of songwriting: what's currently a hit on the charts and what's the key element that makes that song a hit? You need a hook and a good catchy line and so on. I can't write that way, I write from the gut. Green Bottle Lover was like the cliché of a committee designing a horse and ending up with a camel. It had unusual ingredients like a theramin which created eerie noises using sound waves that until then only Lothar and the Hand People had been using. The Beach Boys later used one on *Good Vibrations*. We recorded this little gem, coupled with Nick's very pop-sounding *Down Goes Your Love Life*, at a session the night before we left New York for California. Somewhat predictably, it failed as well.

JOHN KAY: MAGIC CARPET RIDE

Following the session we packed our gear into the station wagon and U-haul trailer and parked them in front of the Albert. We paid the night clerk to watch them overnight, but apparently our tip was deemed insufficient because the next morning most of our gear had been stolen, except for my Gibson guitar which had been tucked under the seat. Fortunately, CBS, which owned Columbia Records, had recently acquired Fender Musical Instruments, and as part of our contract, they agreed to furnish us with brand new Dual Showman amplifiers and Telecaster guitars when we reached LA. When we finally left New York, we bid farewell to $1200 worth of parking tickets we owed to the City of Manhattan. As a going away present, Hank our drug dealing congo player friend from the Downtown, gave us a big bag of amphetamines for the trip. Nick must have taken quite a few because he drove all the way on Route 66, practically non-stop.

When we arrived in LA, we headed straight to Sandy Koufax's Tropicana Motel just west of the intersection of La Cienega Boulevard and Santa Monica Boulevard. The place was a Hotel Albert West kind of establishment, a stopover for folkies, jazzers, and rock musicians but a nice place nonetheless.

Jerry Edmonton: *We checked into the Tropicana Motel and immediately went to the front desk to ask, "Where's Sunset Boulevard?" Being Canadian kids, it was the only street name we knew of in Hollywood. The guy at the desk pointed and said, "Up there." So we walked and walked up La Cienega and I thought, "Jesus Christ, we're walking up a mountain!" When we finally got to the top we looked over and almost in unison shouted, "It's Sunset Boulevard!" We walked down a block and there it was, 77 Sunset Strip, just like the TV show. Satisfied, we turned around and headed back to the motel but we were too stoned to remember how to get back.*

I took some of the guys down to the Troubadour to show them my old haunts. As I was talking with Doug Weston, I looked on the stage and there was Bruce Palmer and Neil Young with the Buffalo Springfield. We hadn't seen either of them since they were playing with the Mynah Birds in Yorkville, so Bruce filled us in on their activities and introduced the other guys in the band. After Rickey Matthews was busted for being AWOL from the US Army in early 1966, the Mynah Birds broke up. Bruce and Neil then left Toronto in an old hearse and met Stephen Stills in an LA traffic jam. Soon after, they formed the Buffalo Springfield. We saw them once or twice after that, at the Whisky and other gigs.

Nick St. Nicholas: *Our first gig was at It's Boss. We went down there in the afternoon, set up the equipment then went back to The Tropicana Motel. When we returned that evening to play, there were no amplifiers. So I contacted Bruce and Neil in the Buffalo Springfield, went down to their management office, and they lent us some Fender Twin Reverb amps.*

When I had gone to Ciro's the previous year, the crowd was chiefly folkies and rockers, but now as It's Boss the place had turned into a psychedelic day-glo dungeon. My beloved Gibson J-45 was gone and I had to use a Telecaster electric. Despite this setback, we went over fine. By this time, the Whisky had become *the* important club, the place where musicians and record company people congregated. We did a week there opening for the Sir Douglas Quintet and again went down well.

Morgan Cavett: *When I came back to LA from San Francisco, the whole scene had changed in the space of eight or nine months. The 'Alpaca sweater smoke a little pot' crowd had moved on. Ciro's was now It's Boss, everybody was taking acid, and quiet little Sunset Strip with its supper clubs was now kids with long hair wandering around, hanging out at Ben Frank's coffee shop. The whole music scene had changed too, and I think the Byrds were instrumental in changing it. A lot of people knew them or were around them, saw what happened and thought, "Shit, we can do that, too." A lot of those bands, like Love, Spirit, and the Buffalo Springfield, evolved from that scene.*

Far from being the hip localized scene it was before I left, Sunset Strip was now attracting kids from outside the area and the local merchants were getting uptight. It was reminiscent of what happened in

Yorkville not long after we left when the city tried to close off the streets. The merchants claimed the kids were keeping customers away and felt threatened by all these wild looking freaks with long hair in colorful garb. On weekends it was a zoo. The freak thing started to spread and with it came more and more kids, mostly bored white middle-class suburban teenagers. Cruising the Strip became the thing to do. All the clubs switched to rock 'n' roll. The Doors were just getting going at Bido Lido's. Pandora's Box, The Trip, Sea Witch were all places where it was happening, as well as It's Boss, the Whisky, and next door to it, the Galaxy. The Troubadour and PJs were still going strong. The traditional straight society and businessmen demanded the police seal off the streets and clean up the area. Patrols increased and new anti-loitering laws were introduced to placate the merchants but both had little effect on the kids who held their ground. A few confrontations broke out and spread like wildfire. The demonstrations grew larger, kids massing on the sidewalks, singing songs, taunting the cops. Celebrities like Peter Fonda joined the demonstrations, drawing further media attention. It all snowballed and the police responded predictably with truncheons in hand. Stephen Stills wrote *For What It's Worth* after viewing the riots on television.

Once the situation got out of hand, a municipal ordinance was passed that no one under the age of twenty-one could be in the clubs on the Strip. With no kids coming through the doors, the form of entertainment at the clubs changed to R 'n' B bands and the older, dance crowd returned. Almost overnight, we had no place to play. We'd only been in LA a month and already it was dead for us.

We met an assortment of interesting people while at the Tropicana, including Randy Meisner, staying there with his band The Poor who had just moved down from Colorado to try their luck in LA. He later turned up in the Eagles. Another was a character named Jimmy Angland and his South American wife Pepa. Jimmy introduced Nick to his first acid trip. As soon as it started to come on, Nick went outside and started shaking hands with trees. Everything was peace, love, and groovy to him. For the guy who had been so down on drugs, Nick took to acid like Timothy Leary and started tripping fairly frequently. We were all tripping then and Goldy kept getting moodier each time. Jimmy loved poppers, amyl nitrate capsules normally used by heart attack patients. When you were really peaking, he'd snap a popper in front of your nose and your heart would shoot through your brain.

To reduce expenses, I split my time between my parents' home and Morgan Cavett's apartment. Morgan hung around with us and came to every gig. Back in 1964 when we first met, he had started writing poetry. By the time The Sparrow arrived in LA, he was into song writing with various partners and had some of his songs recorded through a contract with Liberty Records. So he was coming along, but we weren't. We were almost broke, no management, no gigs, and some of the guys were thinking about going back to Canada. Then Jimmy suggested that Nick go up to check out San Francisco, where he claimed the music scene was thriving. We had heard from various sources that there was something different going on up there, not as limited as LA, a loose and relaxed lifestyle that supported more musical experimentation. The Buffalo Springfield had gone up there to wait out the Sunset Strip problems. What appealed to us, however, was the prospect of finding work. My inclination was still to hold out in LA because the record companies were there. Jerry agreed. But Nick, Dennis, and Goldy went with Jimmy to San Francisco to check it out. After meeting people like Chet Helm who operated the Avalon Ballroom, Nick managed to secure some work at a place in Sausalito called The Ark and phoned Jerry and I to come up. It was December 1966.

Jerry Edmonton: *John and I flew up to San Francisco and back then, the only way you could get to Sausalito at that time of night was by helicopter. It was raining like shit. We flew in and the place looked like crap, this stinking old barge we were going to play at. The whole thing seemed really bad. Someone picked us up in the car and took us to this dumpy little hotel, the Fireside Inn, all damp and stinky. Everybody was sleeping except Jimmy Angland who said, "Take some of this," and of course it turned out to be acid. I was feeling really depressed and bummed out so I had a really bad trip. By the time the sun came up, I was feeling so shitty that I took the station wagon and drove up to the top of this mountain above the cloud level. There was a statue of a jet pilot who crashed on top of the mountain and I looked out as the clouds started parting and*

I saw the valley and saw the bay and there was the Golden Gate Bridge. I was like, "Wow, this is incredible!" I immediately started to feel more optimistic about San Francisco.

The Haight-Ashbury scene was already blossoming though still fairly cool and localized — long hair, hippie clothes, incense, love beads, and a lot of psychedelics. It reminded me of Yorkville in some ways, the Victorian homes turned into headshops, boutiques with colorful drapes and tie-dyes in the windows. Everywhere you went was the smell of incense and marijuana. There was more of a university crowd in San Francisco then in LA — the Berkeley intellectuals and radicals, the Free Speech Movement — who were more open to new ideas and forms of expression. There was very much an 'anything goes' credo to the scene. The student protest, anti-establishment thing was going on but it wasn't the negative 'us against them' thing it later became. The whole scene was still quite innocent. Up in Golden Gate Park you'd see Hell's Angels, hippies in tie-dye stuff, college kids, and some young guys who probably wore hard hats during the week, but there was no real tension between them. They were all there to dig the music. There'd be a guy over here with short hair dropping acid and over there a guy with long hair smoking a joint.

We moved over to the Cable Car Hotel on Lombard Street downtown to get our bearings. Bill Graham's original Fillmore Ballroom had started up along with the Avalon and the Matrix (initially a folk club run by Marty Balin before he formed the Jefferson Airplane) which was on Fillmore Avenue just off Lombard. Other venues included The Roaring 20s around Broadway in the North Beach area, the Gay 90s, and the Ark, an old paddlewheel ferry boat docked outside Sausalito on the way to Mill Valley. Light shows, pulsing psychedelic colors and liquid effects, were an integral part of some of these venues. Bands like the Airplane, Quicksilver Messenger Service, Grateful Dead, the Charlatans, and Country Joe and the Fish were all working this little ballroom circuit, with the occasional outdoor event or free concert. We got to know some of the guys in Quicksilver who helped us out a bit. Big Brother and the Holding Company were held in high esteem on the scene, particularly Janis Joplin, whom we ran into backstage at the Avalon which we played at various times with the Charlatans, Country Joe and the

Fish, Chicago blues harmonica man Charlie Musselwhite and his band, and the Doors.

Quite frankly, I couldn't see what the big deal was about The Doors. I liked the music well enough but I never thought that Jim Morrison was that much of a singer. He was more of a persona, an image, than a vocalist. A couple of years later as Steppenwolf we played with The Doors at the Hollywood Bowl and I thought Morrison was a stone bore. It might have been exciting in Miami when he was arrested for lewd behavior but I fail to see what the Morrison cult of personality was about. Certainly, women responded to his sensuality but I think the outrage from his conduct on stage became the main reason for his legendary status which was further reinforced by his early death — the James Dean 'live fast, die young' legend.

For a gig at the Ark, we moved back to the Fireside Inn, a real barebones place with concrete floors, no frills but cheap. We stayed there about a month until we found a vacant house in Mill Valley up in the hills with a beautiful view overlooking the bay. By that time Stanton was out of the picture, so Nick, ever the hustler, found two young wealthy fur traders to finance the band. They coughed up some money for mattresses and furniture. We were into them for about $1000, which they never saw again. When not gigging we set up our gear in the living room and rehearsed. Things looked promising.

Nick St. Nicholas: *John can't see very well. I remember once at the house in Mill Valley he saw everybody taking turns with a BB gun firing at a tethered tennis ball on a pole in the backyard. So he figured, "Shit, my eyes aren't that bad," and he picked up the BB gun, aimed it and fired. What he couldn't see was that there was a window. The sliding glass door was shut so he shot a hole through the window. Goldy was on acid at the time so John blamed him for it and Goldy apologized.*

We played for Juanita at the Ark and found it an extremely relaxed atmosphere. We could play whatever we wanted, however we wanted to play it. The audiences were mostly stoned and dug different things. The crowd that started coming to see us fairly regularly at the Ark included several Hell's Angels. They were usually high and would lie on the floor in front of us and just listen. Gradually more started showing up and we briefly acquired a bit of a reputation as a Hell's Angels band.

After months of playing tightly arranged sets of three to five minute songs — wham, wham, one after the other — in New York nightclubs we welcomed the opportunity to loosen up on stage. For the first time we ran into groups who were doing twenty minute songs, totally ignoring the typical East Coast dance-band, discotheque formula. We started experimenting more. As the band loosened up we became an attraction at the Ark and the Matrix and our reputation spread around town. The money was never great at these venues, but it kept us going from week to week. Places like the Avalon paid well but at the Ark and Matrix we took a percentage of the door. For the whole duration of our stay in San Francisco, however, we never rose much beyond second billing at the Avalon and the Fillmore. We were accepted by some of the other bands but we never got beyond being considered the new kids on the block who blew in from out of town.

Jerry Edmonton: *At the Ark and the Matrix, we could play original material and do more unusual songs. When it came to instrumental breaks we'd stretch out a lot more. We had the freedom in San Francisco to go longer if we wanted. Nick really got into that. He enjoyed the musical freedom and started to get a little too far out. We would finish a set, go outside somewhere, smoke a joint then go back on and just let it happen. That kind of thing was fairly commonplace with bands there. The arrangements really loosened up and sometimes took an odd turn. John got to be a little harder to work with in San Francisco because he was very regimented. He didn't like too many surprises on stage, I always felt. In the end, I think The Sparrow got too loose in San Francisco, too loose for John. Even though he had tantalized us a little bit into the world of drugs, now that we were all into it he was starting to think, "This is getting too unpredictable."*

We did The Pusher *every night and the intro part before John would get around to singing just kind of evolved as a time for us to do whatever we wanted. One night, Nick came out of the kitchen banging on a pot and pan making weird sounds. He started putting on echo machines and it just went on its own. People started*

talking about the band after that. The Pusher *got people saying,
"There's this band from Canada and they're way out there."*

The Pusher sort of evolved from this stoned, loose feeling we developed and took on a life of it's own. One night at the Ark, Nick came
up with the idea that we not all go back up on stage at once. He
went up first and started messing around with an echoplex, playing
his bass through it, noodling around getting these strange sounds.
Eventually Dennis got up and joined in, then Jerry and Goldy. It
was kind of an Edgar Varese/Stockhausen sounding thing, each guy
grooving on the sounds he was creating, totally unrehearsed, and
chiming in with the others. Sometimes the whole thing took a left
turn and veered off in another direction. It was almost like some
subconscious thing between them, a free form jazz piece not based
on twelve bar blues just experimental sounds. They went on for ten
or fifteen minutes before I joined them on slide and rhythm guitar.
All of a sudden Nick yelled across the stage, "We're going into a
dream, break into The Pusher." Without losing any momentum,
Jerry did a drum roll, I hit that opening G chord, and 'Wham' we
rolled into the Pusher. Well, it blew everybody away, us included.
We got a tremendous reaction because we had taken everybody,
including ourselves, on a trip that was unpredictable until we got
into *The Pusher* which seemed to climax the whole thing. Afterward, we said, "Well fuck man, if we're going to do it that way,
without regimenting it too much, let's do our jam so that it at least
represents on an emotional level certain phases of the shooting up
experience. You know, the rush, your breath being fried."

Word of our elongated version of *The Pusher* got around and
one night Steve Miller showed up to check it out. He was already a
known commodity on the scene. We had seen him at the Matrix
and I thought he was an excellent harp player. Steve watched for
awhile, then got up, grabbed a guitar, and joined in. He started doing
a talking blues about the jam we were into. "One day the bass player
got up and he's doing his thing, then the guitar player got up . . ."
He was making this shit up as he went along, and I thought to
myself, "This guy's really a natural. He's got it in his bones." We
gigged with Steve's band once or twice over the months including
one of our last gigs in San Francisco in June of 1967.

Our twenty minute plus version of *The Pusher* was captured, rather surreptitiously, at a Matrix gig in May of 1967. Unknown to us, the club manager hung a couple of mikes from the ceiling and taped our show that night. What he caught was a pretty loose, stoned set covering our bluesy material as well as *The Pusher*. It wasn't particularly polished or well recorded but it represented The Sparrow in San Francisco. This manager tried to peddle the tapes two years later when we were Steppenwolf and ABC Dunhill bought them, releasing them as Early Steppenwolf. It certainly wasn't Steppenwolf but at the time of its release it gave us some much needed breathing room in our two album a year contract.

Dennis Edmonton: *Taking drugs and becoming aware of other bands like Country Joe and the Fish and Charles Lloyd changed my writing. The bands I saw in San Francisco were much more progressive than the formula rock that I had grow up with. That, in conjunction with taking psychedelics gave me a whole new perspective on music. In my own case, I was never a big fan of the blues because it's basically formula music, three chord progressions. Once you've heard one blues song, you've heard them all in terms of music theory. So I had tended towards more pop music because it had more variety. The blues as a steady diet wasn't my thing. But I witnessed the San Francisco scene and saw there were other areas to explore in music and it really opened my mind.*

We jettisoned the pop ballady stuff in San Francisco that Dennis sang and did either original material or reworkings of obscure blues songs we had found. Cover tunes were totally frowned upon because everybody was into their own thing. As a result, the shift was more towards me, and to a certain extent Jerry, singing lead. Consequently, Dennis's role was becoming less defined.

San Francisco had an impact on my writing as well. My political views had started to gel in the coffeehouses of Buffalo and Yorkville and the topical songs workshops at Newport but found full reign in San Francisco. Songs like *The Ostrich* reflected much of what I observed and felt about the youth culture. Young people were beginning to assert themselves since they did not share the same values as their parents. The concept that the individual is merely a cog in the wheel of society to be a commercial beast of burden with his mind switched into neutral was repulsive to me.

Perhaps because of my background and interest in history, I've always had an anti 'follow authority blindly' and more of a 'question everything' attitude. Perhaps my perspective stemmed also from the fact that I didn't have a father figure or because the Waldorf School gave me an overview of life that was far broader and more humane in its scope. All of the above were the seeds for many of the songs I wrote in San Francisco. I was still idealistic enough to believe that our generation would throw off the bonds of traditional thinking.

We'll call you when you're six years old,
And drag you to the factory.
To train you're brain for eighteen years,
With the promise of security.
But then you're free,
And forty years you waste,
To chase the dollar sign.
So you may die in Florida,
At the pleasant age of sixty-nine.

THE OSTRICH, 1967

My concern for the environment also emerged in early 1967. I had been raised in urban areas but in California I began to view nature from a different perspective. The drug use certainly had a profound impact on my feelings about Mother Earth. Walking among Redwood trees and along the Big Sur coastline while on LSD had seen to that. Observing how some people treated the land made me aware that the 'conquer and subdue' mentality along with the greed factor were rapidly paving the road to our demise. I hoped that a voice in the wilderness might cause others to take note.

The water's getting hard to drink,
We've mangled up the countryside.
The air will choke you when you breath,
We're all committing suicide.

THE OSTRICH, 1967

Since I had a folk/blues background with topical song roots, I used my writing as a means of expressing these views. I had been a fan of the Farinas, Tom Paxton, Phil Ochs, Len Chandler and a good deal of Dylan's early work and was well versed in the troubadour history in the true sense — the traveling minstrel who brought news and commented on events. I remember Robbie Robertson saying sometime after The Band's first or second album that politics and music don't mix, that there is no place for politics in music. I was struck by that because not only does it disregard the centuries-old tradition of the troubadour, but in my mind a lot of what Robbie described in his American heartland, southern culture lyricism was very much influenced by politics. The very nature of retelling much of that history was political. Perhaps he was too much of a romantic to dwell on the underlying political reasons that affected the history he so vividly wrote about.

In the midst of all this tumultuous change both personal and musical, Columbia Records re-entered the picture to try one last time to recoup something from their meager investment in The Sparrow. They sent David Rubinson, a hot young West Coast producer, to check us out. After one set he proclaimed, "You guys are a blues band, not a pop band. This is what you do best and what you should be cutting." Surprise! Sessions were arranged in February, 1967 and we entered the studio optimistic that something positive, something that truly represented The Sparrow's sound and vision would finally come out on vinyl.

By that time, however, the comraderie we had enjoyed in New York and at the Tropicana was falling apart. Rubinson liked my voice because it was gruff and recognizably different. For him, the gruffer the better, but I wasn't happy about forcing my voice. Despite his earlier pronouncements concerning our sound, he suggested we record an incredibly dumb pop song of Dennis's called *Can't Make Love By Yourself.* The result was dreadful. Just like baseball, three strikes and you're out. A few months later to no one's surprise, Columbia notified us by mail that they were releasing us from our contract.

The disastrous session brought matters to a head. Jerry and I remained convinced that the place to be was still LA. Despite the media focus on Haight Ashbury with the kids all wearing flowers in their hair, I didn't think that the Frisco scene and sound were going to break out into a national phenomena. I was thinking on a very practical level: how can we further our career? Sleeping on a mattress in a sparsely furnished house in Mill Valley was hardly my idea of having arrived.

Things were crashing in all around us. Gigs were becoming few and far between and it was back to peanut butter sandwiches and canned spaghetti. Our station wagon was repossessed and Jerry's Dad back in Oshawa got stuck for the $500 we still owed because he had originally co-signed for the vehicle. Goldy's girlfriend Sharon had to haul us and our trailer in her car to gigs. By then our work visas had long since expired, so the four Canadians were now in the States working illegally (as a landed immigrant, I was legally in the US). Nick was sitting at the entrance of the Ark one afternoon waiting for the rest of us to arrive when a dark colored Dodge sedan, a typical undercover car, pulled up and two guys in trench coats got out. They knew everyone's name and gave them ten days to leave the country. Nick was not about to throw in the towel. He went down to the immigration office in San Francisco and ingratiated himself so skillfully that he won a sixty day extension. God knows what he told them.

Dennis had become increasingly unhappy with our dismal state of affairs and his diminishing role in the band. The San Francisco experience had crystallized the differences between his pop sensibilities and the band's blues leanings. The failure of the Columbia session was the final straw for him. In the spring of 1967, Dennis informed us that he was thinking of quitting in order to pursue songwriting full time. At that point the rest of us were still determined to keep the band together. Who are we going to get to replace him? Jerry and I were down in LA during the next incident.

In a panic, Nick thought of a guitar player we all knew from Toronto named Freddie Keeler. Freddie had been with David Clayton Thomas and the Shays before Thomas left for the States to join Blood, Sweat and Tears. He was a fine player but unfortunately he still had the Yonge Street tavern image — short hair and suits. Nick managed to locate him in Toronto and offered to pay his ticket down to San Francisco to check out whether he wanted to join us. He thought it might give Freddie the opportunity to break out of Toronto. Freddie took the bait and agreed to give us a look.

It was early 1967 and the whole peace and love thing was in full bloom in San Francisco. Nick and Goldy picked Freddie up at the airport and instead of bringing him to our place, took him directly to Panhandle Park for one of the Be-ings. Freddie was a very straight guy, soft-spoken, easy going, still living with his mother in safe, middle-class suburban Toronto. He must have thought he had just moved from Earth to Mars. Here he was walking into a scene full of people who looked like barbarians — hair down to their shoulders, beards, bizarre clothes, strange medallions hanging from necks, sandals, faces painted, eyes bulging out, walking around saying, "This is great acid, man. Want some?" This completely blew Freddie's mind. He didn't like it one bit. What we were about musically didn't interest him either. His only desire at that point was to go home, fast.

Goldy couldn't understand Freddie's reluctance to join us. For Goldy, the band had become his extended family. He figured all Freddie needed was to have his mind altered so, without him knowing, according to Nick, Goldy put acid in Freddie's coffee. When it started to hit him, Goldy took him for a car ride around the city. Poor Freddie was peaking and freaking out. Goldy brought him to the Cable Car Hotel where Freddie was so distraught that the manager threatened to call the police. Nick managed to placate him and talk Freddie through his trip. The next day he returned to Toronto.

Jutta had finally received permission to immigrate to the US. There was, however, one hitch: I had to agree to marry her within ten days of her arrival. I already had my green card as a landed immigrant but they gave her the run around for months. Marriage wasn't something we had contemplated before, but we talked it over and reasoned that since we had lived together and that worked okay, if that's what it took to be together, then why not? It was the Sixties so we just said, "Marriage? Sure, who cares." Before she could be allowed in I had to go to a notary public, swear out an affidavit agreeing to marry her, and send it to the American Consulate in Toronto.

Jutta Maue-Kay: *I intended to come to California and be with John, but not to marry him. We were very 'anti-institutions' then. He wanted* to show me everything he knew in California and it sounded great to me being up in Toronto in February. Then I found out the only way I could get my visa was to either have a job sponsored or get married. I broke the news to him and he said sure. Thanks to Solveigh, on February 17, 1967 I arrived in LA. I didn't have the money but Solveigh was already there dating a guy who owned a nightclub on Sunset right next to Schwab's Drugstore. She talked him into paying for my flight and they both met me at the airport. Solveigh had an apartment in Crescent Heights in Hollywood, so I moved in until John came down from San Francisco.

We had to get married by my birthday, February 26th so we arranged to have it done two days before. John was staying at the Tropicana Motel which was five minutes from Solveigh's place. For the ceremony I wore this silver micro-mini dress, very Sixties. John was supposed to come with a ring that some girl had given him or he had borrowed. Angelo DiFrenza was our witness and drove us downtown to the court house for the civil service. John hadn't even told his parents yet. Woody from The Trip back in Toronto had given me his ring and in the car on the way to the court house, I realized I couldn't get it off of my finger. We had to go to a jewelers to have this beautiful white gold ring cut off to put on the cheap ring John had borrowed. Then we discovered that John had lost it, so we found a bubblegum machine and got a ring from it. That was my wedding ring. We stood in line with a whole bunch of pregnant women and their husbands-to-be, paid our $5 and it was, "You do? And you do? You're done. Next." During the vows I called him my "awful wedded husband" (my English wasn't very good). And that was it, we were married. Not very romantic!

Afterwards, we went to Sandy Konikoff's house. Jody, a friend of mine from Yorkville whose real name was Dorothy Scully, had moved to LA and was going with Sandy, a drummer she had met in Toronto. Sandy had worked with Ronnie Hawkins and Bob Dylan and was staying with a band in a house just north of Sunset Boulevard. We had nothing else to do on our wedding day so we went over there. They were so excited that we had just been married they brought out the Acapulco Gold to celebrate. We got very high and when we left, I fell down the stairs and scraped my leg. After that, John and I went to the Tropicana for our 'honeymoon.' We *were in bed when, all of a sudden, Angelo, Morgan, and Marsha showed up at the door. John had told me back in Toronto that he had a son with her and had shown me a picture of the baby she had sent him. I didn't know how Marsha felt because I think she still really liked him. It was very awkward all around but then they left. A strange little scene.*

Later, I brought Jutta around to meet my mother and stepfather and after the initial surprise announcement everyone got along fine. Jutta stayed in LA with Solveigh while I went back to join The Sparrow in San Francisco. Solveigh's boyfriend found Jutta a job as a waitress at the Pink Pussycat, a strip club on Santa Monica Boulevard. She was required to dress like a pussycat in this very revealing outfit with a pink tail and little flashbulbs glowing on her boobs. There were a lot of big tippers there, celebrity types, so she made decent money.

In June The Sparrow were offered a week long gig at the Galaxy on Sunset Boulevard in LA. The riots had subsided and the clubs were back booking rock groups. The Galaxy was right next door to the Whisky and was operated by Rose Deutsch. Dennis had given his notice but agreed to stay on until a suitable replacement could be found. We traipsed back to the Tropicana Motel. There, Nick heard of a young guitar player named Michael Monarch whom he invited down to the Galaxy to check out the band. Michael sat in with us a couple of times. Within a couple of days Michael was playing some of our songs and playing them really well. Then Dennis announced that he was leaving following the Galaxy gig.

Michael Monarch: *I first saw The Sparrow play at the Galaxy and I was really impressed with them. I had only been playing guitar for about a year and was only sixteen when I met them. At that time, John was playing rhythm guitar and singing some of the vocals and Nick was doing some of the vocals so it really wasn't John up front as the leader like it became in Steppenwolf. What really impressed me about the band was that Jerry was just a real kick-ass drummer for those days, simple but very solid, and not a lot of drummers played like that back then. Also, Goldy was great on that old Lowery organ that he had beefed up. He got that real funky sound out of it.*

On the final night of the engagement, we were something like five minutes late getting on stage and Rose got pissed off at us. She and Jerry got into a fight and she tried to slap him. Jerry responded by laying into her calling her every name in the book. Nick got mad at Jerry for blowing any chances of another gig and we all just threw up our hands and said, "It's over." We stored the gear and met a couple of days later to divide it up in fifths (though bad feelings developed between Nick and the rest of us after some of the gear went missing). Dennis was going off on his own, Nick was already planning a new band with Michael Monarch, and Jerry, Goldy, and I were at loose ends.

In retrospect, it seems unlikely that The Sparrow would have been successful if we had remained in San Francisco. I wasn't as comfortable musically in the loose improvisational atmosphere that characterized the Frisco scene, preferring tighter arrangements and knowing where everybody was. When you compare the Matrix recordings of The Sparrow to the sound of Steppenwolf on our first album, there's quite a difference in approach and presentation. Steppenwolf was tight and punchy; The Sparrow loose and improvisational. It seems unlikely that Steppenwolf could have emerged from San Francisco.

Jerry moved in with Nancy Seeling while Goldy and Sharon found a place on Fountain Avenue; they may have even been married by then. Both were trying to make ends meet. Jerry had a one thousand dollar insurance policy that his parents had contributed to which matured when he was twenty-one so he had some money to live on. He eventually moved to Fountain Avenue as well. Goldy had always lacked ambition so Sharon went out to work to support him.

Jerry Edmonton: *Sharon was no rocket scientist but she had a good heart and helped the two of them out by waitressing before we got Steppenwolf together. Goldy had told us that she had done some modeling during that period. Much later, we were checking into a Holiday Inn somewhere in the Midwest and our road manager was looking through the magazine rack waiting for the paper work to be finished. He picked up this men's magazine and was thumbing through it when he said, "Hey, come here." So I looked over and he said, "I swear to God that's Sharon." I said, "Nah, she's got*

*different color hair." "Yeah," he replied, "but they put wigs on
them." We looked at it again and sure enough, that was her all
spread out. That's what Goldy had her do instead of him going out
and getting a part-time job.*

With my return to LA and the demise of The Sparrow, Jutta and I
needed a place to live. Morgan Cavett was living with a woman in
an apartment above a double garage at 7408 Fountain Avenue. It
was a cool little place, $90 a month rent, with a decent sized living
room, a tiny bedroom, and an even tinier kitchen. When the two
of them broke up he moved out but put in a good word on our
behalf with the landlord, Spencer More, and shortly thereafter,
Jutta and I moved in. We didn't have much in the way of furniture
so my parents helped out with a few things, Angie came by with
an old television set, and various friends contributed odds and
ends to turn it into a home. We got a bed and a few other things
from second-hand stores and scraped together a few bucks to
repaint the interior, doing all the doors in different colors to make
it less boring. It was a cozy little apartment. Jutta still had the job
at the Pink Pussycat so we had some money coming in and my
mother would slip us a few bucks once in awhile to help with the
necessities. When my folks purchased a new Camaro, they gave us
their old 1962 Chevy, the same car we drove out to California in a
few years earlier. Gerhard also gave Jutta driving lessons, so we
were at least mobile.

With no band, I needed some source of income. I didn't know
enough musicians in LA to join an existing band but I had some
experience at songwriting. Dennis had secured a writing deal with
Leeds Music and was recording a demo album of his songs.
Morgan and I had already written *A Girl I Knew* during one of my
visits from San Francisco, so we decided to team up and beat the
pavement for our own publishing deal.

Morgan Cavett: *I had been working with a guy named Bernie
Schwartz and we were writing and recording with bands that
played at the Hullabaloo Club. When The Sparrow broke up, John
being very resourceful, was looking at me saying, "You've kind of
made a niche for yourself. You're getting paid for writing songs,*

doing what you want to do." He saw that our songs were being put out by a major label. He and I began writing together and started visiting publishing companies hoping to maybe get a contract and fifty bucks a week retainer between us as a writing team. We would walk in and perform our songs for publishers. I couldn't sing or play an instrument so I needed John to perform the songs. I would write the lyrics and do the sales pitch. This was over a one month period and nothing was happening.

I would go over to their apartment almost every night and write with John. The three of us lived on German pancakes (Jutta makes great German pancakes), apple sauce and potatoes, not a lot of meat, maybe a little sausage, but at least we ate. We would play a lot of monopoly, smoke a couple of joints, drink a little cheap wine then I would go home.

We approached several publishers, none of whom gave us the time of day. One guy asked us to play what we had and afterwards told us that he felt we weren't playing him our best material. Ironically, this same guy ended up running Trousdale Publishing, the publishing arm of ABC Dunhill Records. Some of those very same songs turned up on the first Steppenwolf album, which he then had to handle. Unfortunately, the writing duo idea never panned out. I was at my lowest ebb when Jutta hit me with a bombshell. She was pregnant.

Jutta was adamant she wanted to have this baby. As soon as she started showing she wouldn't be able to work. Who wants to see a pregnant pussycat? I felt a tremendous amount of pressure to come up with something, but what? I couldn't get a straight job, my eyesight precluded that. Then, as it has done so often in my life, fate intervened.

On Jutta's suggestion, her friend Jody moved into the vacant house next door to us on Fountain Avenue, another one of Spencer More's properties. In the intervening months since our marriage, Jody had met a young record producer at ABC Dunhill named Gabriel Mekler and they had been married. Gabriel was born in Israel to an artistic family and raised in Europe. He was an excellent pianist and as a staff producer had worked with a band called The Lamp of Childhood. Jutta and Jody introduced him to me and I instantly found him a likeable, easy-going guy. He was looking for new acts and projects after the collapse of The Lamp of Childhood. When I told him I had been in a band that had recorded for Columbia but just been given its release and subsequently broken up, he replied, "Well, what have you got to listen to?" I played him some Sparrow tapes, probably the Rubinson session and a few other things. He listened intently and then responded, "That sounds okay. Are you still in touch with these guys?" I told him I was in contact with Jerry and Goldy. "Why don't you get a couple of more guys together, rehearse some of these tunes, and let's make some demos."

It was like a fairy tale. Here I was, no work, no money, a pregnant wife and no prospects, then in walks this guy living next door, from a successful record label, saying he thought I might have a shot at a contract if I could get a band together. It was almost like it was all meant to be. Everything seemed to fall into place at the right time.

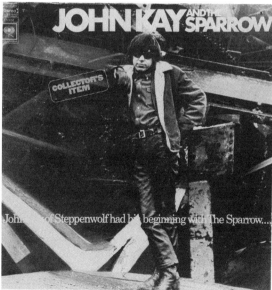

The Sparrow — our first recording session at Columbia Studios, New York, 1966.

Although never billed as "John Kay and the Sparrow," Columbia Records saw fit to release a collection of demos and masters under my name once Steppenwolf became successful.

The Sparrow playing at the Woods Debutant Ball with the Peter Duchin Orchestra, St. Regis Hotel, New York, 1966.

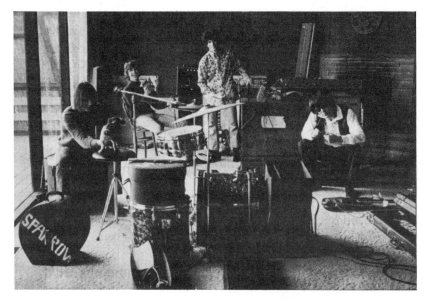

Rehearsing at The Sparrow band house in Mill Valley, California, 1967.

Avalon Ballroom, San Francisco, March 1967.

7408 Fountain Avenue, Hollywood, California (left), the first home for John and Jutta Kay (upstairs) — and for Steppenwolf (garage below). Good friend and Steppenwolf producer Gabriel Mekler lived next door.

SEVEN

BORN TO BE WILD

Get your motor running
Head out on the highway
Looking for adventure
In whatever comes our way

Yeah, darling, go make it happen
Take the world in a love embrace
Fire all of your guns at once and
Explode into space

I like smoke and lightnin'
Heavy metal thunder
Racin' with the wind
And the feelin' that I'm under

Like a true nature's child
We were born, born to be wild
We can climb so high
I never want to die

BORN TO BE WILD, 1967

Dunhill Records, originally founded in the early 1960s by Lou Adler and Bobby Roberts, had recently been purchased by ABC. As a result, Adler and Roberts came away with tidy profits in their pockets leaving Jay Lasker remaining as president. Jay wasn't exactly a musical genius but he knew the business and how to sell records. Unlike someone like Clive Davis at CBS, Jay rarely set foot in the studio. He was a salesman, and a good one at that, who had been with Vee-Jay Records before his post at Dunhill. The label had The Mamas and The Papas, who, by 1967, were drying up on the charts, and Barry McGuire, who'd had *Eve of Destruction* a couple of years earlier but was nowhere to be found. The Grass Roots were paying the label's bills. There was a need for an infusion of new talent.

The folk rock market was waning but labels were still signing anything with long hair. The feeding frenzy over the much bally-hooed San Francisco sound had all but abated after many bands, including our friends the Steve Miller Band, had been snapped up. That scene may have spawned longevity in acts like the Dead and the Airplane/Starship but it never fulfilled the dollar signs that record labels initially perceived across the Golden Gate Bridge. In the summer of '67, ABC Dunhill was attempting to gauge the next big thing. When most labels were merely cashing in on whatever current trend was hot, ABC Dunhill's approach was more forward looking: "Forget about what's on the charts now, because that can change if we get the next new thing."

All Gabriel Mekler was offering us was studio time for a demo session and a shot at ABC Dunhill if the session proved fruitful. There was nothing financial on the table, just a chance to get something happening, something we could do our way as opposed to the way Columbia had tried to program us. Jerry met Gabriel, liked him and the whole idea. Goldy, with little prompting, jumped on board. We considered Dennis and actually contacted him but he was happy doing his own thing writing and recording an album of his own songs for UNI. That album later yielded several tunes Steppenwolf recorded, including *Born To Be Wild* (though we learned it from a separate demo tape), *Tenderness, Ride With Me,* and *The Night Time's For You* written by Dennis and Morgan Cavett. Nick had already assembled his own band, TIME, Trust In Men Everywhere — yeah, right! We called Michael Monarch after Dennis passed on the offer.

He knew half the old songs already and played with a fire and intensity that we felt would contribute to a new sound.

Michael Monarch: *I was really young but I think they needed that, somebody with a rawness and energy. Dennis was a great guitarist back then but he was kind of tame at that point with a clean sound. When I was sixteen, I thought the coolest thing to do was to turn my amp up a little louder than everyone wanted it. And I think that's part of what helped that band get started, a kind of raunchiness for the* Born To Be Wild *lyrics and for the image of the band.*

I've always respected John as a musician not just as a singer, though he is an unusual singer. He had a really different sound with a personality to his voice. The other thing is, I don't think a lot of people realize that John is a good guitar player. He had a big influence on me, things like open tunings, old blues styles, slide guitar playing. He's a real music aficionado as well, especially for American blues, certain types of folk music and even a little bit of country. He had an amazing record collection. I learned a lot about music from him and Jerry. They were turning me on to music that maybe I wouldn't have listened to or hadn't listen to at that point.

Jerry hit on the idea of posting a notice at Walich's Music City at Vine and Sunset advertising: "Bass Player Wanted". In the meantime, I had cleared out one of the garages below our apartment for rehearsal space. The landlord said he didn't care what we did in there. One of the first guys to respond to the ad was John Russell Morgane, or Rushton Moreve as he introduced himself. He set up, started jamming, and it was amazing. He played intuitively, a real melodic style rather than just a thump thump with the kick drum. He loved the Mothers of Invention and brought a non-commercial sound to the band.

Jerry Edmonton: *Rushton came down to the garage and he looked like a pirate. He walked in and he had this velvet Renaissance hat and the same little moustache I had. He looked just right, he was stoned and it was casual. We started playing and it was like 'boom,' like we had been playing together for years.*

With the lineup complete, we began rehearsals in the garage. The sound and style that ultimately defined Steppenwolf on our first album came together in that place, born more out of necessity than any preconceived master plan. All we had were bits and pieces of equipment left over from The Sparrow and some gear remaining from The Lamp Of Childhood that Gabriel borrowed from Dunhill. As I recall, Michael, Rushton and I played through those borrowed solid state Jordan amplifiers, and since I had pawned my Fender amp and Telecaster guitar, Michael lent me his old guitar, a mongrel consisting of a Mosrite body with a Vox neck. Mike, in turn, used a Fender Esquire (one step down from a Telecaster with a single pick-up), while Rushton had a quality Rickenbacker bass. Jerry had his Rogers drum kit, and Goldy was still stuck with his little dual keyboard Lowrey Spinet organ with six foot pedals which, due to its lack of a percussive setting, sounded somewhat vague. As a result of these limitations, Goldy had developed a unique style which consisted of hitting the keys with rapid short strokes in order to achieve some percussive sound from it. He played through a small Leslie speaker cabinet which was so overdriven that it gave it a highly compressed, nasty sound.

With Michael's buzz-saw guitar sound and Goldy's unique organ style, Steppenwolf had a much wider, fuller, nastier, darker sound than The Sparrow ever had. Later, after signing with Dunhill, I retrieved my Fender gear and we all played through Bassman heads and Dual Showman cabinets with Mike using a Mosrite fuzz-tone that sounded so compressed that his guitar parts at times came out like a tape recording played backwards. The raw, heavy sound on the first Steppenwolf album emerged from that hodgepodge of equipment we had junked together. The ironic thing was that once we could afford better gear, the sound on our subsequent albums changed into something else. It wasn't the same.

The band rehearsed most afternoons, running through a few Sparrow things we wanted to keep like *The Pusher, Hootchie Kootchie Man, Sookie Sookie, Tighten Up Your Wig,* and *Baby Please Don't Go* as well as new things I was writing like *Desperation* and *Your Wall's Too High.* As tunes were written, we'd kick around ideas for arrangements. That's where Jerry proved to be a major influence. He had a keen ear for finding the best way to deliver a song. For instance, he came up with the suggestion to turn *Desperation* from 4/4 time to 3/4, creating a whole new feel that gave the song its strength. The sound was blues-based but we were moving beyond simple twelve bar blues figures. It was a tougher, tighter sound than The Sparrow.

One song we tried out in the garage was a tune Dennis had suggested to Jerry, a recent creation of his entitled *Born To Be Wild*. I thought it had killer lyrics and an interesting guitar riff but sounded somewhat puny on Dennis's demo.

Dennis Edmonton: *The demo tape that Steppenwolf originally heard of* Born To Be Wild *was not from the demo sessions for my solo album that Jerry and a few others played on. It was just one guitar and one voice. There was a guy who was kind of like John Kay, a solo blues player named John Hammond Jr. and I liked his style of guitar. I was fooling around with some of his riffs and guitar patterns, changing them around into my own thing. One of those riffs became the foundation for* Born To Be Wild.

I was walking down Hollywood Boulevard one day and saw a poster in a window saying "Born to Ride" with a picture of a motorcycle erupting out of the earth like a volcano with all this fire around it. Around this time I had just purchased my first car, a little second-hand Ford Falcon. So all this came together lyrically: the idea of the motorcycle coming out along with the freedom and joy I felt in having my first car and being able to drive myself around whenever I wanted.

I put it together with a reworking of a John Hammond riff, borrowed a tape recorder from Morgan Cavett, and put it down on tape. In my tiny apartment on Yucca in Hollywood, I couldn't make much noise because the other residents complained. I still had my Telecaster but I couldn't plug it in to an amp, so I did the demo tape with the Telecaster dry, unplugged. When Jerry asked me if I had any songs because he and John were getting back together, I took the tape over to Jerry and Nancy's place but they weren't home so I dropped the tape through the mail slot. Nancy had this big dog and afterwards I worried that the dog would eat the tape before Jerry got back.

Born To Be Wild *didn't stand out initially. Even the publishers at Leeds Music didn't take it as the first or second song I gave them.*

They got it only because I signed as a staff writer. Luckily it stood out for Steppenwolf. It's like a fluke rather than an achievement though. For me at the time, it was just another song of many that I was writing and I liked them all. It isn't the writer or the artist who make it a hit, it's the public, and they liked it. The music business has a tremendous amount of luck to it. It's not always who's the best or works the hardest, it's just this tremendous luck factor and being at the right place at the right time. Born To Be Wild *had those factors going for it.*

At that point, I had started calling myself Mars Bonfire. I had watched a bunch of James Bond movies at one sitting in a theater and for some reason I just got the idea for the name. It was Bonfire not Bondfire as it was misspelled on the first album. The Mars part came from a book I was reading at the time on Greek mythology and I read that Mars was the god of war and the image appealed to me. Years later, I went to Europe and discovered that mars is a common word in several languages. I didn't legally change it until I became a US citizen in 1987. My birth name is now my middle name, so I'm Mars Dennis Eugene McCrohan Bonfire, aka Dennis Edmonton.

Michael took Dennis's riff and made it his own, playing it with distorted guitar in a much more aggressive manner. We picked up the tempo a bit from the demo and found a key that worked for me; Goldy supplied that sort of organ answer thing to the guitar and Rushton added a melodic bass pattern that gave the song something extra. The intro snare drum crack to set up the song and drum fill at the end of the instrumental break were Jerry's idea. I don't remember spending more than an afternoon transforming it from the demo to our version, but once we were through, it was ours.

Jerry Edmonton: *I was used to hearing songs with just acoustic guitar and voice. That's how John used to play new songs for me. I put Mars's tape on and thought, "This is great! This sounds like the band." I took it over to John and Jutta's place and put it on his tape machine. Everybody listened to it twice through with Michael copping that guitar riff right away. As soon as he started playing that riff, the band just fell in behind him. It took about twenty minutes and that was it. That's the way the song has always been,* *never changed. When John started singing, it was almost like Mars couldn't have written a better song for John's voice. That sound was classic Steppenwolf.*

The funny thing was, the song didn't stand out to Jay Lasker at Dunhill Records or his group of guys when we played it to them. When we recorded it and played it back for ourselves we went ape-shit. We said, "This is it, that's the single." Gabriel was telling them this was it and twice they turned it down as the single. I couldn't believe it. The song was ready, it just took the executives another half a year to be ready for it.

The Sparrow had recorded a version of *The Pusher* in New York at the demo session for David Kaprilik but what came out was still fairly folkie sounding and tame. We had transformed the song into a *tour de force* while in San Francisco, but in Steppenwolf we arranged it with more bite, less trippy without the long intro. The Steppenwolf version was slower, raunchier, grinding and that was definitely Michael Monarch's influence. He gave it that raw edge.

I always liked Chuck Berry's writing, so I thought it would be fun to write a tribute to him using as many of his song titles as I could. The result, *Berry Rides Again,* was done in a half hour at our apartment. In the early days, Chuck was the only lyricist in rock 'n' roll who told a story in a hip way with themes that kids related to. Goldy had all the chops in the world to do any style once his ear grabbed onto it. For *Berry Rides Again,* Goldy listened to Johnny Johnson, Chuck Berry's original piano player, and nailed that real rock 'n' roll piano down.

In theory, we were a five man band; all for one and one for all. Each of us was talented and capable as a musician in his own right but we didn't really try to push the soloist-as-focal point idea. By '67-'68, the big deal was the virtuoso guitarist or soloist, like Hendrix or Clapton, with a band built around that individual. It was the era of the long, rambling solo and frankly I found a lot of it tedious, the twenty minute 'Pass the No Doze' guitar break. From our inception we sought a group sound rather than building the thing around one of us. We were a band, equal and democratic in theory. There was no effort made to feature one of us prominently.

In terms of the financial stakes, the original five were equal partners in this venture. But the reality of any group dynamic is that dominant personalities will assert themselves, grab the rudder and determine the direction. That was basically what happened from the beginning. Jerry and I were the strong personalities. The two of us took care of the business end because we were a little more pragmatic and we wanted to play our music without compromising. We were willing to put up with certain aspects of the music business in order to achieve that goal. Jerry had an intuitive feel for how a song should be arranged. I would introduce material to the group, usually just guitar and voice, letting the other guys find their own parts. This procedure often brought a fresh left turn to the way I had heard a song in my head. Rushton and Michael would find parts right away. At times Jerry would give suggestions to Goldy and as soon as he had a direction, he was fine. As the drummer, once the groove was there, Jerry was always thinking, "What else does this song need?" He was definitely responsible for contributing some of the better arrangements on our songs but never received the proper credit due to him.

We rehearsed in the garage through August of 1967, a typically hot summer in LA, too sweltering to keep the garage door closed. The sound was ricocheting off the houses, bouncing around the neighborhood. Kids on the street started showing up, digging what we were doing. Gabriel came by periodically to offer his assessment and thought it sounded promising. The volume was loud enough to bring out the LAPD who threatened, "We're gonna give you guys a noise warning once. If we have to come here again, you guys are going to jail." So we now needed a new rehearsal space. Somehow, we learned of a lounge out on Venice Boulevard that had recently gone under and was available for nothing. We hauled our gear down there and resumed practicing. Not long after that, Gabriel came by once more, listened, and pronounced, "I think you're ready."

He booked some time for us at Sun West Recorders, a small demo studio on Sunset Boulevard and Western Avenue. The plan was to do a direct-to-two track demo tape, eleven or twelve songs, everything we knew. When the day arrived it turned into a bad comedy script where everything goes wrong. Goldy and I headed over to the rehearsal hall on Venice Boulevard to pick up the gear, pulling an open U-Haul trailer. We had called the lounge owner ahead of time to ensure that he was there to let us in to collect our equipment. My hair was fairly long by then and so was Goldy's, which drew the attention of a passing cop car. He pulled us over, checked the vehicle's registration, then, pointing to the trunk, inquired, "Got any contraband? Any explosives in there?" Not satisfied with a simple no, the cop asked us to open the trunk, but before he would look inside he called for backup. God knows what he was expecting to find in there. Within a couple of minutes three or four more cops arrived on the scene and tossed the car, pulling seats out, looking everywhere. After wasting our precious time, they waved us on our way.

When we arrived at the lounge we found the rest of the guys but no owner. We waited and waited but he didn't show. Taking matters into my own hands, I climbed up on the roof, crawled over to the skylight, jumped down into the darkened building, and made my way to the exit. I pushed open the doors, no alarms sounded, so we started hauling our gear out. Within five minutes sirens wailed as a police car screeched to a halt in front of the building and cops jumped out, guns drawn. Silent Alarm. There was no arguing with these guys but I managed to explain the circumstance and suggested they check with the operator of the liquor store next door who had gotten to know us from our frequent visits for snacks during rehearsals. The guy verified everything. As we frantically lugged our gear into the studio, the engineer yelled at us, "You guys are late."

We finally calmed down enough to run through our tunes, no overdubs, just a live set. Gabriel seemed pleased enough with the results, took the tape box and asked, "What about a name?" Surprisingly, up until then we hadn't given much thought to a name. We definitely did not want The Sparrow. A few silly suggestions were thrown around like the Humble Fumbles, then Gabriel suggested the title of a book he had recently read, Herman Hesse's Steppenwolf. We weren't exactly thrilled with it, but no one had any better ideas on the table so Gabriel scrawled 'Steppenwolf' on the tape box and assured us that if Dunhill wasn't interested we could change the name and go elsewhere. Later, people naturally assumed a connection or some preconceived plan since Hesse and I were both German. Life often being stranger than fiction, it was simply the case of an Israeli-born guy reading a German book and suggesting the name to an American/Canadian/German rock 'n' roll band. No divine intervention or superior insight on our part to choose that name, just pure coincidence. The name certainly turned out to be good for us, creating an identifiable image and the whole wolf mystique. And I don't feel the name has dated the band like others typical of the Sixties such as "The Plastic Subway" or "The Electric Grapefruit".

Steppenwolf is a fairly common word in the German language and quite literally means 'a wolf of the Steppes', the prairies of eastern Europe. It wasn't concocted for the title of the book. Hesse's character was a loner, a man drifting in the no man's land that separates true idealism and individualism from a comfortable bourgeois lifestyle with all its hypocrisy, never being totally at peace in either camp. I thumbed through the book when the name was initially suggested by Gabriel but never read it entirely until several years later. I was then surprised to discover that I empathized with the Steppenwolf character as I'm sure many do who see themselves as lone wolves trying to remain true to their ideals. Raised as creatures of comfort and materialism, we seem to be fighting an endless tug of war trying to balance the needs and desires of the body with our higher aspirations. To quote Hesse:

"There was the wolf in him, the free, the savage, the untamable, the dangerous and strong. . . . but the wild and wicked wolf was also a man and had hankerings after goodness and refinement, and wanted to hear Mozart, to read poetry and to cherish human ideals. . . ."

The name Steppenwolf just seemed to go with the look and sound of our band — aggressive, kind of wild, intense, urgent.

Gabriel played our tape for Jay Lasker. He couldn't make heads or tails of our harder rock sound, so wisely deferred to others who could. "I don't understand this stuff but let me play it for my daughter Marcy and Steve Barri to see what they think." Marcy was sixteen and, like most teenagers, had an intuitive feel for rock 'n' roll. Steve was a pop record producer at Dunhill and a hell of a nice guy with an open mind to something new. Both responded favorably, with Steve recommending Jay sign us to the label.

The next thing I knew, Gabriel and I were sitting side by side across from Jay — burly, glasses, cigar dangling from his mouth — who proposed a standard recording agreement. We had no money for a lawyer, nor did we even have a manager. "John, what do you want?" enquired Jay. "Two things we need Jay," I responded. "We need a small advance to get our equipment out of hock, about $1500 will do, and we want it in writing that you will release an entire album of our work because we just came off Columbia where their approach was single, single, single until you get a hit then an album." Jay's response: "No problem." Having enjoyed hit albums by The Mamas and The Papas, that was his approach from the get-go. With those conditions embodied in an agreement, all five of us signed with ABC Dunhill and Trousdale Publishing, their publishing arm.

I breathed a little easier after that. Jutta was now far enough along in her pregnancy that she had to quit her job. With a band, a record deal, and the rest of my equipment out of hock, we took on a few dates around LA before recording our album. We played the Blue Law out near the Harbor Freeway, a concrete psychedelic bunker where the sound ricocheted all over. It was awful but there was one interesting thing I remember. The other band on the bill, whose name I can't recall, featured a girl drummer who was pretty good. Her name was Karen Carpenter and her brother Richard was also in the band. A few years later I was surprised to see them as The Carpenters. We also performed at the Buckley School, an exclusive private school where Morgan Cavett's future wife was in the audience. On another occasion we played a birthday party for actor Barry Sullivan's daughter up in the Hollywood Hills. We also did the Pasadena Civic Center, a place we playing several times in the early days. These gigs put some money in our pockets and got our name around.

From the outset, ABC Dunhill let it be known that they expected us to have management. Gabriel expressed an interest but Jay discouraged it. He suggested a company in his building, Reb Foster and Associates, whose big act had been the Turtles. The company was fronted by Reb Foster, a popular DJ at KRLA radio, and his cousin from Texas, Bill Utley Jr. The two were later joined by Burt Jacobs who had managed The Standells. Reb was the DJ with the radio connections, Bill was the mastermind who dealt with the record companies, and Burt handled the day-to-day affairs working directly with the bands. Burt was quite a character and we took to him right away. He had a very brusque business demeanor and could be gruff to booking agents but with us he was like a football coach — his boys could do no wrong and there was nothing he wouldn't do for us. Unfortunately his rough exterior sometimes made us more enemies than friends in the business. That only came to light years later because we were sheltered from any negative reactions at the time. When we signed with Reb Foster and Associates, they had to pump $30,000 into us right off the bat for lawyers to draw up contracts, equipment, a van, clothes, getting rid of our personal debts, and promoting us on personal tours.

Not long after signing the management deal we were ready to record our album. By now it was December 1967. The band had been together only a matter of months but things had accelerated at a brisk pace compared to the years of slogging it out in The Sparrow. United Western Studios was ABC Dunhill's studio of preference, a traditional multi-room studio — television work, jingles, and albums. The Mamas and The Papas had recorded their hits here. But once we got started, it was like being back in Toronto again — "Turn down, I'll turn you up in the booth," — older, union guys punching in and out who knew nothing about loud rock 'n' roll, freaking out every time the meter went in the red. We got through only four tracks in ten days and all we had to show for it was a wimpy, tinny sound. After the fourth day I went home disgusted. "That's not how the band sounds. We're ballsier than that!" What could we do? Gabriel hadn't been to a lot of studios to know any better.

Morgan Cavett: *The band had already started recording their album at United Western but weren't happy with the way it sounded. I had just cut a three song demo for Judy Fine of the Womenfolk at American Recording Studios, this little hole in the wall studio in the Valley. I had hired Jerry and Dennis to play on it. Judy got a deal at Verve Records on the strength of that demo. John heard the tape and said, "Man, listen to that bass sound, so full and wide. And that kick drum!" It wasn't hard rock but it sounded really good. So he said, "Let's go play it for Gabriel." John and Gabriel figured maybe they could record the album there instead.*

Richard Podolor ran the studio but it was a real family affair. Mrs. Podolor, Richard's mom, was the receptionist and did the booking, his Dad did the sweeping up. Richard's big English sheepdog was always around. Richard and his friend Bill Cooper did all the engineering. It was mainly a demo studio but they booked the band in and they recorded the whole album there.

On Morgan Cavett's recommendation, we booked studio time at the American Recording Company. The studio was in a converted Chinese restaurant in Studio City, all stuck with acoustic tiles and a homemade echo chamber. They had installed big thick old meat locker doors for sound isolation. It had a tube board with rotary pots and an eight track machine.

Richard Podolor had been a child prodigy on classical guitar, touring Europe in the Armed Services Special Services before opening up the first American Recording Company with his parents on Sunset Boulevard in 1958. There, he recorded several hits with Sandy Nelson (including *Teen Beat*) and the Hollywood Argyles (*Alley Oop*). Richard often played on these sessions. Longtime friend and bass player Bill Cooper came on board as an engineer in the early 1960s before Richard moved the studio to the San Fernando Valley, becoming one of the first independent studios in the Valley. There, they recorded The Hondells, The Turtles, The Standells, Electric Prunes, and many others. Richard and Bill knew that studio like you know your own living room because they built it. They knew every wire because they put it there themselves. That initial booking resulted in a successful professional relationship lasting several years and earning eight gold records for us.

We brought in our gear, set up, and played live with some sound separation and a guide vocal. We laid it all down on eight track, leaving a couple of tracks for vocal and the odd percussion overdub. On the first day we knocked off seven songs in a row. They all sounded killer. We were ready. We knew those songs inside and out. We had our whole lives to get ready for this album, we had rehearsed the songs over and over in the garage and had played them at our gigs as well. Each song was done in two takes at the most with the attitude, "Make each part count and pull its weight." You'd be hard pressed to find any instrumental overdubs on that first album except maybe tambourine.

On the second day we did four more tunes, a couple of hand-clap and tambourine overdubs, and I put down a few vocals. I finished all the vocals on the third day and on the fourth, we mixed the whole thing. After only four days and $9000, we walked out with the first Steppenwolf album. Amazing!

Bill Cooper: *The original band had that kind of chemistry together that allowed then to come in and crank something out in four days. There was a real cohesiveness. Groups are weird. It's not necessarily the five best musicians, it's the five best pieces that form a jigsaw puzzle. Each guy has his own individual personality. I mean, nobody played like Goldy or Jerry or Michael, and Rushton was an inventive bass player, really clever and deceptive in his style. Some of the riffs that Michael came up with were so original. Jerry had a definitely different sound and I thought he was great. I had never heard anything like them before. Michael had an old Esquire and they had some Fender Showman amps. Everyone thinks they must have been using Marshalls for that sound but they would just crank those Showman amps up to ten and stand on the other side of the studio and let it go. That was their sound. They had a really fresh sound, more energy, more ragged than some of the pop stuff that was out then but like a breath of fresh air. It didn't sound manufactured, it was real.*

There was a lot of personality in that band. At that time, nobody dominated. They played as a group on that first album. It wasn't until later that the dominant personalities came out, John, and to a lesser extent Jerry. John is a very forceful person. He definitely became the leader.

During the mix down, that's when Richard really takes over. He knows what he's doing and doesn't take a back seat to anyone. For example, on the drum break in Born To Be Wild, *the band thought it was just a part of the song but Richard, who's a real excitable guy, started jumping up and down screaming that it was great and punched it up putting echo on it. And he was right. It was an important feature of the song. He's real intuitive and honest. If he likes it, he'll tell you and if he doesn't, he won't mince words.*

Gabriel Mekler came at it more from a musical standpoint

rather than from a technical thing. He wasn't a guitar player, he was a keyboard player but he had a rock 'n' roll attitude, a street attitude. He wasn't one of those straight-laced company types. But I don't think he had much to do with the Steppenwolf sound. He got them the contract and named them but he didn't mold their sound or anything. When John and the guys had their direction and knew where they were going, at that point there wasn't an enormous amount of input from Gabriel that they needed. They knew what they wanted and we put it down on tape. John's attitude to recording was very serious, very business-like. He rarely allowed outsiders into the studio and avoided any kind of distractions.

Once the album was completed I took a tape of it home, played it on my machine, and really dug it. The sound was full, the drum sound was right there, solid, and there was some off-the-wall riffing between Michael and Goldy. My voice sounded the way I wanted it to come across. Reb Foster came over one night to hear it and listened straight through twice in a row before declaring that it was definitely happening. This was in early January 1968. Things looked promising for the new year.

The first album did two things for us right out of the starting gate. First, it established Steppenwolf as a raw, ballsy band leaning heavily on blues and hard rock influences. Second, it showed that we were a band that concerned itself with issues beyond 'I love you, you love me, oh how happy we could be' in songs like *Take What You Need, The Ostrich* and *The Pusher*. That paved the way for what came later with *Monster*. There were those who considered us a thinking man's band. All this was fine with me.

When the album was released in the spring of 1968, the cover photo shot on infrared film showed the five of us among the plants at the Cactus Garden in Beverly Hills all decked out in the latest psychedelic outfits. The whole San Francisco flower power thing had spilled down to LA, everything was colorful, paisley, beads and brocade. Goldy's wife Sharon and Rushton's girlfriend (who he referred to for some reason that I never understood as Animal Huxley) were both seamstresses and made some outfits for the photo session. I had on a Mod shirt and a paisley tie. The other guys had the obligatory beads and Nehru jackets. For both shots I removed my sunglasses because I didn't think the label wanted the band to appear too mysterious. The original pressing of the album cover was printed on silver foil, giving it a unique, shiny surface that caught attention.

While we were still recording the album at American Recording studio, ABC Dunhill released the more pop-oriented *The Girl I Knew*, written earlier by Morgan and I, backed by a shorter version of *The Ostrich*, both from the disastrous United Western sessions. It stiffed almost immediately. Once the album was out, they released *Sookie Sookie*, which earned some regional attention, especially on both coasts, until programmers in the Bible Belt began speculating on just what "Let it hang out, baby, everybody work out" might mean. After that, they dropped it like a hot potato. *Sookie Sookie* did receive considerable airplay at KRLA and KHJ in LA though. Jerry and I were driving down Sunset Boulevard one day, the radio was on, and out of the speaker came *Sookie Sookie*. We pulled over to listen, all goose bumps. For the first time we felt we had broken through the barrier that separated the band from the public by having radio accept us.

We filmed a promotional clip of *Sookie Sookie* (this was long before MTV and rock videos became *de rigeur*) at an old airport near Pomona with the band positioned around some old B-29 bombers and a go-go dancer on the wing. The screening of that clip triggered the demise of Jerry's relationship with his girlfriend Nancy who, upon seeing the go-go dancer, lost it completely and started swinging at Jerry in the parking lot. Voices were raised to the top of their lungs and finally teeth went flying. Some people were just not meant for the rock 'n' roll life. On April 4th, we made our national television debut on *American Bandstand* miming to *Born To Be Wild* and chatted with Dick Clark who seemed relieved to discover that, rather than being stoned out hippies, we were fairly intelligent and articulate. Other local television work included *Boss City*, an LA rock show on KHJ, the *Della Reese Show, Steve Allen*, and a new program called *Playboy After Dark*, where we actually played live doing bits and pieces of *Berry Rides Again* and *Born To Be Wild*. There we met Hugh Hefner, a congenial guy who invited us to visit the Playboy Mansion if we ever passed through Chicago.

As the album picked up momentum, we resumed gigging

around LA, playing more high profile dates, including the Santa Monica Civic Center supporting Cream along with the Electric Prunes and a folk singer named Penny Nichols. Ticket response was so overwhelming that a second show was added for the same night. Cream had been touring the US extensively and seemed somewhat fatigued during the first show. We were hungry and ready. Everything clicked for us and the response was great. I suspect that that was at least part of the reason why Cream came out for the second show with both guns blazing. We learned we still had a long way to go before we could consider ourselves headliners.

Jerry, Goldy, and I had made our return to the Whisky when Steppenwolf opening for Hugh Masakela and a few weeks later for John Mayall's Blues Breakers. The Whisky and the Troubadour became regular hangouts for Jutta and I. Even later after we became successful and toured internationally, we would often meet friends and/or catch a performance at either place whenever I was in town. One night in 1967, Jutta and I were at the Whisky to see Sam and Dave, whom I had always dug but had never seen live. The place was packed and, sure enough, they had a full blown horn section and the two of them were dynamite. After the show, roadies began setting up equipment on the dance floor in front of the stage, a drum kit and twin sets of Marshall stacks. I figured it must be a trio but had no idea who it was. Mario, the club manager, came up to the mike and announced, "And now ladies and gentlemen, direct from the Monterey Pop Festival, the Jimi Hendrix Experience!" Out they came, Jimi, Mitch Mitchell, and Noel Redding — Afros, wild clothes, the whole bit — and proceeded to lay waste to the room with their guest set including *Foxy Lady, Hey Joe,* and *Wild Thing.* I was completely blown away! Jimi was a guitar wizard, totally unique with his look, demeanor, and sort of half singing, half talking vocal style. We didn't meet that particular night but our paths crossed again over the next year.

Throughout this whole period, Jutta was dealing with her pregnancy. She was very supportive with respect to my band activities but she was having some problems. Despite all the promising signs, four days of studio time and the odd gig didn't yield a lot of revenue for us so we were still largely living hand to mouth. One day she passed out in the kitchen as the result of an iron deficiency. The best we could do on our limited budget was to qualify for subsidized medical care at the UCLA Medical Center. Despite these problems, on March 29, 1968, Jutta gave birth to our daughter Shawn Mandy Kay at UCLA Medical Center. Gabriel drove Jutta to the hospital because I was out of town. Morgan was there, too. It was one of the first out of town gigs we did as Steppenwolf, the Avalon Ballroom in San Francisco. Management felt that because we had been somewhat of a known entity in San Francisco as The Sparrow, there was a market for us. We were on stage and Chet Helm interrupted us to announce that I was the father of a baby girl. The crowd cheered and applauded me. It was quite a moment. Morgan still enjoys reminding me that he held Shawn before I ever did.

By early summer the album was in the Top Ten, still without a hit single. ABC Dunhill was crying, "What's the next single?" We were getting heavy FM exposure on the album, especially with *The Pusher* and *Born To Be Wild*, but AM still wanted a single. Reb Foster had received positive feedback from his radio friends that *Born To Be Wild* was a definite contender, but Jay Lasker was promoting the idea of *Everybody's Next One*. I wouldn't have minded the latter because I co-wrote it with Gabriel but I wasn't convinced either way. Finally a compromise was reached: they would press the two songs back to back with neither designated as the A side. Let radio determine which was the hit. Within two weeks it was obvious that eight out of ten radio stations went for *Born To Be Wild*. ABC Dunhill jumped on the bandwagon to promote that song.

There were a number of factors at play that contributed to the success of *Born To Be Wild*. Certainly, it had a drive, an urgency with solid drumming and great guitar riffing. Another key factor was timing. It was summer time, kids were out of school and wanted to hear more exciting, get-it-on, high energy music. The single was released in June and soon became an anthem that summer for any kid tooling around on the highway or hitting the road. It came out at a very turbulent period, the summer of 1968 — the Vietnam War on television every night, student demonstrations on campuses, the King and Kennedy assassinations, urban rioting, the Chicago convention. The song's lyrics and message spoke to a generation which craved some excitement and some escape from the downer that America had become that year.

On July 5th we performed at the Hollywood Bowl with The Doors and the Chambers Brothers and went over very well. We caught Mick Jagger backstage checking out Jim Morrison. Our first foray beyond California was our memorable summer of 1968 bus tour. Someone in our management had come up with a special excursion bus from the Council Bluffs, Iowa Transit System. A few modifications had been made: removing the standard Greyhound type seats, installing a clothes rack, curtains on the windows, an ice box, a couple of tables mounted between the seats, and bunks for eight people. No luxuries, standard army-style cots and no central air conditioning just bus air. Our equipment, big Sunn amplifiers given to us through a sponsorship deal, was stored underneath in the baggage bays of the bus. We took along one roadie and a fellow named Lance Corey, a former blackjack dealer from Lake Tahoe, hired by our management as road manager. Lance was a novice to touring with a rock 'n' roll band but managed to learn the ropes along the way.

We headed out across the country playing a combination of ballrooms and psychedelic dungeons like the Electric Factory in Philadelphia. Much of the tour concentrated on the South, which became a major market for Steppenwolf over the years. Driving through that part of the US was a strange experience for me, a very different way of life that I had only read about — very rural, and the color bar was still in evidence. The tour lasted the better part of the summer and as we proceeded from city to city, we discovered that our album had already penetrated much of the country, largely as a result of the extensive airplay we received on the so-called underground FM stations. At that time, these stations could virtually play whatever they wanted and took a liking to us. We were delighted to find that people at our shows were familiar with our songs and lyrics. Most of them were our peers — we looked more or less the same, were roughly the same age, and seemed to have similar beliefs and concerns. Watching their reaction it appeared that they shared a feeling of solidarity through our music, the same sort feeling I experienced at the Newport Folk Festival: "I'm not alone, others think like I do, it's growing; here's a band that's saying things I care about." We would talk to our fans as much as we could wherever we went, listening to their complaints and concerns.

These informal encounters helped us keep in touch with what was happening in America. Many of these conversations came to influence my writing that summer. Later when we started flying to gigs and playing arenas, I think we became isolated from our peers, the people we were playing for.

What a tumultuous year 1968 was. Here we were launching our group out on the road and there was so much anger in the land. The whole youth revolution counterculture was in full swing by then. The government's resolve remained firm to stick it out in Vietnam, and by mid-year our commitment had peaked at 500,000 troops. Sixteen thousand would be killed that year alone with over one hundred thousand wounded. The country was seriously divided with animosity festering on both sides. The Tet Offensive was a massive jolt to Middle America who up until then seemed convinced of the government line that we were winning. Horrific images of Tet, My Lai, and saturation bombing every night on the news were turning the tide of public opinion away from the war. Lyndon Johnson, gauging that mood shift, dropped out of the running for the 1968 Presidential election, dividing the Democratic party and the anti-war movement between Eugene McCarthy and Robert Kennedy on the one side and old HHH, Hubert Humphrey, on the other. With Robert Kennedy's assassination sapping all promise of hope for the anti-war movement, the real fight was not to be found on the floor of the Democratic National Convention in Chicago but in the streets where the law and order establishment's main man, Mayor Richard Daley, served notice in the most merciless manner that democracy belonged to those with power, not the masses. Once again, America sat stunned viewing vicious brutality on their television screen, this time in their own nation.

Student demonstrations were on the rise on university campuses across the land, Columbia University being brought to its knees by the SDS, Students for a Democratic Society. The assassination of Martin Luther King in April unleashed decades of frustration for blacks as dozens of American cities burned and troops were called in. Out of these ashes came the more militant Black Panther Party professing the opposite ideals of King's non-violence. Then, like the phoenix, Richard Nixon rose from political oblivion to gain the Republican nomination and the Presidency a few months later. With him came his crowd of myopic, repressed, vindictive types, the ugly underbelly of American politics that put the final nail in the coffin.

I believed in Bobby Kennedy's and Martin Luther King's ideas. I was rooting for them and in both instances, like most young people, I was devastated by their deaths. Those two events along with the Democratic Convention were what often caused people of our age to say, "A change has got to come. Something has to be done about those who are permitting this and are doing nothing about it." And the rock 'n' roll rebellion was a backdrop to all this. Unfortunately, when it later became an 'us against them' situation, the tragedy was that the idealism, the energy, the optimism, the motivation of the younger generation was completely deflected into a negative direction by the establishment's petrified stance towards any change. Here was a generation of people who felt attacked. So it became a confrontational deadlock.

Oddly enough this reaction was rooted in the young people's fervent commitment to what they had been brought up to believe, namely that America stood for human rights, equality, democracy. And now they expected America to live up to those ideals. But instead of using that idealism to everyone's common advantage, both sides became polarized. As things deteriorated, these young people became more and more disillusioned until the whole thing started to turn into the escapism that came to characterize the late 1970s: "Well, we can't save the world anyway so I may as well throw on my fancy duds, go to the discos and 'boogie 'til I drop'." The disillusionment that took place from the mid Seventies onward eventually culminated in the Me generation yuppie attitude and the greedy Eighties.

As Steppenwolf's singer and principal songwriter, the requests for interviews were often directed towards me. I became the spokesman and I usually gave a reasonably decent accounting of myself. Given the nature of some of my lyrics, I was frequently asked to give my opinion on the state of affairs in the country. If I feel strongly about something, I'm not afraid to speak out about it, right or wrong. Thus the tag of Steppenwolf being a thinking man's band came out of both the lyrics I was writing and my public comments. And my views for the most part were supported by the other guys in the band. These views were set forth a year or so later on the MONSTER album.

Danny Goldberg: *John Kay has a mind which comprehends much of what ails America, and an ability to mouth the sentiments of millions of young people.* (Circus Magazine, *1969*)

In Albuquerque, New Mexico, I was interviewed by a young man named Michael Blake, who, to my surprise, knew our album inside out and related to our lyrics and philosophy. He was just getting his start in journalism and we did an extensive interview together that eventually turned up in an underground publication entitled *Hard Times.*

Michael Blake: *What the audience doesn't know is that, through his extremely weak eyes, John Kay has formulated a vision of America and mankind that makes him one of the most significant social commentators of our time. He has the rare ability to view tangled, vast problems with sure clarity but he simultaneously avoids black and white conclusions.*

Michael and I hit it off and over the years kept track of each other's activities. In the early 1980s he came out to LA to try his hand at writing movies. He had sent me a script he had written years earlier that had a part for me as an itinerant musician who blows into town and talks with young musicians there. It never came to anything but he ultimately wrote *Dances With Wolves.* Michael was one of our earliest supporters, and when he won his Academy Award, I jumped out of my chair screaming, "Alright, Michael!" Through all the years of struggle, he stayed true to his dream.

We played some pretty strange places on that first tour. In Slidell, Louisiana, we pulled up to a psychedelic bunker, an old warehouse with walls spray painted with garish colors. Lance Corey went to open the door but the hinges were broken and it fell off nearly knocking him out. The power in this place must have been wired for Lawrence Welk because it kept going off all evening during our set. We discovered that the promoter had extension cords running to a nearby hotel through a tunnel. We finished our set but it had been interrupted so many times that the promoter demanded another set. Our contract specified only one show. It turned out that the sheriff in town who was standing off in the wings with his big Colt revolver on his side was in partnership with the promoter. He ambled up to us as we were heading for the dressing room. "Y'all doing another set ain't ya?" he queried, patting his revolver. When we refused, he handcuffed Lance Corey until we agreed to go back on.

Heading north, we arrived in Chicago, and following our gig, we took Hugh Hefner up on his offer to drop by the Playboy Mansion. It was an enormous building in the middle of town with several floors, an indoor pool, and everything a playboy could possibly want, gorgeous girls everywhere. Hefner was awaiting the delivery of his DC-9, all black playboy jet at the time, and he showed us a large scale model of the plane, replete with rotating round bed in his private state room plus other amenities. Presumably as a result of our relationship with him, we ended up appearing on *Playboy After Dark* several times and being guests at his various facilities on a number of occasions.

In Cleveland, we a did guest spot on the *Upbeat* show, a local rock showcase hosted by a Bobby Vee lookalike still stuck in the Fifties, totally out of the picture. The director was on another planet as well. In some brainstorm of his he decided to have us mime to *Born To Be Wild* with Goldy seated at a grand piano and me sitting on the piano with my legs crossed Marlene Dietrich style. To them what was the difference between Steppenwolf, James Brown or the 1910 Fruitgum Company? It was all just pop music, right? (We even played a date with the 1910 Fruitgum Company sometime later — imagine *Simple Simon Says* meets *The Pusher*!) We reluctantly acquiesced. Goldy sat at the grand piano, legs crossed, hands folded primly in his lap until the organ parts, then, with a flourish of his hands, gave his best Liberace imitation. I mimed the lyrics atop the piano looking as bored as I possible could. It was the first television show we had done outside of LA and we were aghast at the idiocy of it. We made a return appearance on the show a year later wherein this same host proceeded to compare Steppenwolf's music to progressive jazz! By the end of the summer the first album had gone gold.

Shooting a film clip at the Air Museum, Ontario,
California, to promote the release of the single
Sookie, Sookie, *1968.*

The original lineup of Steppenwolf, close
together, one last time.

Celebrating Steppenwolf's first gold record on the rooftop of the ABC/Dunhill building (left to right: Goldy McJohn, Gabriel Mekler, Nick St. Nicholas, who replaced Rushton Moreve, Jerry Edmonton, Marv Heffler of Dunhill, and John Kay, with Dunhill president Jay Lasker seated).

EIGHT

MAGIC CARPET RIDE

You don't know what we can find
Why don't you come with me little girl
On a magic carpet ride
You don't know what we can see
Why don't you tell your dreams to me
Fantasy will set you free
Close your eyes girl
Look inside girl
Let the sound take you away

MAGIC CARPET RIDE, 1968

During that summer tour of 1968 we attempted to write songs on the bus, in hotel rooms, in dressing rooms, preparing for the next album. We had already recorded a couple of tracks before we left for the tour but we still needed more material. That well-worn cliche about having twenty years to write your first album and six months to do your second was ringing true for us. In this business you're only as good as your next record.

We were really pushed for time on the second album. This one was done piecemeal. We came to a deadline and it was still taking longer. With more money we could afford better equipment — guitars, amps, Hammond B-3 organ — but we couldn't recapture that initial raw sound that characterized the first album. Also the studio had now upgraded from eight to sixteen tracks which meant that recording took longer. Added to that was a dearth of good songs. *Magic Carpet Ride* and *Don't Step On The Grass, Sam* were the powerhouses that carried STEPPENWOLF THE SECOND up the charts, with *Magic Carpet Ride* becoming an instant hit, bigger than *Born To Be Wild*. The album did very well out of the gate but in the long run it wasn't as strong as the first. It lacked direction, wasn't as aggressive, raw or raunchy.

Jerry Edmonton: *John's ego was suddenly catapulted after that first album. All the things we had hoped to do as The Sparrow that hadn't jelled suddenly came together with that first Steppenwolf album. But we didn't have quite as prolific material for the second album as we had on the first one. The record company wanted another album. Money, money money. We weren't really prepared for that second one, so we had a couple of 'off the wall' tunes on it. Gabriel Mekler had to write some things and I had to do a vocal on one song that John didn't want to sing,* Faster Than The Speed Of Life, *one of Dennis's songs.*

In the studio, John was always open to my ideas for arrangements, maybe because he knew he needed them. But on the other hand, I needed to express myself and I had an easier time arranging and writing with John than anyone else in the band. Working with John was fun. We never crossed that line. We would push each other only so far. To this day, we have never had a falling out.

A new song is like a new pair of boots. You have to work them in until they fit just right, and you only do that by wearing them a lot. You play a song over and over again on the road exploring the phrasing and meter until it feels right. When you're writing in the studio, you don't have that opportunity because you record the new songs right away, often before they get a chance to became comfortable. If you've played a song on the road for six months, you can knock it off in one take in the studio and it'll be killer. That's why the first album took only four days. It was like a live album without the audience. But from then on it was write, record, play and this made the studio albums sound like *studio* albums. We were vaguely aware of that but there was nothing we could do. We were on the music business treadmill — album, tour, album tour . . .

Magic Carpet Ride evolved out of something Rushton had been messing around with, a simple but catchy three note bass figure that he played whenever we were setting up or doing soundchecks. We were in the studio recording the second album and Rushton came in, sat down with his bass, and said, "I wrote this song and it's really great." So we said, "Okay, play it," because everyone played their songs to the band. He played this three chord pattern 'Domp domp, da da da domp domp; domp domp da da da da-domp domp' on his bass and sang, "I like my job, I like my baby." That was it. Mars Bonfire was there because we had cut one of his songs, and when Rushton started playing this bass figure, Mars joined in playing the three chords to it. Richard Podolor is a very excitable guy and he heard them messing around with this pattern and hollered over the intercom, "That's great! Don't forget that. We'll put it on tape. Bill, run the tape." At one point, Mars started doing a kind of Bo Diddley rhythm, adding a sixth note to the chords, but Richard came over the intercom and shouted, "Don't do that. Keep it straight." It was Mars or Jerry who suggested that it break out at one point into a climbing chord pattern, then back into that three chord thing, then climb into a long jam in the middle of the tune. In an hour we had cut the instrumental track. I asked Bill Cooper to make me a copy of the tape because I had some ideas for it. I felt there wasn't enough to "I like my job."

I took the tape home and put it on my new sound system. We were still living on Fountain Avenue but it was after the first album so there was some money rolling in. One of the first things I had done with some of my royalties was to go down to The Sound Center and purchase my first real hi-fi system, brand new. I had the system in the apartment for no more than a week when I brought home this tape. Out came this domp domp, da da da domp domp thing and I just sort of let my mind flow. "I like to dream right between my sound machine" — the sound machine being the hi-fi system. Twenty minutes later the whole thing was finished. At the studio the next day I started singing it and Gabriel said, "That's great. Let's do it." We added a falsetto harmony on the chorus of "You don't know what we can find" and "You don't know what we can see." We still had this jam sequence in the middle that went on forever, so Jerry, Michael, Goldy and I went into the studio and made some instrumental sounds and noises on the track to sound cosmic, like a magic carpet ride to god knows where. Michael was getting feedback sounds, I was making scrapping noises with my pick and a bottleneck, and Goldy was doing sweeps on the organ. Bill milked this hodgepodge through echo to create a real sound picture. We then used a cloned piece from the first chorus that Bill edited to the end of the jam. The whole thing hung together.

One problem still remained: the intro was too vanilla and needed something that would set up the song more interestingly, like a magic carpet taking off. We went back into the studio and really went crazy with feedback and Jimi Hendrix sounds. Michael was hitting his pick-ups with a pick, just pounding on his guitar. Bill cut it all together, we went into the booth to listen to it, and it was goosebumps all over. Everybody in the room knew it was a hit. When we played it for Reb Foster and Associates, they were convinced it was going to be a monster. ABC Dunhill were equally thrilled. The song came out in the wake of *Born To Be Wild* and went right up the charts to number 2. It moved faster than *Born To Be Wild* and initially outsold *Born* in singles sales. It saved the second album. Writing credits were assigned to me and Rushton; regrettably, it turned out to be the only song he ever contributed as a songwriter.

With a shortage of quality material and the clock ticking, we were forced to lean on others to get through the album. Gabriel contributed a couple of tunes, notably a song that Jerry sang called

28. Mars had come up with *Faster Than The Speed Of Life,* and although Jerry was all for it, I didn't like it. I thought it was too contrived — Mars trying to create a follow-up to *Born To Be Wild.* As a result, I refused to sing it. Jerry ended up singing it as the opening cut on the album which became a point of confusion for some fans. For those who bought our first album, I was the one recognizable voice of Steppenwolf. I sang all the songs on the first album and, for better or worse, people identified my voice with the band. When people bought STEPPENWOLF THE SECOND, there was a different voice on the lead-off track. That was partly a carryover from The Sparrow days where we had multiple singers. Gabriel was an easy going guy who didn't view things in a rigid context of a Steppenwolf sound being defined by the first album.

As a songwriter, you learn very early that you are not going to please everybody, but you have to please yourself when you sit down to write or record a tune with the conviction and passion that may in turn touch your listener. My simple philosophy was to write what moved me and to say what I felt, guided by my inner voice, rather than analyze the musical fashion of the day in an attempt to get a hit. I had often seen Dennis try this with The Sparrow and it did not appeal to me. There has never been a point since where I have felt obliged to change my approach. Naturally, nobody wants to stand still. I'm subject to the influences of new developments and conditions that arise. But ultimately, it still has to be something that I care about. The basic questions for me remain: who are you, what do you stand for, and what matters to you? They are at the root of it all every time I sit down to write a song.

If I'm not intensely involved with what I'm writing and consequently have to perform, I can't write it. Singing about Incense and Peppermints in 1994 would be a tough chore for me. I need some substance to sink my teeth into. On the second album were a couple of tunes that I felt I had something to say. One was *None Of Your Doing.*

> *If I could show you where I've been,*
> *Perhaps you'd know and never ask again.*
> *Could I forget the things I've seen,*
> *Perhaps I'd smile and we would be the same.*

I can't return to where you're going.
What I have learned, it can't be undone.
Don't blame yourself, don't you know,
It was none of your doing.

NONE OF YOUR DOING, 1968

The song was about a young vet returning from Vietnam trying to deal with his new viewpoint on the world, finding that his attitude had changed so radically while away that he can't even relate to the woman he left behind. He tells her: "I'm a different person and that change is not of your doing, it's me." The song came from my conversations with people who had been in Vietnam or who had friends over there. I learned of the difficulties they had adjusting to a society that really didn't want to hear about the war. Guys were coming home and being spat on, neglected and scorned because they weren't heroes like the GIs returning from World War II. The Vietnam veterans really suffered at the hands of American society, from both sides. It was something I felt was important.

The Steppenwolf sound had been labeled by some as 'white blues.' There was no denying our roots were in the blues, but with a few exceptions, notably *Hootchie Kootchie Man* and *Tighten Up Your Wig* (our tribute to Chicago bluesman Junior Wells), we had evolved a sound less derivative of straight blues while still packing some of its structure and punch. Prior to the completion of the second album, I had made some statements to the media that I wanted to leave the blues behind us. Still, I had a concept in mind for the album, a suite that would chart the evolution of the blues from field music through urban electric blues to a more modern blues-derived rock style. I intended it to cover the whole second side of the album and give us the opportunity to, once and for all, lay the blues to rest. We didn't completely succeed in fulfilling that concept. It started off with a solo acoustic slide guitar doing an authentic rural country blues on a porch setting (we even had birds chirping in the background). It progressed from there to a more or less standard blues band instrumentation joining in with the same guitar part picked up by an electric guitar. From there it went into various stages where the organ came in to create an R 'n' B groove instrumentally moving into a dance kind of R 'n' B club setting with simulated live audience participation. A certain amount of the initial premise was followed but the real problem lay in trying to communicate what I was after, what I was hearing in my head, to Gabriel, Richard, and Bill as well as the band members in order for all of us to pull in the same direction and contribute ideas to make it happen. For various reasons we just ran out of juice right around the time we recorded it. It worked well, however, in our live show.

We were more successful with *Don't Step On The Grass, Sam.* Everybody just clicked on that one. The song was based on something I had watched one night on the *Joe Pine Show.* He was the Rush Limbaugh of the late Sixties, an ex-marine, exceedingly right wing type who verbally abused and insulted a variety of guests. He was a really nasty person and his audience would cheer him on, most of whom were either emotionally disturbed or intellectually challenged. He manipulated the ignorance and shortcomings of his audience for self-promotion and profit. These people needed something to hate because they had to blame somebody for what wasn't going right in their lives, and Joe Pine simply exploited that sentiment by providing them with scapegoats.

One night his guests were a government official and a representative of the counterculture who discussed the pros and cons of marijuana use. The latter advocated the theory that marijuana was no more harmful than alcohol and should be decriminalized, while on the other hand, the government official favored tougher laws on marijuana, blaming most of society's ills on it. I thought, "Oh boy, here we go again." Having personally been hoodwinked by Reefer Madness, I naturally assumed that thousands of others had also discovered the big lie. I felt very strongly that marijuana was completely misrepresented in terms of its potential harm. The song came as a direct response to this constant distortion by the authorities. My concern was that young impressionable people might not know where the lie ended and the truth began. If they had been lied to about marijuana, might they not assume that they had been misled about drugs in general? Would someone experiment with say heroin thinking its dangers were greatly exaggerated? I really believed that a disservice was being done by those who, under the guise of protecting the public, simply created the big lie.

Well, it's evil, wicked, mean and nasty.
Don't step on the grass, Sam.
And it will ruin our fair country.
Don't be such an ass, Sam.
Well, it will hook your Sue and Johnny.
You're so full of bull, Sam.
All will pay that disagree with me.

You waste my coin, Sam, all you can,
To jail my fellow man.
For smoking of the noble weed,
You need much more than him.
You've been telling lies so long,
Some believe they're true.
So they close their eyes to things,
You have no right to do.

DON'T STEP ON THE GRASS, SAM, 1968

As it turned out the song became, along with the Jefferson Airplane's *White Rabbit*, a target for that illustrious shining example of morality, Vice President Spiro T. Agnew himself in a speech to a political convention in Las Vegas. Robert Hilburn, writing in *The Los Angeles Times*, stated the following in response to Agnew's allegations:

Another drug song mentioned by the Vice President was Don't Step On The Grass, Sam. *Written by Steppenwolf's John Kay, the song is a socio-political comment on court and government attitudes toward marijuana. Rather than being a glorification of drugs, it is an argument for treating marijuana differently from hard drugs. It is a position widely held inside the rock community and in many areas of the rest of society. Kay's reaction to Agnew's charges: "It makes me a little sad, I suppose. Here is a man who is listened to so much by his generation and he doesn't even take the time to study the subject enough to avoid enlarging the generation gap by spreading half-truths and other forms of distortion. By making these kind of comments, he is doing precisely what he accuses us of doing — being irresponsible."*

The song became a concert favorite. Jerry and I sang it in a call and response manner, like the Joe Pine discussion. We added a 3-D element with a simulated drug bust and the toilet flushing at the end which went down well with fans who could relate to it. Unlike the blues suite, *Sam* worked because everyone was involved.

Magic Carpet Ride was released in the fall and by November the single and STEPPENWOLF THE SECOND, were lodged in the Top Five, earning us two more gold disks to accompany the two for our first album and *Born To Be Wild*. As 1968 drew to a close, it seemed as though we had the Midas Touch.

That fall, we had played the Fillmore East in New York, opening for Mike Bloomfield's Electric Flag. The next night, we started at Steve Paul's Scene, a New York basement club, not a whole lot to look at but for some reason it had become *the scene.* Our first night happened to be the last night for The Crazy World of Arthur Brown whose record *Fire* I really liked at the time. This guy was strange!

We hung around to watch his set, it was just Arthur Brown singing and a trio — organ, guitar, drums. The Scene had a postage stamp sized stage with pillars and heating ducts running through it and little tables scattered here and there. As we watched, the organ intro started up and out of the little storage room behind the stage appeared Arthur. He was dressed like Kufu the Magnificent Pharaoh with a long gown/drape outfit down to his ankles, huge bell sleeves, and a metal crown that was on fire. He stepped up to the mike and shouted, "I am the God of Hellfire and I bring you . . . . . . Fire." And he launched into the song. He was flailing about and kept waving these enormous sleeves above his head when the lower part of one of them caught fire. There he was in a frenzy and hadn't noticed these little flames licking up towards his arm because he was too busy hollering, "Fire, I'll teach you to burn!" Meantime, one of his roadies spied what was happening and on his hands and knees started crawling toward him, trying to beat out the flames every time Arthur's sleeve flew by. Arthur, oblivious to the fact that his sleeve was in flames, gave his roadie one of those 'Get away from me. Have you lost your mind?' looks. Finally he realized he wasn't just singing Fire, he was *on fire* and stood still long enough for the roadie to extinguish him. We were beside ourselves howling at this whole scene.

The next night we shared the bill with Mose Allison. He did all those great songs like *Parchment Farm* and *I Live The Life I Love* with this neat scat growl thing he had. During our break, Jimi Hendrix walked in with Buddy Miles and the keyboard player from the McCoys. "Can we jam?" they asked. So we let them use our equipment. Jerry was really shitting because Buddy's a pretty hefty dude and really slammed those skins. It was Jimi's jam, so we didn't sit in, but he came back a few nights later and did it again.

Michael Monarch: *Hendrix had the maitre d' come over and grab me after we had played. He and Nico from the Velvet Underground were together and he told me he liked my guitar playing, which was pretty good for a kid who had only been playing for less than two years. He invited me up to his apartment after. At The Scene he jammed with my equipment but unfortunately I didn't play with him.*

As we were leaving the club I met Jimi. He was sitting in a Corvette and someone said that Jimi wanted to say hello. I went over and he said, "Hey man, nice to meet you. I like your sound. Let's do some jamming sometime." Months later I was back in LA and Jutta and I had been invited to The Factory, a private club in West Hollywood, for a party thrown by Mama Cass and, of all people, Kirk Douglas in honor of Donovan who was commencing a major US tour. Jimi was there and invited us to join him at his table. We got to talking about music and found that we both had been frustrated at times by our inability to accurately reproduce the sounds and music we heard in our heads. After a while, the conversation became semi philosophical and eventually turned to technology and how someday perhaps we would be able to simply attach electrodes to our foreheads and spontaneously create music unencumbered by the limitations of our hands and voices. The party was winding down so we all went over to the house Jimi was renting in one of the canyons.

That night, Jutta and I had taken something new, THC, a tablet form of cannabis, and I had been drinking Black Russians. Shortly after arriving Jutta decided to take off her clothes and go for a swim in the pool, while Jimi and I talked and noodled around on a guitar in one of the rooms. He had some albums on a table, one of which was STEPPENWOLF THE SECOND. "That song *Don't Step On The Grass,*

Sam," asked Jimi, "did you write that guitar riff?" "Yeah," I replied, "It's just a simple thing." And he responded, "Yeah, I know, but I kind of like it." I told him my reaction the first time I heard The Experience. It was quite relaxed and subdued, no bodyguards around, very casual. Acknowledging and admiring each other's work was the closest we ever came to getting to know one another well. That night he was open and gracious, soft-spoken, almost shy. He was then and remains to this day one of my favorite musicians.

In subsequent visits to New York, Noel Redding, Jimi's bass player, looked us up a few times and we hung out. Once we went to see Jimi at a recording studio in Manhattan, probably the same place he later bought and renamed Electric Ladyland. In any case, when we arrived Jimi was playing guitar and singing by himself in the studio. He finished his take, came into the control room, said hello and we chatted briefly, then after inviting us to hang out he got behind the board to listen to the playback. Later, Noel mentioned that at times he and Mitch Mitchell would overdub their parts on things Jimi had cut by himself. This was towards the end of "The Experience" days and I guess the writing was already on the wall. We stayed for a little while but with Jimi's mind on his work and ours on a party somewhere, we took our leave and said goodbye. That was the last time I saw Jimi alive. Of all those we've lost over the years (aside from Wolf members), I miss Jimi, along with Lowell George and Bob Marley, the most.

Following the second album, what solidified our success was the inclusion of *Born To Be Wild* and *The Pusher* in the film *Easy Rider*. After *Magic Carpet Ride* had been a hit, I received a phone call from Burt Jacobs who told me that Peter Fonda and Dennis Hopper were making a low budget movie about two guys who ride their Harleys across the country "in search of America," sort of a late Sixties hip version of Route 66. Fonda and Hopper wanted a non-traditional soundtrack but were out of money so decided to use existing songs by the Byrds, the Band, Jimi Hendrix, Bob Dylan, and Steppenwolf, among others. Their hope was that these artists would be sufficiently impressed with the movie to agree to some kind of compensation based on its success. All those involved were invited to a private screening on a back lot in Hollywood. We saw the film and were simply blown away by it. Back then it was the first counterculture movie to openly deal with drugs, bikes, acid, sex, and the counterculture. I arrived a little late and caught the tail end of *The Pusher* scene with Phil Specter, and then heard *Born To Be Wild* with Fonda and Hopper riding across the screen. We thanked them for considering our songs and offered to work something out for compensation. Rumor had it that Dylan wanted to write some new stuff which he felt would be more appropriate, but they said they would rather use *It's Alright Ma, I'm Only Bleeding* because it fit perfectly. Dylan didn't agree so on the soundtrack album Roger McGuinn sang the song. We also heard that The Band wanted to do the entire soundtrack but again Fonda and Hopper passed. I think that's why Smith sang *The Weight* on the album. We just said, "Cool movie. Thanks for thinking of us. Send us the check."

What *Easy Rider* did for us was to spread the Steppenwolf name worldwide, paving the way for us to tour internationally, especially in Europe. It also solidified an image that, although not incorrect, was somewhat incomplete. Although the movie was beneficial in spreading the band name, it would ultimately become a hindrance to our ability to progress. By 1972 we found ourselves tied up in a straightjacket image of a macho, leather, biker band.

Since The Sparrow days I had worn leather and sunglasses, but once my personal image connected with the biker thing in *Easy Rider, Born To Be Wild* and all that, a macho swagger, sado-masochistic perception suddenly reared its head. I remember one female interviewer in New York who told me that the first time she saw the band in concert she thought I looked as if I would jump off the stage and kick the shit out of the first three rows. She was nervous about doing an interview with me for that reason.

Bill Cooper: *John has successfully created this image that he is one guy you don't want to mess with. But he is definitely not what he appears to be, quite the opposite in fact. He's a very thoughtful person, very nice, very rational, and very complex.*

Crawdaddy Magazine (1970): *While it may come as a disappointment to some of his audience, John Kay does not live in a dungeon below Sunset Strip surrounded by instruments of torture, Doberman Pincers and cages of bruised but willing groupies. When I met him* *he had the kind of tan you don't get beating up people in dark bedrooms, and he spoke in well articulated English on subjects more* humanistic *than animalistic.*

After *Easy Rider*, many people assumed that the band was closely associated with the biker lifestyle. The ironic thing is, due to my bad eyesight, I have never driven a motorcycle in my life. The fastest thing I've ever ridden is a bicycle. Occasionally, when bikers would approach someone in the band and ask, "What kind of bike does John really have?" the response would be, "Oh man, he's got a garage full of them. Ten or eleven. They keep giving them to him over the years so he's got one for every occasion." And they'd go away happy. I remember at the Agora in Columbus, Ohio a few years back I came out after the show and there was a biker with a beautiful, immaculate motorcycle with god knows how many layers of candy apple red paint on the gas tank. He pulled out a buck knife and thrust it into my hand. "Go on, autograph my tank. Scratch your name in it." Astonished, I said to him, "You sure man? This bike is beautiful." But he remained adamant. "Don't worry, I'll shoot it with clear lacquer afterwards." So I stood there scratching right down to the metal of this beautiful paint job and the guy went away absolutely thrilled.

We've always had bikers at our gigs going right back to The Sparrow days at the Ark. Bikers and biker clubs still come out regularly to our concerts throughout the United States. We have also played over the years numerous times at biker rallies, from regional meets to Sturgis, South Dakota and Daytona Beach, Florida bike weeks as well as the 1993 Harley-Davidson 90th birthday bash in Milwaukee, Wisconsin. Sometimes the crowds were gigantic with thousands upon thousands of riders as far as the eye (even someone's else's eye) could see. It's an awesome sight to behold, acres and acres of chrome, almost dangerous to look at in bright sunlight. No matter where — Canada, Scandinavia, Australia or at home — bikers have always supported the Wolf. Not once, to the best of my recollection, have they ever started any trouble at our shows. We appreciate their loyalty and their desire to live their own lifestyle. They will always be welcome at our concerts.

Just as our success was solidifying, Rushton was given the boot from the band. Always an eccentric individual, the rest of the band knew very little about his private life. We had just played the Hollywood Bowl when Rushton was accused of stealing steaks from a market in LA. He was becoming increasingly paranoid of the police and would relate to us these wildly imaginative tales of being arrested and beaten by the LAPD. He became a kind of wild child.

Besides, by the second album Rushton was often at odds musically with the rest of us. Early in 1969, we were flying out to Colorado for a weekend gig. Rushton arrived at the airport with his girlfriend, a disproportionate amount of luggage for a weekend trip, and a few of his friends in tow. He gave us some innocuous story about going to visit relatives and we left it at that. The next day, after the gig, I received a phone call from him saying he wasn't returning to LA with us, offering another convoluted tale about his relatives. We were expected back in LA that day for a television show taping. Michael phoned one of his friends who substituted for Rushton, faking his way through the taping. By this point I was seething.

When Rushton finally surfaced in LA, the truth filtered out. He and a number of his friends had been convinced that a cataclysmic earthquake was going to take place that particular weekend, dumping California into the ocean. When nothing of the kind occurred, he returned, hoping to resume his place in the band. At that point, what I should have done was sit him down, tell him what he did was wrong leaving us high and dry, and warn him not to do it again. Because of the pressures on me as a result of the band's success, coupled with the drugs I was taking, I was volatile at that point. Everything was either black or white, no grey areas: Rushton fucked up, therefore he's out.

Jerry Edmonton: *Rushton did some dumb things like getting caught stealing steaks at the Farmer's Market. Or, once John was late for practice in the garage because he and Jutta were out somewhere and the rest of us were just standing around outside when Rushton had the desire to smoke some weed. He knew that John kept his stash in the bathroom in a little jar so he climbed up the side of the garage scaling along the wall like a cat burglar, snuck into the bathroom, rolled a joint and climbed back out. He did that more than once.*

When John got hip to this it pissed him off. Little things like that irritated John about Rushton but John tolerated him because he liked his playing.

When he skipped the TV show in LA, Rushton broke the code of honor. In those days, there was one side of John where he would growl, "Grrrr, fire him!" In retrospect, the record company and the management should have sat us down and worked it out. Instead, we broke up the band that created that sound and those hits.

Our first album, that's the best one; there was a magical sound between all the instruments. That's maybe one mistake that was made, and I'm not blaming anyone, but I don't know why we had to change. I know John liked to change. He'd say, "We can't just do the same old thing," and I kept arguing, "We can do the same thing because its selling a lot of records." That sound, the first album and to a lesser extent the second one, was the sound everyone remembers. That was the Steppenwolf sound. Unfortunately we started changing too many people in the band and lost that sound.

Instead of taking time off and auditioning a new bass player, looking to see who was out there, we called Nick. With pressure from the label for a third album and tour commitments pending, we had no time. Nick became a kind of 'devil we knew.'

Jerry and I hadn't kept in contact with Nick since The Sparrow split up a year and a half earlier. His band TIME, with a hot young guitarist from Alabama named Larry Byrom, had recorded an album that had not done well but they had some heavy money behind them, so much so that Nick was driving around LA in a Jaguar XKE. We had heard via the grapevine that Nick had become a decent bass player because the guys in TIME had pushed him to sit down and practice. After Rushton was dismissed, Jerry was keen on Nick joining and I must admit I thought it would be interesting with another ex-Sparrow in the band. Although there was an element of sentimentality, the decision was undertaken for practical reasons: we needed a bass player immediately. Nick leapt at the offer.

Nick was a born entertainer on stage and that was a further inducement to bringing him into the fold. Once he got into the spotlight, though, it was "Hey folks, I have arrived." He had dreamed of this all his life. Soon after joining, we performed on *The Smother's Brothers Show* on an elaborate set consisting of mirrors and crystal chandeliers. Nick showed up wearing a floor-length kaftan and would put on this 'spaced out' look whenever he caught the camera focusing on him. He soon took to appearing in concert sporting kaftans and mu mus. He was a little strange but nothing threatening, he was just being Nick St. Nicholas the rock star.

Nick came on board at the peak touring period for Steppenwolf — America, Canada, Europe. We started flying out on weekends to perform, going out Friday morning and returning late Sunday night, thus allowing us more time at home. Nick also entered the picture as we were preparing to record our third album. Unfortunately, we discovered that everything we had heard about Nick's improved bass playing wasn't true.

With the third album, STEPPENWOLF AT YOUR BIRTHDAY PARTY, others in the band, especially Michael, were beginning to see that royalties from songwriting on a hit album were fairly lucrative. A light went on in their heads: "I can write songs, too." At times, their songwriting ideas were an inspiration for me, providing the seed for a song which I would finish writing. *It's Never Too Late* and *Jupiter's Child* emerged from ideas offered to me. Nick had come up with the line, "It's never too late to start all over again." I liked it and immediately wrote the rest of the song. Jerry gave me a couple of lines about a fiery wizard, I think the idea of a Jupiter's child was Gabriel's, and again ideas started popping into my head. There were, however, a number of tunes on the third album where I had to bite my tongue because others felt they were now writers too. I didn't want to aggravate what had already become a source of irritation, namely the dominant role Jerry and I had in directing the band. There was some pressure from within to be more democratic. Besides, on the third album Jerry and I didn't have an overabundance of material because of the schedule ABC Dunhill had set for us. They wouldn't wait for us to write more suitable material. It forced me to defer to the songwriting contributions of others in order to meet a deadline. As a result the album suffered.

The worst thing we ever did was allow ABC Dunhill to insist that we write, record, and deliver two albums a year plus tour to support each one. We never considered the drawbacks when we signed. Like any hungry young band we were just relieved to have a contract offer. What our management should have done had they been attentive enough to read the writing on the wall was to say to the label, "Times have changed. We don't want to kill the goose that lays the golden eggs. Let the band take a break, go their own ways, finish the new house, be with their families, replenish their batteries, and when the creative spark returns then they'll go into the studio and make some fresh music." Our management didn't have the balls to say, "They're not ready. You don't get an album." Other artists were beginning to do that, and although in some cases it produced self-indulgent crap, in other instances it gave an artist enough breathing space to create something worthwhile away from the treadmill. Unfortunately, the men in suits still viewed rock 'n' roll bands as a fleeting thing. Get in and grab as much money as you can before it dies.

Jerry Edmonton: *After the second album, John hinted he was going solo. That's why the third album had such a hodge podge of writing on it. After two hit records, John was getting that ego high and probably hearing things from some people like, "You did all this, you're the voice, look at all the songs you wrote." There are a lot of people like that in this business.*

The sound of the band was the band with John's voice, not just his voice. I talked to Burt and Bill and told them John wanted to be this solo guy and they said, "What?" That was the one time our managers did do something because they saw money going down the tubes. They called John in and had a talk with him. From that day on things were different. Everybody still got their vote, unless the vote wasn't exactly the way John wanted it because he had that leverage. He could just say, "You guys can be Steppenwolf." I think John knew that inside. He had control without putting it in writing. It was, "I'm not leaving the band but I can have this unspoken way of manipulating the band."

I was prepared to go it alone if things did not work out. I had been on my own before and I could do it again if I felt trapped in an unhappy situation. Much of the friction between us during the BIRTHDAY album sessions was really the result of my belief that several of the songs written by other band members were weak. I was further frustrated by the fact that I had been run ragged and did not have as many tunes written as I would have liked.

Still, there were some bright spots. Prior to recording STEPPEN-WOLF AT YOUR BIRTHDAY PARTY, I had been approached by the producers of the movie *Candy,* based on the staggeringly popular paperback book that every teenage boy in North America had read underneath the covers. Richard Burton, Marlon Brando, and Ringo Starr were in the film. The producers had a rough cut which they invited me to view with the idea of using *Magic Carpet Ride* and one more tune they wanted me to write for the soundtrack. I was skeptical at first but they convinced me to come on board once they told me The Byrds were contributing as well.

Not long after that I found myself back in New York at the Hotel Albert. We had decided that staying at our by then customary suites at the Plaza Hotel was isolating us from the street scene and we wanted to see if returning to our old hangout in Manhattan would bring us back in touch with our roots and inspiration — sort of a 'stay hungry' approach. Regrettably, we discovered it didn't work. Once we'd moved on from our humble origins, pretending nothing had changed was useless. There were few distractions at the Albert so I took my guitar and banged out *Rock Me.* It's about girls like the character in *Candy* who are trying to navigate through the labyrinth of growing up and learning how to deal with their own sexuality while the entire male population is trying to get next to them. We cut the track and it went into the film. Dunhill also released it as a single and it climbed to number 7 in Cashbox. Jerry came up with an inventive percussion groove in the middle that really nailed the tune down. We still hadn't completed the third album, so *Rock Me* filled the void for AM radio.

Along with *Rock Me, It's Never Too Late, Jupiter's Child,* and *Happy Birthday* (a little song that Gabriel wrote featuring a grinding organ sound, female backing vocals, and my gravelly vocals) were my favorites on that third album. They had some spark and emotion. Songs like *Sleeping And Dreaming, God Fearing Man, Round And Down,* and *Mango Juice* were a total waste of time as far as I was concerned. Compared to our previous two efforts, the third album bombed at the time and represented a significant step down. Over the years it eventually surpassed gold but sales figures don't mean a thing to me if an album is weak. There are other albums I've done since it that sold fewer copies but I'm more proud of than the BIRTHDAY album.

As *Rock Me* was exiting the charts, we released *Jupiter's Child,* but radio didn't care for it. The only thing we could think to pull from the album was *It's Never Too Late,* our first sort of ballady single. It scraped into the Top Forty but failed to give us the hit we had hoped for, which was too bad because it would have broken the streak of rockers and opened up a few new doors for us. Its release coincided with our appearance on *The Ed Sullivan Show,* the foremost variety show on television that virtually everybody in North America watched each Sunday night. For our April 17th performance, all of about four minutes and change, we had Bill Cooper edit together a medley of *Born To Be Wild, Magic Carpet Ride,* and *It's Never Too Late* from the records. The band would mime to this while I sang live over the original vocal tracks. We flew out to New York and began rehearsals the next morning at seven.

Backstage at the theater was like a circus: half dressed people and animals going in and out, Topo Gigio the Italian Mouse, Yugoslavian jugglers, the Peter Janero Dancers. It was like vaudeville. We got on stage for the run through and discovered to our dismay that the monitor speakers through which we would hear the playback of our music track were totally inadequate. We had become quite proficient at miming to a pre-recorded track by then, but it required loud playback levels enabling Jerry to hit his drums hard without the real drums drowning out the pre-recorded track. Otherwise we'd be out of sync. These speakers were okay for crooners but damn near useless for rock 'n' roll. Jerry struggled through a couple of run throughs and then locked into it as did the rest of the guys. I was dealing with an additional problem. Over the months since the songs were recorded, my phrasing had altered slightly from the original versions from singing them live, so I was floundering trying to get in sync with the music track.

By evening we were prepared for Ed to announce, "Right here on our sheeew, for all you youngsters out there, here's Steppenwolf." To Ed's surprise, girls were screaming for us, not as much as for the Beatles, but there was a loud response nonetheless. Apparently, you never knew ahead of time who Ed would call over to speak with him, so the producer told us to be ready just in case. Well, we finished our medley and Ed motioned us to come over to where he was standing. There we were in all our rock star regalia standing beside Ed Sullivan. Stuck for something to say, he proceeded to ask us who our favorite acts were. I said something like Hendrix and the Rolling Stones. He went through all of us until he arrived at Nick who responded in his own inimitable way, "My favorite band is right here in New York, the Fugs." Ed, who was completely taken aback and wasn't quite sure what Nick had just said, replied, "The Frogs?" To which Nick pressed on with, "No man, the Fugs! You know *the Fugs!*" Rolling his eyes in horror, Ed quickly ushered us off stage.

"Why don't you come with me little girl on a Magic Carpet Ride . . ." Performing at the Newport Pop Festival, 1969.

Dueling Rickenbackers, Nick & I at Newport '69.

Photo shoot for the cover of STEPPEN-WOLF AT YOUR BIRTHDAY PARTY *in* *the debris of the burned out Laurel Canyon home of Bob Hite (Canned Heat), 1969.*

Talking about The Fugs with Ed Sullivan
following our performance, April 17, 1969.

Off the road again, with Jutta and Shawn at our Nichols Canyon home in Hollywood Hills, 1969.

NINE

MONSTER
ON THE LOOSE

The police force is watching the people
And the people just can't understand
We don't know how to mind our own business
The whole world has to be just like us
Now we are fighting a war over there
No matter who's the winner we can't pay the cost
Yes a monster's on the loose
It's put our heads into a noose
And just sits there watching

America where are you now
Don't you care about your sons and daughters
Don't you know we need you now
We can't fight alone against the monster

MONSTER, 1970

Hippies with money. That's what Jutta and I were once the money started coming our way, though vats of money weren't rolling in immediately after the first album went gold. Steppenwolf's success was incremental not instantaneous like Guns 'n' Roses, whose first album went triple platinum and they're all multi-millionaires in eighteen months. The first thing Jutta and I bought besides the new stereo system was a cool little second hand Volkswagen Bug convertible, the first material benefit from Steppenwolf.

Gabriel Mekler had suggested hiring a business manager for the band, an accountant named Don Sterling. Don was an aggressive guy on our behalf, right off the bat negotiating a reduction in the percentage we were paying to our management which we then used to pay for his services. For the same percentage we now received personal and business management. We had heard horror stories of managers turning up in Ecuador with rock stars' money, but with Don scrutinizing every dollar we felt more secure.

Jutta and I were still living in that $90 a month apartment on Fountain Avenue when I returned from the 1968 bus tour that summer, but we now started thinking, "If this keeps up maybe we can afford to rent a house." With a baby now to look after we definitely needed more space. Back then for about $250 a month you could rent a comfortable unfurnished two bedroom house in Laurel Canyon. That was our thinking when I approached Don whose response was: "Don't rent, buy." I said, "Buy? Me? Twenty-three years old and buying a house?" "Yeah," countered Don, "it establishes your credit and you'll build up equity." I went home and told Jutta what Don had suggested. She was as surprised as I was.

I asked Don to give me some idea of how much we could afford and I was overwhelmed. So Jutta and I started looking around at homes in the canyons of the Hollywood Hills where we knew we wanted to live. One was a little gingerbread "Bird house," supposedly built by an architect named Byrd, a bungalow in Nichols Canyon off Dresden Drive with little bird hole openings in the gables, two brick chimneys, one a spiral round design, and a cedar shake roof. We weren't quite certain what we wanted initially but over the course of a few weeks we went back to it, drawn by its rustic charm I suppose, and eventually decided to buy it. We added a loft to the living room with a library ladder up to it. My stepfather helped me build a work room in the double garage where I could write and record. The property had a little creek running through it that gave the place a country feel with possum, raccoons, coyotes, and even deer. We added an electric gate and a black-bottom pool that was so natural looking that years later a wild mallard built her nest and hatched her ducklings there. Tucked away in the hills, it was almost totally private. There we were with our new house, nice furnishings, Shawn was growing up healthy, we had a nanny/house-keeper, and plenty of money.

Jutta Maue-Kay: *We both came from working-class backgrounds so we never thought we could own a house like that. We gradually furnished it the way we wanted it, mostly from auctions because it was cheaper. We decorated it into our own trip with Persian carpets, cushions, a hookah, and a bedroom like an Arabian tent (which was John's fantasy). The peacock feathers idea came from Pam Morrison's boutique, Jim Morrison's wife. Every room was a sort of trip, our fantasies.*

Shawn Kay: *Mom and Dad had some weird things in our house, I must admit. It was sort of a hippie pad. Mom had glued peacock feathers to the loft ceiling, feathers everywhere, and there were wolf skins in the loft. I was the first one to freak out about that, so they got rid of the skins. Nowadays, they can't believe they had them. Mom had a big mirror inlayed with a Buddha. And we had a wrought iron ladder that went up to the loft. Dad had a little display on top of the wall in the living room with medieval swords, morning star with the pikes that he had brought back from England, some old rifles, and a shield. Our hallway had black and white psychedelic wallpaper. It was weird. Our little den was Moroccan, and we sat on pillows at an original antique gold Moroccan dining room table where we ate. The room was lit with Persian lamps. It was a real little canyon Sixties hippie house. They got rid of all that stuff in the late Seventies. I guess they grew out of it.*

We followed the blueprint of the lifestyle of the successful rock musician: we started going to nicer places, wearing nicer clothes, hanging out with people in the same circle. The first time the band went to England we went crazy bringing back antique cars and other paraphernalia. Jerry had a 1937 Bentley and a 1952 Allard sports car, Goldy picked up a 1952 Rolls Royce Saloon car, and I purchased a 1938 Lagonda, the dumbest thing I've ever done. It was a monster to drive and was always in the shop for repair. Poor Jutta was the one stuck driving it; the thing maneuvered like an army truck with the steering wheel on the right side. It took two people to turn the wheel. Later I bought her a rare 1955 Mercedes Gull Wing for her birthday. She loved that car. We took vacations in places like Hawaii, though those were rather rare in the first few years due to the hectic pace imposed upon us by our management and label.

Later I realized many of these things were merely distractions, the consolation prize, toys to be enjoyed that provided some momentary pleasure. We indulged ourselves but the material possessions certainly could not replace or fill the void if you were frustrated or unhappy. And they can get in the way of what you are supposed to be focusing on, the music. We lived in the fast lane, no denying it, but it was a bit of a facade for some underlying problems.

Jutta Maue-Kay: *I was not very happy those first few years. I sort of got lost for awhile. Our lives changed alright but it was more John's life, and I felt like I was just tagging along. There were a lot of good times but I felt stuck. He was out on the road and I stayed home. We took some wonderful vacations but on a daily basis somebody had to be at home. Guess who? And I started to resent that sometimes. It was the first time in my life that I wasn't working and I felt very insecure so I tried to keep busy with Shawn and the house.*

The guys were playing their rock star roles out there on the road and I had my suspicions, which later proved to be true. That was when we were the least happy with each other. I was cooped up while he was on the road, and when he would come home, I wanted to get out. He wanted to stay home and enjoy his privacy, but he understood and did compromise with me.

Many times I was tempted to go out and get a job. I had a period of time when I had very low self-esteem. John was out there and it sounded so exciting while I was at home raising a baby. I was very unhappy, jealous and the drugs didn't help either. It took me quite awhile to figure out that it was really my problem. I had to work that out and John was very helpful.

Jutta and I were both going through some changes — the money, the hectic lifestyle, the escalating drug use. Jutta and I were using cocaine fairly liberally, not to excess by any means, but for a time it was a daily routine: You wake up, you had a long night, you drank too many damn Black Russians the night before because the coke you were doing kept sobering you up, so it's "I'm feeling a little dizzy with this alcohol let me have a toot here. Hey, hey, I'm feeling great. I think I'll have another drink!" It was this yo-yo effect so that when you did get some sleep after maybe smoking some grass to come down from the coke, you were comatose for twelve hours. Then you wake up and it's: "Oh man, I'm really groggy. A hit of coke would fix me up just right. Do we have any in the house? No?! Well, we'd better call and get some." Jutta and I were also smoking cigarettes so among the nicotine, the alcohol, cocaine and grass we were going from one thing to another everyday. My temper was a bit more prone to flair ups, I became less patient with people, and I became more frustrated, but the coke made me feel enthusiastic about a lot of things.

Bill Cooper: *Richard and I had been pretty straight about the whole drug thing in the studio until Jerry Edmonton started coming around. He was the first one to start polluting everyone. Musicians tended to view drugs as a tool: "If I take this I can stay up an extra twelve hours and do two more tracks." But there wasn't a lot of stuff going on in the studio with the guys in Steppenwolf. We weren't involved with them socially so I don't know about that side but nothing ever got crazy in the studio where everybody got blasted and sat around doing nothing for eight hours. John would never have allowed that. The only thing John would have in the studio was his Kahlua. He loved Black Russians especially when he was doing vocals. He had this Steppenwolf portable bar that he carried around with him.*

Our public relations firm, Gibson and Stromberg, was one of the hottest in LA. Gary Stromberg was a funny man to be around who knew all the right people in LA. Jutta and I began hanging out with him. We'd go to the Whisky, the Troubadour, the Candy Store and stay out until all hours of the night. We were out practically every night when I wasn't on the road, talking that shit, drinking too much, snorting coke. Upstairs at the Rainbow with Robert Plant or whoever, everyone doing lines. We were having a ball and figured we could afford it. There was good food (I started gaining a little weight), good music, good drugs, good company, we were driving some of the hottest cars in town. The people around us made us feel special. "How can I say no to my favorite yes man." There was a lot of action and it was very seductive.

By the early seventies coke was everywhere and it was no longer just the rock stars who were doing it. The accountants, managers, lawyers, record promotion guys, the people in the suits were all into blow. I remember Alice Cooper's coming out party, a promotional party thrown by his management. Everybody who was happening was there. Outside into the hall were phone booths covered by a large Chinese folding screen so you couldn't see the booths. Everybody in the booths was going, "Yeah, so I told this guy, snort, I'd call tomorrow, snort. . . ." At all these posh parties, everyone was in the lobby tooting, everyone in their pop gear at their tables tooting. That shit was everywhere, just like the old *Saturday Night Live* sketch with Bill Murray: "Hi, Jerry Aldini, Poly Sutra Records. Tootskie, baby?"

Jutta and I still dropped acid for recreational purposes, going up to Big Sur for a weekend, camping out under the stars, doing acid, wandering through the woods and frolicking on the beach. It was still a time when grass and acid were taken as a form of relaxation the way that people use alcohol. Beyond that, many people used them to unlock the other side of the brain and encourage the creative flow. My own personal line that I would never cross was sticking a needle into my body as a means of getting high. As far as I knew, nobody in the band was ever a junkie. I would have thrown them out immediately.

I saw the casualties. One of our sister acts at ABC Dunhill was Three Dog Night. They had some guys who were straight, others who were burning the candle at both ends, dangerously close to having a serious drug accident. Over the years, various people I knew or had seen like Jimi Hendrix, Janis Joplin, Al Wilson and Bob Hite of Canned Heat, Lowell George of Little Feat, all allegedly died as a result of drugs. Looking at it now, if you count the people who died from drug-related circumstances it's a rather shocking number.

I think we were all too busy or in a state of denial: "I'm able to control it. I can stop whenever I want." You bullshit yourself because you're young and think you're immortal. I don't think that any of us thought we saw people around us who were candidates for a quick death. When it did happen it usually came as a great shock.

I invited my mother and Gerhard to come to our first headlining concert at the Forum in LA. She had seen me play on an amateur level with the German church group back in Toronto but never saw me perform again until Steppenwolf was already successful. The concert was sold out and she was all a twitter. The enormity of our success truly amazed her. Here were twenty thousand people screaming for her boy and his band. She was proud of my success and, I suspect, also relieved that she didn't have to worry about me anymore.

My mother had a typical hardworking immigrant response to my success — she was very proud of me but it didn't alter her life in any way. She continued to work at Bulloch's and live in the same place. Nor was she interested in lavish gifts from me. I asked if they'd like a new house but they were happy with what they had. My mother did like vacations by the sea, so we rented a beach house in Malibu, and my relatives Tuta and Robert from Toronto flew in, and the four of them, along with Shawn, spent two months there. Jutta and I joined them a couple of times. Another time I sent them to Honolulu and we rented a house on Diamond Head Road, close to the Atani Estate where the band had stayed once before. I was glad that I could do something special for them after all their years of supporting me.

In 1969 we began our most successful and wildest touring. Initially, we flew to our gigs by regular airlines, often a Delta 747 flight. The upstairs lounge was divided by a partition with six swivel captains seats and a games table. If you booked six first class seats, you could reserve this private compartment. The road crew would occupy the lounge seats on the other side of the partition so no one else could get in. When people would wander up to the lounge, they'd usually beat a hasty retreat.

Jerry Edmonton: *Once we could afford it we always traveled first class. The most important thing is your state of mind when you walk out on that stage. It's only an hour or two but if you're* *temperamental, which a lot of musicians are, and if something throws you off, the show suffers. And it's those twenty thousand people out there who see it suffer. We used to have the Playboy limo cruise by and pick up John and I and another limo pick up the other guys at the same time. We'd meet at the airport, go to the TWA ambassador lounge, have free cocktails, pre-board, get off the plane, limo's waiting right there at the steps, go to the hotel, check into a suite, limo takes you to the sound check, you go back to the hotel, the promoter buys you a wonderful dinner, you go to the show and it's a great show. No distractions, nothing to piss you off before you take the stage. It cost more but it made for a good show. Sometimes, however, if you get too jaded with it and something doesn't go smooth you can become a bitch. Bitching because the limo was white when you wanted a black one. But that didn't happen much with us. Compared to the riders in contracts nowadays, all our rider said we required was a private dressing room, some soft drinks and beer and some towels. That was about it. No M&M's with the brown ones taken out or a vegetarian chef in the middle of Idaho.*

Later on we started renting private planes and it became like a search and destroy mission: swoop down in our plane, limo service, suites at the best hotels, do the gig before thousands of fans, partake in the drugs, alcohol, girls, then fly on to the next town and lay waste to it. We had taken on a road crew that included Bob Tomasso as road manager and Jerry Sloan as stage manager.

Jerry Sloan: *John looked like a junkie to me when I first met him, with the dark shades, the leather, this whole image he portrayed, yet he turned out to be one of the most mild mannered persons I ever met. He played up the whole rock star image, the coat over his shoulders, the leather pants and snakeskin boots. But he was the ultimate professional and kept a pretty tight reign over that band. He didn't say absolutely no drug use but he didn't want it to be too blatant. He was the authority in the group and it was best for everybody that he was. They couldn't have found a better leader. They all knew that if he walked out there was no Steppenwolf.*

It was a wild time. Each band member had his own custom

made velvet lined case with compartments to carry his favorite liquor. It was their survival kit with condoms, penicillin, pills, everything they needed on the road. And everywhere they went it was party time. They'd often take an entire floor in a hotel with all manner of illicit activity going on from room to room, spilling out into the hallways.

The lifestyle implied by my dark glasses, leather, the roughness of the voice, the aggression in the music, the raunchiness of the sound of the band, the fact that in those days I didn't smile a lot in photos, and all that 'take no prisoners' young bravado — I lived it to a certain extent. We may have been called the thinking man's rock band by some but we were nevertheless out there enjoying our success. During those years I expected some of the spoils of victory. There is no denying that there were transgressions on my part with respect to my fidelity. You go out there, do your show, your adrenaline's rushing, the crowd is going wild and afterwards, they're there. And you're ready. My energy level on stage was directly affected by sexuality. If you had attractive women in front to play to, you were more into it. That's one of the reasons why young guys pick up a guitar or drumsticks in the first place. At no time, however, did my sexual activities on the road threaten my relationship with Jutta. She was the only person I wanted to be with. Although I met some nice women on the road, none of them constituted a threat to Jutta.

Still, I deceived her and that was absolutely unforgivable. I knew who I loved but by the same token the life out there — the adulation, drugs, temptations — was extremely alluring. I got used to, in the words of a bad country song, having my Kate and Edith too. I was living a very good life at home; we had a great relationship as sexual partners. I was living a double life and the danger of losing the woman I loved through these other activities was pushed to the background because I didn't want to give anything up.

Bob Tomasso had a knack for arranging demos of private planes for us. Once we tried out Elvis's Viscount out of Las Vegas. Another time we took out two Lear Jets and John Lear Jr. piloted one of them. Someone foolishly asked him how fast the plane could take-off. We were practically pinned to the back of our seats, hair flying backwards as he proceeded to demonstrate the virtues of the Lear Jet's almost vertical take-off. He followed that death defying feat with a roll that almost brought back everyone's lunch. After each flight, Bob would tell the owner that we would evaluate the plane and call him next week. Invariably he would call back to say we had found a better plane. We tried Lode Stars, Lear Stretch 25s, Gulfstreams, all kinds of different planes. There was a plane that we considered purchasing, an old four engine Mohawk Airline Convair 440. It had been gutted inside, there were no seats, and we had to throw air mattresses in to sleep on. The damn thing would hardly start. There was oil leaking from the engines. We did a weekend tour with it as a demo and had to make an emergency landing.

Jerry Edmonton: *I remember one plane we were demoing we brought back some young girls with us over the state border. They had said, "Can we go to LA with you?" So we said sure 'cause they were kind of crazy and so were we. Once we got in the air our managers said, "What the fuck are you guys doing? You can't transport these girls across the border, it's against the law." One of them thought for a second then added, "Unless you pay them." They would be like stewardesses and working. So the management gave them some money. There was a poker game going on and Nick didn't want to lose so he put up his house. Our manager was still winning so Nick put up his wife, Randee. Anyway, it ended up Nick didn't lose her.*

Once while over Lake Michigan on our way from Chicago to Duluth we got caught in a blizzard. We had rented a two engine plane that sat twelve. When it started to get bumpy and we saw it snowing outside, we started thinking, we're going to join Buddy Holly. The plane was bouncing up and down, shuddering and shaking so severely I had sore elbows and a bump on my head from hitting the fuselage. The pilot came on the intercom to inform us that we couldn't turn back — and that the airport we were heading for was closed. But we had no choice, either land or run out of fuel. To his credit, the pilot got us down on an instrument landing to the snow covered runway. When the plane finally hit the tarmac it bogged down in the deep snow and only rolled a quarter of the normal distance. We knocked the door open and looked out. The wind was blowing so strong we couldn't see the terminal building. Here we were in all our pop gear and snakeskin boots with a huge snowbank in front of us. One of our crew had to jump out into two and a half feet of snow, hike to a phone booth, and call two taxis who couldn't believe we were at the airport.

Around this time we noticed that Goldy was changing from the happy-go-lucky guy we had known to a brooding, morose, unhappy personality largely as a result of his drug use. He started to become unfriendly with stewardesses and sometimes caused problems on flights. Jerry and I were at times embarrassed by his behavior. From the time I had worked selling crackerjacks and Coca-Cola at Maple Leaf Gardens to my time at the New Balladeer and Troubadour, I was aware that people could treat you like a door mat. As a result I always tried to remember those experiences and be courteous to people. I was not in the habit of regularly playing the big shot. Jerry and I hadn't forgotten or lost touch with our humble beginnings but Goldy had, always playing the role of a rock star around limousine drivers, doormen, or waiters: 'I'm a rock star so I'm expected to be obnoxious.' To a great extent his obnoxious behavior was the result of his own insecurity. His musical contributions also started to need a lot more direction and supervision.

Jerry Edmonton: *When Goldy would get a little stoned he used to do things he thought were funny. When the stewardesses in first class would come around, they'd ask your name just to make it more personal on the flight when they were serving you. Goldy would say, "Mr. Ough, that's spelled O U G H, but you can call me Jack." They would fall for it for a minute and then they'd glare at him. Another time, I was sitting across the aisle and he looked at me and said, "Watch this." He took his dick out of his pants, put the unbuckled seat belt just over it and rang for the stewardess. She came by and asked if she could help him. "I'm having the darndest time getting the buckle done up. Can you help me?" So she reached down and picked up both ends and there was Mr. Ough. She screamed. The next thing we knew, the captain came down and looked at all of us together and told us to behave on the flight.*

Prior to our first trip to San Antonio, Texas, we were told that The Who's drummer and resident loony, Keith Moon, had been thrown through a plate glass window somewhere in the South by unappreciative "fans." Since San Antonio had a large military-based population, many of whom did not care for guys with long hair, we hired two off-duty cops, five dollars an hour each, one a motorcycle cop replete with aviator glasses, uniform and holster and the other a descendant of Davy Crockett, to protect us. The only limos they could get for us at the time were from a funeral home. The cop on the bike led the way, the two limos put their lights on, and we rode through San Antonio in a nice orderly procession. We approached an underpass where a clutch of servicemen were walking. They looked up to see this procession, stopped in their tracks, took their hats off, and held them to their chests. They figured it was a funeral.

We were occasionally picketed in the South outside the venue by church groups protesting our song *The Pusher*, insisting we were taking the Lord's name in vain. Once, in Winston Salem, North Carolina we were scheduled to play the War Memorial Arena, 9,000 people, sold out. At the airport we were met by the mayor, police chief, and the fire chief who were very pleasant and congenial but who had come to inform us of the following problem: a fundamentalist Baptist preacher currently running for one of the city council seats had heard that Steppenwolf was coming to town. He had gone out and bought every one of our albums, listened to them, and came to these three civic leaders with the following demands: either we were not to play at all in the War Memorial Arena paid for by taxpayers' dollars or we must delete certain songs, one of them being *The Pusher*. We were getting a vibe from these people that they thought this preacher was an asshole but they had to throw him a bone. Finally they concluded that we couldn't sing the line "God damn the pusher."

Just prior to this incident, we had received an excerpt from an article written by a clergyman for one of the Baptist publications explaining that *The Pusher* was not only anti-drug but that the phrase "god damn" was being used in the true biblical context — may God damn the pusher for doing what he does. He was the first one to have the insight to see the obvious. But that didn't cut it with these guys. In the end we told them that we could not delete *The Pusher* from our set because that was one of the songs the crowd would definitely expect from us. "All I can tell you," I offered, "is that I will most likely not sing 'god damn.' " They responded, "We'll have a cop on stage who'll shut you down and arrest you if you do." We went on that night, the crowd was really into it, boisterous and loud, and we went down well. When it was encore time, we went back up and I addressed the crowd: "Unbeknownst to you, there was a good chance that we would not play tonight. You guys would have all had to get your money back and it would have been a real drag for everyone. There were certain demands put on us by the municipal power structure here in terms of what we could or could not play. Now there's a man running for office and his name is [such and such] and some of you may be old enough to vote so you might want to keep this in mind. He's the person who started this whole thing. Now I have more or less promised that I will not sing two very important words out of *The Pusher*. But you guys didn't promise anything like that. It's up to you." We started into the song and every time I was supposed to do "god damn" there arose nine thousand screaming voices shouting at the top of their lungs, "GOD DAMN THE PUSHER." You've never seen so many red faces backstage. They didn't have to arrest me, I didn't have to cop to their power game, and the crowd got a buzz out of it.

Another incident occurred in Monroe, Louisiana when the local sheriff had someone pull the plug on the equipment after we started playing *The Pusher*. A scuffle broke out behind the stage between various roadies and local officials. Jerry Edmonton was waving a drumstick in the guy's face shouting, "You shouldn't have done that." Frank Rojo, our equipment man, leapt through the crowd backstage, grabbed this guy by the throat, and pinned him on the ground. The sheriff waded through all this, his baton in hand about to beat Frank senseless, when Jerry Sloan pulled Frank off the guy. The sheriff came up to us and bellowed, "You cain't do that boy, you in Monroe, ya hear? You in Monroe." Eventually the power was restored and the show continued.

We were thrilled to be booked for a sold out concert at Maple Leaf Gardens in Toronto, the place where I used to sell Coca-Cola and crackerjack in the town that had been the home to four of us in the band. We were going home to show the folks that we'd made it. The show was sold out two weeks in advance, but we never made it and it remains one of my greatest regrets. Two days before the gig I came down with strep throat and tonsillitis. Laid up in bed, the pain was so intense that even the act of swallowing saliva brought tears to my eyes. No amount of medical care could resolve the problem. Sly and the Family Stone were brought in at the last minute to replace us. A year later we had our chance to make up for the cancelled show by appearing at the Toronto Pop Festival at Varsity Stadium as part of a three-day festival with us closing the event. One of our favorites, The Band, was also on the bill. However, once again factors beyond our control intervened to mar our intended triumphant return. It was raining and cold and the show was running late. People were already starting to leave because it was a Sunday night and they had to go to school or work the next day. When we finally took the stage, we found puddles everywhere. I put on my guitar, stepped up to the microphone, and immediately fried my lips because I was standing in water. For the remaining part of the show I attempted to sing a few inches away from the mike. Once in a while the electricity arced across and zapped me enough to take my mind off what I was doing for a couple of minutes. We kept at it, though, because we figured that if we quit playing, it would appear like we were wimping out. We'd look like a bunch of whining pop stars. It ended up being a rather perfunctory performance. Hardly an auspicious return.

Jerry Edmonton: *I used to get this feeling every time we played Toronto, no matter where it was, that the people there had a bone to pick with us. Kind of like, "Aw, how come you guys left Canada?" But if we hadn't left, we wouldn't have gotten anywhere. I guess they figured we should have come back more often.*

When we took Three Dog Night on tour as our support act to help launch them, it caused some problems. We discovered that while we were getting a little road-weary and were also by then having to deal with Michael Monarch's immaturity and indifference on stage, the Dogs were ready and able to steal the show, and did so several nights in a row. We had gotten sloppy and complacent on stage. Finally we had had enough and at a band meeting it was decided that the next night, I believe it was in Sacramento, we would go out and kick butt, playing with the intensity we were capable of. The old Musketeer spirit was back, if only for a brief period. We were headliners in every sense that night.

We made our first visit to Europe in early 1969 and received a warm reception everywhere we went, especially in Germany since the band included two expatriate Germans who had gone on to become successful in North America. The media promoted the idea that Germans could take a bit of pride and credit in the fact that Nick and I were native sons. In the years since our success, Solveigh had returned to Germany and she met us when we arrived in Munich. It was like old home week. The press was well pleased that I could conduct interviews in German, and I even introduced the songs in German to the surprise of the audiences. Some people who didn't know of my heritage were confused. Others who did know apparently told the promoter that somehow it broke the mystique of the band as American. For the rest of the tour I spoke in English on stage. We appeared on several television shows there, including *Beat Club* in Bremen with go-go girls in fringed bikinis boogalooing up a storm on a screen behind us. In London, we made our British debut at the legendary Marquee Club in Soho where bands like the Yardbirds and the Who had played in their early years. We shared a bill that night with a fine new band called King Crimson.

The European tour brought things to a head between Michael Monarch and the rest of us. Between the hectic tour pace, too little sleep, too much drinking, drugs and cavorting about, Michael was burning out. His temperament became a problem — moody, sullen, uncooperative. In Sweden we played with rented equipment from England, and Michael got so furious with this gear that at the end of our concert he pushed the stack of amplifiers he had been using over the poor roadies. He had become a heavy user of downers. I confronted him on that once and his response was, "You don't understand. These things are me. When I wake up and take one of these reds, I'm taking one of me. That's what I function on." He and I were frequently at loggerheads both in the studio and on the road, even getting into shouting matches on stage.

Nick St. Nicholas: *Michael got so mad once that during the instrumental part of* Born To Be Wild *at a major show, he handed his guitar to one of our roadies who came out and did the solo from*

Taxman while Michael was off to the side smoking dope with his friends. Another night, he just leaned his guitar against his amp and walked off the stage. Michael also didn't like it when John would come out and hold these long lectures and tell people what was wrong with the country. That just annoyed him. He would say, "We're a rock 'n' roll band, let's rock 'n' roll."

Michael Monarch: *A lot of the problem was that I was not a seasoned musician in that band. Those guys had done a lot more and probably appreciated the success at the time more than I did. To me, it was just what happened, we were successful, no big deal. If I had been through what they had been through, I may have been more diplomatic or understanding about what was happening with the band and what it took. On the other hand, I might not have had that crazy and wild abandon to my playing which helped the band in the first place.*

John had gone from being just one of the guys in the band to being a strong front man and writer and there were ego problems. He was very strong willed. His German character and his hard life probably shaped his attitude towards things. All this made John quite hard to deal with and I think everybody at one time or another felt it.

They were kind of like big brothers to me and I think I rebelled against it. I felt they were trying to keep me under their thumb in a way and maybe I didn't really know what I wanted to do but I wanted to assert myself. So that got on their nerves and they got on my nerves, John more than anyone. I got on well with Jerry and hung out with Nick after he joined. But the final straw for me was THE BIRTHDAY PARTY *album photo session that I didn't show up for and I guess I was losing interest by then. There was a lot of political stuff happening, who's siding up with whom, that kind of thing. There was a pecking order in Steppenwolf that was already developed and mainly it was John and Jerry who had been his sidekick from way back. I wasn't at the bottom or anything but the band was really controlled by John with Jerry's help. The others realized the best thing to do was to keep the main nucleus of the band together, so I was out.*

Jerry Edmonton: *Michael was too young. The difference between seventeen and twenty-two is huge. Also, Michael didn't like John's attitude or his philosophies on life. They'd sit on the plane and start* *in on each other. John would say, "You're being a spoiled little brat." Then Michael would tell John exactly what he thought of him, "You pigheaded Nazi." It was like two totally stoned people having a street fight in the first class section. They'd argue all the way to the next gig. They were both egoed out and Michael was becoming really asinine. It just got to the point where I knew what was coming and I knew I couldn't do anything about it. John did his thing, his unwritten, unstated power play of "Either he goes or I go."*

Although the BIRTHDAY PARTY album had already been recorded with Michael in the band, it was yet to be released and we still hadn't shot the cover. In Michael's absence, Gabriel Mekler had to stand in for him at the photo session.

With Michael gone and commitments once again pending, we had no time to consider adequately auditioning a replacement. Fortunately, Nick recommended Larry Byrom from his old band TIME. Larry brought to the band new energy, musical ideas, creativity, and his own distinctive guitar style. He was a true musician, very talented on several instruments, a good singer, congenial, easy-going, enthusiastic. With Larry, we moved forward rather than laterally and found a new vitality and fire.

Coinciding with Michael's departure and Larry's entrance was the release of EARLY STEPPENWOLF, a collection of live recordings from the Matrix two and a half years earlier when we were still The Sparrow. The sound was atrocious, recorded without our knowledge or consent by the club manager on a cheap little tape machine and two microphones suspended from the ceiling. There was very little that could be done to improve the sound quality due to the way in which it was recorded. Once the club manager discovered we were successful he decided to peddle the tape to the highest bidder. Columbia, who had us signed up at the time this stuff was recorded, passed on the tape. They had already foisted an album of old Sparrow demos on the record buying public culled from our 1966 New York sessions entitled JOHN KAY AND THE SPARROW. They even went so far as to cleverly airbrush the other four guys out of the front cover photograph, an old Sparrow publicity shot from Toronto, and feature only me.

Somehow Jay Lasker got wind of this tape and ever the marketing wizard figured, "I can get this for next to nothing and we'll make it a collector's item. It'll plug the gap between products and give the boys a little more time for the next one." He was right about that. How good, bad, or indifferent the recording quality, it bought us some much needed time to regroup with Larry and have the breathing space to put together our next record. We needed something strong to pull us out of our nosedive following the BIRTHDAY album debacle.

By the end of the 1960s, there was a mounting degree of frustration on the part of the young in general and college crowd in particular towards the establishment and the Vietnam War. The positive idealism of the early part of the decade had turned ugly and confrontational, the catalyst being the Chicago Convention of 1968. Everything seemed to be coming to a head, and I felt it was time for us to take a stand and speak our minds. On previous albums we had occasionally taken a position on certain matters with songs like *The Ostrich, The Pusher, Don't Step On The Grass, Sam, Take What You Need,* and so on. This time, however, we decided to use an entire album to state our case, sort of our view of the state of the union, even the state of the world, for that matter, since the US was messing around in South East Asia and had deserters in Sweden and Canada. The idea for the MONSTER album was born out of a conversation between Jerry and I in a limousine ride to the airport. We were searching for a concept to build an album around and Jerry said, "What's going on with this country? It's gotten to be this monstrous thing. How did it get to this point?" We kicked around the word 'monster' and came up with an image of the United States as a multi-faceted, multi-tentacled beast, an image artist Rick Griffin picked up on for the cover art. We continued exploring this idea on the plane flight back to LA and Monster, the concept, was born. We then proceeded to compose songs that would express those feelings musically and lyrically. The concept demanded a bigger, heavier sound, and Larry and Jerry came up with some strong ideas. Jerry had written the melody line for "America, where are you now" a year earlier noodling around on a guitar during the bus tour, and I constructed the rest of the song to fit it.

America, where are you now?
Don't you care about your sons and daughters?

Don't you know we need you now,
We can't fight alone against the monster.

MONSTER, 1969

Larry offered some great instrumental ideas, more melodious, almost orchestral at times. Everyone in the band seemed stimulated into a new energy level. Nick had enough respect for Larry's musical talent to take direction from him, so that worked, too.

Doing a concept album on America offered us the opportunity to get a lot off our chests and out of our systems. For me, an amateur student of history, I was able to express my views on America, past and present. My early childhood experiences in both Germanies and Canada allowed me to see America from a different perspective, that of an outsider looking in, seeing many of the problems that plagued it. I had grown up admiring America from a distance, envying what it offered, influenced by its creative output through music, movies, and books.

I viewed the United States as the most recent human attempt at progress in terms of how it conducted itself, structured its society, elected its leadership, what it stood for and what it attempted. Even though the United States had many shortcomings, it still had at its foundation the Jeffersonian ideals. It had always come back to that touchstone: "Yes, we strayed off the path and veered away from our goals but that dream, that aspiration of humanity as exemplified by those underlying beliefs is still there." By 1969, America seemed to have lost that path, and many of its young, ourselves included, felt it needed to be reminded it was still within reach.

The spirit was freedom and justice,
It's keepers seemed generous and kind.
It's leaders were supposed to serve the country,
But now they don't pay it no mind.
'Cause the people got fat and grew lazy,
And now their vote is just a meaningless joke.
They babble about law and about order,
But it's all just an echo of what they've been told.

MONSTER, 1969

What happened to the dream espoused in the Sixties that fueled the various movements? We had emerged from the fairly boring but prosperous Fifties into the Sixties with Kennedy and that whole Camelot analogy. Everything appeared so promising. Then all of a sudden we lost the dream, partly as a result of the three assassinations of people who meant something to this country and its people. The optimism turned to anger, particularly among the young. Straight society resisted the youth movement and their call for change, meeting it with cynicism and negativity. Instead of acknowledging the need for re-evaluation, the reaction was to entrench and protect the status quo in any way possible.

Perhaps the biggest tragedy of the Sixties was the opportunity missed by not harnessing the wisdom and experience of the older generation and combining it with the enthusiasm, energy, and optimism of the young, joined like two horses on the same wagon pulling in the same direction. It was regrettable that the two couldn't join forces to move forward and not repeat the mistakes of the past. Instead it became a finger pointing exercise. "You old bastards screwed this place up and you're not letting us get to the helm because you think we're too young and crazy." I felt that at that point it came down to either get on with the job of improving the situation or, like an old truck driver of ours once said when he had eaten too many bennies and couldn't stand to see a mechanic fiddling around with the engine while he was late for a delivery, "Boy, hand me that wrench, stand back and fan me." I wanted to say: "Look, if you're going to just sit on your butts, smoke cigars and talk about the old days, then get the hell out of the way because we, like every new generation, are having to deal with the world we inherited." In the song *Move Over*, I was expressing that impatience.

> *Don't make me pay for your mistakes,*
> *I have to pay my own.*
> *Yesterday's glory won't help us today.*
> *You wanna retire, get out of the way.*
> *I ain't got much time,*
> *Young ones close behind.*
> *I can't wait in line.*

MOVE OVER, 1969

It's hard to believe that during the MONSTER album days I considered becoming directly involved in politics myself. I felt that speaking one's mind through song lyrics was all well and good but I also wanted to test the system by participating in the electoral process. There was a vacancy on the Board of Trustees of the junior colleges. The voting district in which I lived, the Hollywood Hills-Laurel Canyon area, was well-populated with people of my ilk, so it seemed possible to get elected. The board only met twice a month and therefore posed no problem to my music career. The idea of being a young person on a board that made decisions affecting other young people appealed to me. Besides, I felt that if I were successful it might give some encouragement to other young people to run for office. If we couldn't get someone elected on the rather modest level of the board of junior colleges, then it was rather doubtful that change could be brought about through the traditional avenues which, in theory at least, were supposed to be open to everyone.

The whole idea became academic, however, when I discovered that my American citizenship would have to be obtained prior to the filing deadline of my intention to run for office. In spite of my lawyer's best efforts to set my naturalization on the fast track, we were unable to meet the deadline. Management had jumped the gun with a premature publicity release and the press had a field day with the episode, one even going so far as to refer to me as "Steppenwolf's singing councillor." After some time, we were far too busy with the Wolf to give any further thought to elected office, and in hindsight, I'm glad it never came to pass. I'm far too outspoken and lack the proper temperament for the political arena.

On the MONSTER album we dealt with themes such as the state of American society (*Monster*), the Vietnam War (*Draft Resister*), the power elite (*Power Play*), even organized religion (*From Here To There Eventually*). I was brought up and confirmed in the Lutheran Church and believe that organized religion, when it doesn't go overboard or get stuck in the metaphor, can serve a very positive function in our society in terms of being charitable towards those less fortunate. Someone like Mother Theresa I admire because she is living the true life of a Christian and doesn't care whether she's taking care of Hindus, Muslims, or Christians so long as the people are in need. At the time I wrote that song, though, I viewed organized religion as part of the skeleton of society in which rigor mortis had set in. It was one of several pillars that held up the mausoleum we called American society.

The Wolf was on top again in 1970 with a hit album and succesful tours. MONSTER stemmed our downward slide, going gold right out of the chute and holding its own without the benefit of a hit single, though *Move Over*, released prior to the album, went Top Forty. Listening to the MONSTER album, Jay Lasker had asked, "Which of these songs is the hit?" The label was still stuck in that AM mode. I replied, "Well, I don't know if you're gonna get a hit single. This is a record that hangs together as an album. It's not merely a collection of songs." They eventually released an edited version of the title track that charted reasonably well at #39. Jay realized there was a huge college market out there who could relate to what we were saying on the album. Besides the usual trade papers, ABC Dunhill advertised in college newspapers and underground publications, even printing the lyrics to *Monster* in the ads. We played several college dates and met with an overwhelmingly positive response from the students. We even heard from history teachers who had used the lyrics in class as a means of getting through to kids bored with the idea of history but who liked Steppenwolf. Despite the fact that our critics generally assailed the album ("What? A politically-conscious motorcycle band?"), it gained us a much wider audience and a whole new respect.

We debuted the Monster concept in concert before 100,000 people at the Miami Pop Festival in early 1970. Since the album was a socio-political concept, we went down to Western Costume in Hollywood and rented some appropriate duds for the event. Each band member would dress in the uniform of some segment of the establishment/authority/power structure and these symbols would then be destroyed by fire at the end of our set. Production wizard Chip Monck tried to accommodate our request for fire on stage but in the end his efforts were thwarted by the local fire marshall (where is Arthur Brown when you need him!). Instead we used flash pots which failed to convey the idea as effectively as we had planned. In any event, we arrived at our dressing room and started changing. Jerry picked an admiral's uniform, Goldy wore professorial robes, Larry had on a business suit and tie and Nick was Uncle Sam. I had chosen a California motorcycle cop's uniform replete with helmet, gun holster, cuffs, the whole nine yards. With my long hair tucked underneath the helmet and with my shades on, I looked more than the part.

While still in our street clothes, three black musicians had walked through our dressing area into the adjacent sauna which had been designated the official 'smoking parlor' since the wafting aroma of marijuana smoke could best be contained in the air-tight enclosure. When these three musicians emerged a few minutes later in a highly altered state of mind, it just happened that I was standing there in full police regalia playing with my billy club. I've been color blind since birth but I swear I saw black skin turn ashen. These guys froze in mid sentence, one of them still pocketing his bag of grass. Not quite grasping the situation I said, "It's okay guys . . . It's John Kay . . . from Steppenwolf." Total silence. Then I removed my helmet, my hair spilled out and the three almost collapsed in relief. I apologized for being the cause of their visibly aging several years.

With my helmet back on, we got into the limo to take us to the outdoor stage. It was amazing to witness the power of a uniform. I was the first one out of the vehicle and played the part of a hired police escort for the band. The security force, some of whom were local police, immediately sprang into action, parting the sea of humanity in front of me like Moses. Once on stage it was a different story. With the stage dimly lit to allow the guys to check their instruments, I approached the microphone. The first few rows were able to see that there was a cop on stage, no doubt there to make some unpopular announcement or stop the festival altogether. Word spread to the back of the crowd and quickly the sound of hissing and then booing grew to a fever pitch. The guys launched into *Sookie Sookie* but still there was no sign of John Kay, just a cop at the mike. Right about when my vocal started, I threw down my helmet, and in an instant of recognition the crowd exploded into a roar.

While touring with the MONSTER album, we played the Bath Blues Festival in Britain alongside Led Zeppelin and Frank Zappa where the British Hell's Angels were the security, complete with chromed Nazi helmets and pool cues. We also played an anti-war festival at Shea Stadium in New York which Peter Yarrow of Peter, Paul and Mary had organized. We returned to Germany and played in Hannover again. Following the show I received a note backstage from some of my childhood friends who wanted to see me. We spent a wonderful time together reminiscing. On that trip we filmed a German television special for a very progressive German producer who put us on a turn of the century train, a locomotive and a parlor car with chandeliers, velvet drapes and tassels, Persian rugs, mahogany side panels and a semi-circular bar at the end of the car. He arranged for exclusive use of a twenty kilometer section of track on which we shuttled back and forth as he filmed both inside and out. We had been given Winchester rifles and were shooting from the car at symbols of the German establishment. We fired at a bear that was the symbol of a German condensed milk company. He also had us chasing a nun. We then played a few tunes in the parlor car. In Munich, we played at the Circus Krone, a circular venue designed to resemble a big top, which served as the winter quarters for the circus. Nick came across this big bell and for a lark decided to ring it. The damn thing turned out to be the fire bell. Circus people came running to rescue all the animals in their stalls before realizing it was a false alarm. A couple of gypsies really chewed Nick out for that.

Jerry Edmonton: *After a gig somewhere in Germany, Frank Rojo and I were hanging out in the hotel bar. Then we went up to my room and were drinking something called Vodka Gimlets, getting totally wacko. Frank opened the door to go back to his room and said, "Wow, what's this?" In the hallway were dozens of pairs of shoes left outside to be polished by the hotel service staff. We started walking down the hall tripping out over all these shoes. Then Frank got this idea, "These German guys gotta lighten up. It's summertime. They should be wearing sandals. Let's do 'em a favor and give 'em sandals." So we gathered all these shoes, got the exacto knife from the electrical repair kit and did some custom leather work. We cut them up and put them back, all in the wrong places. Some of those guys could have been going to important business meetings the next morning, and when they opened their door there'd be two different ladies shoes. By the time they found their own, they had been customized, soles flapping and air holes cut in them. The hotel never said anything to us when we checked out.*

Back in the States we recorded a benefit concert at the Santa Monica Civic Auditorium that spring for a live album. The idea was to release it as a 'best of live' album because we generally had a good stage show. Putting it out would again buy us some breathing space for the next studio release. However, when the live album was recorded, it became apparent that we had too much material for a single album and not enough for a double. So we went back to the well and dug up *Twisted* and *Corinna Corinna* from The Sparrow days and recorded them in the studio, adding them to the album by mixing in the audience applause. We also tagged our current single *Hey Lawdy Mama* onto the album in a similar fashion. It was a bit of a con job. STEPPENWOLF LIVE maintained the momentum of that year reaching #7 on the charts and going gold with *Lawdy Mama* scraping the Top Forty. The album captured a rather sub par performance and revealed that Nick's playing was way out of tune in *Magic Carpet Ride*. To this day I can't stand to listen to that album.

The public perceived Steppenwolf as a macho, 'balls to the wall' group, but Nick's robes on stage didn't exactly fit that image. Granted, it was a time of sexual ambiguity — Donovan wore robes then — but in Steppenwolf? I didn't have any problems with homosexuality or bisexuality, but Jerry and I felt that Nick's mode of dress was sending confusing signals to our fans and the public in general. We also weren't sure what Nick's sexual orientation was or had become. Larry expressed some reservations about working with Nick under these circumstances. Everything came to a head on Easter weekend 1970 at the Fillmore East in New York.

It was the second night for us at the Fillmore. Nick was really loaded on THC that night and had a bunch of his friends with him, some of whom we suspected were homosexual or at least bisexual. We got into our limousine and Nick brought his friend Tony with him. Tony and Nick were really high and becoming embarrassingly loud. Tony started playing the name game song in the car. "Nick, Nick, Bo bick, Banana fanana fo Mick . . ." Then he went to "Jerry, Jerry Bo berry, banana fanana fo merry . . . ," then to Larry. I'm sure he knew that this was pissing me off but he just kept on going. Tony then paused and went, "And now . . . let's do . . . John! John John bo bon . . ." As Jerry tells it, "I could see John sitting in the front seat steaming and he's thinking of how to take over East

Prussia right about then and invade France and England as well. I figured we were in for an interesting night." He wasn't far off.

At the Fillmore East, a projection screen was often lowered on stage to entertain the audience with a cartoon or two while the crews changed equipment for the next act. So it was on the night in question. The cartoon ended, the screen went up, and we were standing in the wings ready to the take to the stage, the lights went down but Nick was nowhere to be found. He was hiding something from us until the last possible moment. Finally he showed up, we took the stage, Jerry counted in *Sookie Sookie* and the lights went on . . . and there was Nick in a sequin jockstrap and bunny ears!

Jerry Edmonton: *I can appreciate Nick's creativity but it was the wrong band and the wrong moment to pull that off. He didn't want us to know he was wearing that until it was too late to stop him. Otherwise we would have wrestled him to the ground and told Bill Graham we had technical difficulties. Anyway, the lights went on and we launch into* Sookie Sookie *and I hear this excruciating sound coming from the bass. John turned around to me and said: "What the fuck is going on?" He can't see that well, so he started moving closer to Nick. Now, besides hearing Nick, he could now see Nick in his sequined jock strap and bunny ears. I knew we had to stop. The audience was stunned. Someone in the audience yelled out, "Get that fag off the stage!" John heard that and was getting madder and started walking towards Nick. It was dead quiet out in the crowd. I just put my feet up on my drums and thought, "Maybe they'll think it's a part of the show." John walked over and snarled to Nick, "Take those fucking rabbit ears off and tune your bass, you're out of tune!" Then he turned and walked back to his place not saying a word to the audience. I figured someone had better ease the tension so I leaned into my mike and announced, "Trix are for kids." The audience chuckled nervously but John was ready to kill Nick.*

When the show was done, I went looking for him. I was stomping around backstage looking to put a serious hurt on him but he made his escape. Following that incident, Jerry and I decided Nick had to go. We told him so at the airport waiting to fly home. He took it badly, shouting back, "People are gonna know. The audience is gonna expect a blond bassplayer," to which I responded, "Well, we can always dye his hair."

Larry suggested George Biondo, once again from the group TIME, to replace Nick. When we took George out of TIME their managers said, "That's it. No more band. You guys do what you want. We're tired of being a farm team for Steppenwolf." George, like Larry, proved to be a worthwhile addition to the band, a fine bass player and singer who worked well with Larry. He played tight with the kick drum, and although not as adventurous as Rushton Moreve, was much steadier and more inventive than Nick.

By this time, after five albums, Gabriel Mekler was less interested in producing. Over the previous two years he had been dividing his time between us and Three Dog Night with a number of side projects including Janis Joplin's COSMIC BLUES album that Jerry and Goldy played on. But he was burned out, felt there was no challenge left. He was also fed up with Three Dog Night, finding it difficult dealing with seven people. After the MONSTER album, Gabriel and Richard Podolor had a falling out and refused to work together. For our part, we liked working with Richard and Bill Cooper in their studio. We didn't want to move. *Screaming Night Hog*, a good song that blatantly pandered to the motorcycle crowd but failed to make much of a dent in the Top Forty, became our last production with Gabriel. When Gabriel backed out, Richard offered to step in and fill the breach. Richard had always been an integral part of our sound and took over production.

With Richard Podolor at the helm and George Biondo recruited on bass, we entered the studio with a renewed vigor to record what would become our strongest album since the first.

Performing during the Monster Tour at the Miami Pop Festival, 1970 (my shirt was supposedly worn by Rod Steiger in the film In the Heat of the Night).

*Tuning up backstage, with Jutta in her
snakeskin coat, at the Santa Monica Civic
Auditorium, for the performance recorded
for the* STEPPENWOLF LIVE *album, 1970.*

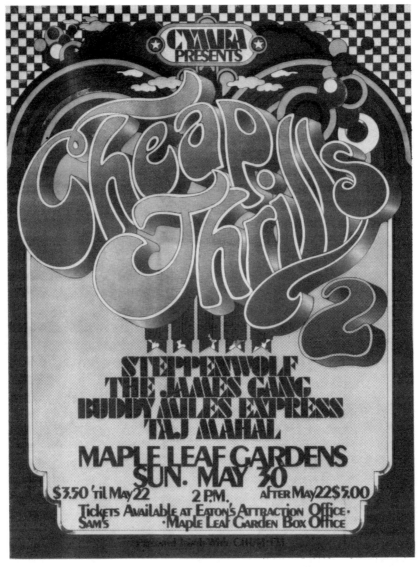

Our long anticipated return to Toronto as a successful band — and my return to Maple Leaf Gardens where I once sold peanuts and popcorn — was thwarted by a case of strep throat.

TEN

ROCK ME

Don't know where we come from
Don't know where we're goin' to
But if all this should have a reason
We would be the last to know
So let's just hope there's a promised land
And hang on 'til then
As best as we can

ROCK ME, 1969

Artists tend to create their best work when they're lean and hungry. It's that blind determination, raw energy, 'us-against-the-world' cockiness that drives you to take risks, to push the envelope because you have nothing to lose. Back in '67 in the garage on Fountain Avenue, we had that attitude, that hunger, and our first album captured it and in only four days of recording. There was no need to do those songs more than two or three times, we knew every note. We'd lived those songs, sweating them into shape in the garage, working out the kinks on stage. That was Steppenwolf, pure, raw rock 'n' roll energy. The problem was that by late 1970, after several gold records, world tours, everything we could possibly imagine at our fingertips, we had lost our edge. There was a distance that had grown between us and the real world. The first class travel, fancy suites, limousines, parties, the best drugs, the whole rock star trip — all these indulgences had become the preoccupation that distracted us from what we should have been focusing on, the music. We had fallen into a rut of inconsistency — good album, weak album, personnel change, better album again, and so on.

Those people who had been our real fans, who bought all our albums and knew all the lyrics, stayed with us through thick and thin. The fans who had jumped on our bandwagon when we had hits on the radio and were on their favorite television shows, who followed the flavor of the month pop group, had moved on to the next big thing. We had lost that contingent but that was okay; they were never the following we sought. By 1970, we were still in the race and had something to prove. The LIVE album had sold well, and like EARLY STEPPENWOLF it served to buy us some time to regroup. Artistically, the album was definitely lacking so we felt that our backs were to the wall to produce something substantial. We had pulled ourselves up with MONSTER and we could do it again. In terms of the players, with Nick out and George in, the band was at its strongest since the first album. Morale was high, the live shows were better than ever, and attendance was healthy. We had a new-found confidence and commitment. In the studio Richard and Bill pulled out all the stops to make STEPPENWOLF SEVEN the most consistent album since the first.

The MONSTER album was intended to get certain things out of

our system. We had done songs before about particular issues but right then with the Vietnam War, we felt the need to make a statement. Once that was done, I didn't have anything else I wanted to get off my chest. So on SEVEN we went back to a purer rock sound. After a year in the band Larry had hit his stride. Though he had been the new kid on the MONSTER album, he had given the band the spark which helped make the album successful. By SEVEN, Larry was at his creative peak. For me it was a relief because he and the others were bringing me good tracks to write lyrics for.

Larry Byrom: *That album marked the most creative period of my life. A lot of times Jerry and I were left in the studio and we were full of ideas, mostly guitar riffs. Almost all the musical ideas on SEVEN were riff ideas of mine. I had never experienced that approach to writing before where it's your baby and you give it to someone else and a week later they bring it back and you're surprised at what happened. John was a master at that. He made every arrangement idea we had work perfectly. For example, I wrote the riff and music to what became* Ball Crusher *and had no idea that John would turn it into the ultimate sexual macho song but it worked.*

With a few exceptions, I rarely brought in completed songs anymore. Out of the usual time pressures we had evolved a recording routine whereby the other guys laid down tracks based on instrumental ideas they came up with and presented these to me. They'd be in the studio working on tracks while I was working on the melodies and lyrics, either somewhere else in the studio or at home. More often it came together but sometimes it was, "Oops, that's in the wrong key, you'd better go down instead of up with that melody." Those times were terribly frustrating because it meant agonizing hours up until four in the morning going, "Shit, I've heard this music sixty times in a row and I'm still not happy trying to construct a melody to fit this thing." Once in awhile, by having to go left instead of right, I was forced into something that ultimately sounded fresh to my ears, a melodic twist I might not have thought of otherwise. At times, the pressure to meet absurd deadlines straight jacketed me into accepting some changes or keys that I didn't particularly like but couldn't be altered. Admittedly, it was not the preferred way of songwriting but it did have some positive payoffs, especially on the SEVEN album.

Anyone who has ever worked with me in the studio can attest to the fact that I take recording seriously. There's a constant struggle in the studio not only to achieve the desired sound that I hear in my head with everyone interacting but also to grab those moments of inspiration or the germ of an idea before it zips through my brain and into the void — to hear something and say, "This, now, that's it." What is destructive to that process is when I'm trying to articulate an idea that I'm unable to play and therefore have to describe to another player while the other guys sit around, get bored, and start telling jokes, for instance. When that happens I've been known to lose it. "God damn it. We're here to do music and you just broke the spell." The intensity can be overwhelmingly powerful to someone walking in cold.

I take songwriting just as seriously. Around the time of the SEVEN album, Danny Hutton, a friend of mine from Three Dog Night, and his girlfriend dropped over to our house one evening for a visit. We chatted for awhile, then I excused myself and went off to my studio to finish working on some lyrics to a track the guys had given me. Danny was surprised by what he considered my self-discipline. Like most people, I'm constantly in danger of being distracted by other things — family, free time, business, and just plain laziness — but I think there's still a bit of the working class ethic in me that coerces me to knuckle under when the pressure is on and get the job done. It's a tug of war sometimes.

STEPPENWOLF SEVEN opened with *Ball Crusher* setting a macho swagger tone. We pulled *Forty Days And Forty Nights* from an old Muddy Waters album. I always liked the feel of it. *Hippo Stomp* was basically saying that we're all in this river of life trying to make the best of it as we float downstream. We tend to be carried along by what's happening around us without thinking sometimes. *Fat Jack* was just Jerry, Larry, and George poking fun at the little hot dog stand next to the studio and some of its patrons. One of the highlights on the SEVEN album for me was *Renegade*. The instrumental track Larry had written and laid down with the others had a certain mood to it opening with the acoustic guitar, frantically building in the middle, then coming back down again. It triggered a mental

image in my head the first time I heard it. The music almost emotionally conveyed the subject matter to me, and once I locked on to
what I wanted to write about, the song virtually wrote itself. That
doesn't happen that often. The song marked the first time I wrote
about my early childhood, sort of a catharsis.

> *It's a mighty long way out of the darkness,*
> *To where the sun is free to shine.*
> *Well, the truck came by and pulled us in the back,*
> *And left us where the railroad tracks crossed the line.*
> *And the border guide took us by the hand,*
> *And led us through the hole into the promised land beyond.*
> *And I can hear him now, whispering soft and low.*
> *When you get to the other side, just you run like Hell.*
> *And it's "Hey, you, keep your head down.*
> *Don't you look around. Please don't make a sound.*
> *If they should find you now the man would shoot you down."*

RENEGADE, 1970

Snowblind Friend was written by Hoyt Axton about an ex-guitar
player of his who died of an overdose. When I came out to California in 1964, this guy (whose name I shall not mention in defer-
ence to his family) was one of the first musicians I befriended, an
easy-going, gentle guy always willing to share his knowledge and
love of music. It was he who originally taught me the guitar riff I
played in *Power Play* on EARLY STEPPENWOLF and the MONSTER
album. He also introduced me to the music of blues great Robert
Johnson, for which I am forever in his debt. When I learned of his
death through Hoyt's song, I felt it was a song we should do. Oddly
enough, at the same time Hoyt, who was working with our management along with Three Dog Night, had a song called *Joy To The
World.* The Wolf chose *Snowblind Friend* and the Dogs took *Joy To
The World* — which turned into their biggest hit ever.

We chose the right song for us, an anti-hard drug statement
and, uncharacteristically, one of our softest cuts ever. When we
released the song as a single, radio ignored it. Its release coincided
with a period when the FCC had written a directive to all radio

stations informing them that they were monitoring whether or not radio was playing drug-glorification songs. Many programmers backed off on *Snowblind Friend*. These same people had the balls to call our management company and ask me to record anti-drug public service announcements. My response to them was, "*Snowblind Friend* is about the best thing that I've heard come out of the music community about the pitfalls of excessive drug use. You guys shunned this record and now you want me to record a statement saying, 'Please kids, don't do drugs?' Forget it!"

Over the years since the SEVEN album, I've often been approached by fans curious about the spoken passage at the beginning of Larry's instrumental tour de force *Earschplittinloudenboomer*. Larry wrote it and played almost every instrument, including the horns (as a kid, he had been Alabama state junior bugle champion). The guys finished the track and phoned me at home asking me to say something in German about a high school joke I had told them involving English syllables to approximate a German sounding word. They liked the made-up word "Earschplittinloudenboomer," a dumb play on words, and planned to have this huge explosion at the end of the track. Over the phone I said in English, "Today, we have good news and we have bad news." Then in German I continued, "The first half won't have understood what I just said. And the other half still won't know what an Earschplittinloudenboomer is —" meaning those who speak English won't understand what I just said and those who speak German won't know what an Earschplittinloudenboomer is because it's just a made up word to sound German.

Despite lacking a solid hit single, STEPPENWOLF SEVEN went gold, denting the Top Twenty. After the failure of *Snowblind Friend*, *Who Needs Ya* got some airplay and posted a modest chart showing. We were proud of SEVEN and it received favorable reviews, such as this notice by Steve Rosen in the *Los Angeles Free Press*: "Steppenwolf was elevated from the wild and raw animal as presented on their first album, to a thinking creature capable of creative thought on MONSTER, and finally to a fully developed being, capable of expressing the range of emotions from nadir to zenith on SEVEN." I would agree.

We filmed performance videos for *Screaming Night Hog* and *Snowblind Friend* at American Recording Studio as well as a location shot for the latter on El Capitan in Yosemite National Park. For the shoot, we flew up to San Francisco, then took a smaller plane from there to Mariposa airstrip, a little shack on a plateau with a steep drop on one side. Our road crew had flown up earlier and were waiting for us. We then went up the mountain in a Winnebago and did a couple of takes right at the precipice of El Capitan. We thought we were going to fall 5,000 feet to our death for this video. The wind was howling so much we had to put sandbags on the drums to keep them from blowing away. They told me to climb over the wire barrier that blocked tourists. The producer kept saying, "A little further, a little further, that's perfect." I couldn't see very well and ended up sitting on a rock hanging over the cliff playing my guitar with no safety ropes. We had the roadies with us on the plane ride back and the pilot didn't think we could take off with the extra weight. Finally he decided he would take an extra long run. He then proceeded to back the plane onto the dirt way back off the runway. Off we went. At the far end of the runway it just fell off into the wilderness below. We were all yelling, "Jesus Christ, get this thing off the ground!" When we got to the end of the runway, the plane went off the plateau and straight down, then it pulled up and up trying desperately to get over the mountain peak looming in front of us. The engines were straining, the plane was shaking, and so were we. Finally, after clearing the peak, we breathed a sigh of relief and made our way home.

Following a brief vacation in Hawaii we went back out on the road in early 1971 with renewed confidence to promote the album. There was even some talk of us doing a movie tentatively entitled *From Here To There* with live concert footage to be shot at the Winterland in San Francisco but nothing ever materialized. We once again toured in Europe, this time bringing our wives along. One of the most memorable Steppenwolf gigs for me was performing at the Royal Albert Hall in London. The show was a sell out and the crowd response was phenomenal. Between the extreme heat on stage and the intensity of our playing, our performance was exhausting. Fans were standing along the edge of the low stage pounding it with their fists and singing along. It was another one of those perfect moments, lasting over an hour and a half. When we finished with *Born To Be Wild*, Larry blacked out from heat exhaustion and fell flat on his back right there on stage. The crowd went crazy and brought us back again and again until finally we had nothing left to play and I believe I told them so. It was one of those nights you don't ever want to see end. What made it even more enjoyable for me was that Jutta was there to share the thrill of it all. At times like that you know you've got the best job in the world.

Other European highlights included shows in Copenhagen, Amsterdam, and Helsinki. Jutta accompanied me to Germany, where we played Hamburg, her hometown. A Hamburg newspaper made mention of the fact that the wife of Steppenwolf's lead singer was a local girl. We visited with her family and friends, then she took me around to her old stomping grounds, places like the defunct Star Club and the very much alive Top Ten Club where she had seen the Beatles ten years earlier.

We returned to New York on the Queen Elizabeth II ocean liner. During the voyage our head waiter inquired whether we would consider playing a set for the crew in their lounge several decks below. He told us Ringo Starr had done so on a previous voyage. We decided it might be fun. There was a tiny stage area with some band gear so we made the best of the situation and played a short set. Word had spread that we would be playing and the place was packed to the point that it was hard to breathe. We were somewhat relieved to get some fresher air topside.

By the SEVEN album, our management company, Reb Foster and Associates, had become a power in the music business. They handled Steppenwolf, Three Dog Night, Smith, Edgar Winter's White Trash, and Hoyt Axton, among others. There were, however, some problems developing between management and our label, some accounting irregularities based on the poor contract the band had initially signed in 1967. We were earning a low royalty rate divided among five guys with both personal and business management taking their commissions off the top. Bill Utley, who acted as liaison with Jay Lasker at the record label, mobilized a campaign to bring ABC Dunhill around to seeing things more equitably. First Steppenwolf sued the label, followed by Three Dog Night, both bands withholding any further product pending settlement of the dispute. Bill marshalled all his public relations savvy on our behalf with articles appearing in the various trade papers and saw to it that our PR company kept feeding the media on the conflict. With a lawsuit tying up revenues on existing stock indefinitely, ABC Dunhill decided it was time to release a Steppenwolf greatest hits album. Jay was the master of repackaging. He had done it over and over with The Mamas and The Papas and went on to do so with Steppenwolf product over the years. With no input from us, they put out STEPPENWOLF GOLD featuring our hits with a gawd-awful cover of a woman painted gold looking like a second-rate hooker covered in Woolworth's jewelry. Our dislike of the cover notwithstanding, the album went gold practically right out of the box and continued to sell well for many more years to come.

ABC Dunhill's plan was to withhold our royalties in an attempt to starve out the two bands. Between Steppenwolf and Three Dog Night, we represented over sixty percent of the label's revenue. It was a war of nerves to see who'd crack first. We kept up the pressure until the big guys from the ABC head office in New York came out to see what was going on. Assessing the potentially staggering revenue loss, Jay was told to relent and renegotiate. In the end, both bands came out of the dispute on the winning side — improved royalty rates, rights of approval, minimum promotion budgets, and the reversion of the masters to us (we surrendered back to ABC Dunhill the rights to our masters three years later in order to get off the label, a move that I now regret). We won but it proved to be a hollow victory. After finally getting our just desserts, we then delivered our weakest album since STEPPENWOLF AT YOUR BIRTHDAY PARTY.

Just as the legal battles were being settled, Larry Byrom suddenly announced his departure from the band. It was a disappointing turn of events, for we were feeling a sense of renewal largely as a result of Larry's contributions. He was going through some private upheavals in his personal life that regrettably involved certain band members. Larry was always a country boy, and I think the LA fast lane was becoming too much for him. He was barely twenty when he joined and it was a case of too much too soon. It was a loss that proved costly to our creativity.

Larry Byrom: *I loved working with Jerry but he and I developed a bit of a personality conflict. He could be very cutting, very cynical in his remarks, trashing people for fun and messing with their heads. I* *was reared in the South, so I was used to good old boys with manners and hospitality, and there was a really different attitude coming from Jerry that I found difficult to deal with. As for Goldy, he ran off with my wife so I couldn't work with him any more.*

Richard Podolor had recently produced the hit *Ride Captain Ride* for a south Florida band, Blues Image. Just as the record was charting, the band broke up. Richard had been impressed with their guitar player, Kent Henry, and recommended him to replace Larry. I invited Kent over to my studio and jammed with him a bit. He was a tasty slide player, more than adequate on lead, though not as spontaneous as Larry or Michael. With pressure from the label for product, we grabbed Kent.

The FOR LADIES ONLY album was a good idea that never really jelled. Jerry's idea for this concept album was positive, but much of the material was weak. And I have to take the blame for much of that. After Larry left, I did not contribute with the same degree of dedication and energy I had done in early years when it was do or die and get things done because there were bills to be paid and a family to take care of. Jutta and I were pretty comfortable after the SEVEN album, so the hunger wasn't there. Four years on the treadmill of writing, recording, interviews, tours, trying to find time for my family — all this was no longer fun. It was a grind, a job in the negative sense. My songwriting had dried up at that point and I was running out of ideas. I contributed only a few things to the album, and we had to depend on Mars Bonfire for three tunes. I relinquished the reins to a certain extent to Jerry who sort of steered this one through. Without Larry to provide a spark of creativity, the album suffered from lackluster material and performances. Kent was a reasonably talented guitar player but not a creative songwriter. The album had its moments but overall it was inconsistent.

Bill Cooper: *Recording the FOR LADIES ONLY album was like pulling teeth. It just didn't sound as strong as their other stuff. There was a real energy on SEVEN because it was fun doing it. Richard and I had taken over the reins on it and had full access to do what we wanted. But on the FOR LADIES ONLY album the writing didn't seem up to us. It was a darker period and it sounded rough and* *ragged and there seemed to be no purpose behind it. There was not the same feeling at all and I knew we were really stretching it a bit.*

Jerry Edmonton: FOR LADIES ONLY *should have turned out better. It was an attempt to go back to something like the* MONSTER *album and do another concept. I think the song* For Ladies Only *is great and so are* The Night Time's For You *and* Ride With Me, *but once again we ended up doing a couple of fillers. But it may have been a concept that our audience wasn't ready for yet. We thought it was kind of humorous, Steppenwolf, this 'balls to the wall' motorcycle band, singing about women's perspectives; however, our audience missed it. We had a lot of males in our audience and they went "Huh?!" They didn't get it so the album stiffed. We thought the photograph of the dickmobile in the gatefold cover was hilarious but figured the label would axe it. Jay Lasker saw it and didn't get it so he okayed its use.*

We were getting tired of all the personnel changes and were just a band coasting on its own weight down a slow hill because of the name Steppenwolf. John was burned out, Kent wasn't Larry, and Goldy had reached the point where he had no new ideas.

We should have shelved that album and gone to Hawaii — stop and take stock, re-assess, get a perspective on what we were doing and what we wanted to do — but instead it was the endless ride back on the road to promote an album we knew was weak. At that point there was no talk of splitting up, but the writing was on the wall. It was becoming increasingly difficult on stage. We weren't filling the arenas. Some nights the audience only tolerated things like *Renegade* and *Snowblind Friend* while waiting for *Born To Be Wild* and *The Pusher*. It was like playing to five thousand downer freaks shouting "Play *The Pusher*" all night long. I felt we were locked into an image that we couldn't break out of. As much as *Easy Rider* served to boost our early career, in terms of the media it caused problems. Whenever we tried to break away from our motorcycle/political image with new songs like *Renegade* and *Tenderness*, our audience was still only interested in hearing *The Pusher, Monster, Born To Be Wild,* and *Magic Carpet Ride*. They wanted no deviations from the norm. It was a straightjacket.

I didn't have the energy needed to pull the band together again and there wasn't anyone to pick up the banner and say, "Here's what we need to do." So I opted out. I wasn't satisfied with the album, the make-up of the band, and what I felt was the load of holding it all together falling on the shoulders of Jerry and me. And I started to question the time spent with the band away from my family and resented that time because it was no longer fulfilling on a personal level. My head wasn't into hard rock music at that stage in my career; I had been working on some ideas of my own in a softer, more personal vein. I wanted to make some decisions on my own, take my own time, do material that didn't have to be justified within the context of Steppenwolf. Being together with Jerry and Goldy for seven years, we had almost exhausted the musical combination of ideas that one group of individuals can create.

In August of 1971, we played our last concert for the summer. We usually took September off before playing college concerts in October and November. I decided after the summer tour to have the October and November concerts cancelled in order to do my own album. After I wrote it, I liked it well enough to want to make the inactivity of Steppenwolf permanent. In the meantime, Jerry and Goldy had been working together with other people from a group called Damian and were excited about what they were doing too. So Jerry and I agreed to put Steppenwolf to rest. With hindsight what I should have done was say to Jerry, "Let's sit down and talk about whether or not we want to continue working together because if we do, I personally want a year off. I may not call you or see you, but I want some time off; I want to think, I want to see if the fun comes back." That's what I should have done. Instead it was, "Ah shit, I'm tired. It's not jelling. Let's pack it in." Everything was either black or white, no gray area. I thought I had a decent shot at pursuing my own musical preferences and ideas. Still, I could have done so without having to say goodbye to Steppenwolf.

Jerry and I discussed the split and informed Goldy of our decision. Nobody tried to talk us out of it. After the LADIES album, ABC Dunhill wasn't that interested in the band and stated they didn't want a Steppenwolf without John Kay. Our management company indicated that they preferred to stick with me as a solo artist. The band could have tried it without me but it would have been a long shot.

We decided not to release a simple press statement but to retire the name with some sort of honor by informing the media at a Holiday Inn reception, an appropriate venue given that it had been our home often enough on the road. Someone in our management finagled Los Angeles Mayor Sam Yorty into declaring the day, 14 February 1972, Steppenwolf Day. In true showbiz style, the Holiday Inn reception was merely a public relations ploy to thrust forward Jerry and Goldy's band Seven and my solo album on the coattails of Steppenwolf, like two phoenixes rising from the ashes. My album was done and the John Kay Band had been put together. Rather than announce the breakup, then later promote both projects, we set it up to coincide with the launch of both bands. In reality, Steppenwolf had been deceased for months. After five years, eight gold records, $42 million in record sales, and playing to more than two million people in concert, Steppenwolf retired.

*Steppenwolf live at Royal Albert Hall,
London, 1971.*

On stage with Kent Henry during one of our last shows before Steppenwolf disbanded, 1971.

Taking a break with Shawn during the photo session for the cover of FOR LADIES ONLY, *1971.*

WOLF GOES TO PASTURE—Steppenwolf is hanging up its rock & roll shoes. Following the group's announced plans for retirement, the members received letters of commendation from many high ranking officials in the recording business and Los Angeles Municipal government. Los Angeles mayor Sam Yorty declared Feb. 14 (Valentine's Day) as "Steppenwolf Day" in his city, citing the group for bringing added revenue to town with over $40 million in record sales, and for serving as "a musical ambassador for Los Angeles to the world." Group leader John Kay has announced plans for a solo LP, "Forgotten Songs And Unsung Heroes," while the remaining original members, Jerry Edmonton and Goldy McJohn are forming a group, Manbeast, with ex-members of Damian. In this pose, the group's mementos are displayed by Jerry Edmonton, Burt Jacobs of RFA, Goldy McJohn, RFA's Bill Utley, John Kay and Reb Foster of Reb Foster Assoc., Inc.

Billboard *Magazine announced the retirement of Steppenwolf.*

An invitation for a "Special Kind" of party to bid farewell to the Wolf.

ELEVEN

MOVIN' ON

The big eight wheeler movin' down the track
Means your true lovin' daddy ain't comin' back
'Cause I'm movin' on, I'm rollin' on
You're flying too high for my little sky
So I'm movin' on

I'M MOVIN' ON, 1950

In the fall of 1971, I had assembled a group to record my solo album. Rehearsals had been held in a relaxed atmosphere at my home studio and I found myself buoyed with enthusiasm. I was taking a risk and it felt good. For the project, I recruited George and Kent from the Wolf and brought in two Canadians, Penti "Whitey" Glan on drums and Hugh O'Sullivan on keyboards. Penti had been a member of The Five Rogues and The Mandala, one of Canada's best late Sixties groups, back in my Toronto days before arriving in LA in Bush, a short lived group under Reb Foster's care. Bush's guitarist Dom Troiano, the original replacement for Robbie Robertson with Ronnie Hawkins back in 1963, had written a few tunes for Three Dog Night. I didn't know Penti personally, only by reputation, and he in turn brought in Hugh O'Sullivan, another former member of The Mandala. The five of us kicked around some arrangements for a few cover tunes I wanted to record as well as four highly personal songs of mine written since the last tour that didn't fit the Steppenwolf mold. All tolled we took about eight weeks to rehearse and record FORGOTTEN SONGS AND UNSUNG HEROES with Richard and Bill at the controls. I loved making that record. It was a well-recorded album, very warm sounding and personal.

The FORGOTTEN SONGS album was more the result of my folk, country, and country blues influences than rock 'n' roll. During the preceding year, I had been wrestling with the whole burnout syndrome involved with my membership in the band. We had been creating albums and music based on record company deadlines and that's not always the most conducive way to be creative. I wanted to express other thoughts and feelings of a personal nature. I was also suffering a bit of an identity crisis. My initial career as a singer/songwriter in the early Sixties had not had sufficient time to mature. Right around the time that I had started to get into my own style of playing, singing, and writing, The Sparrow came along. I never really reached the stage as a solo act where I had a label deal and was pushing the limits of my writing talent to see where it would go. So that first solo album was a step back to that period and the people who influenced me — Hank Williams, Robert Johnson, Hank Snow, Richard Farina. The cover tunes on FORGOTTEN SONGS AND UNSUNG HEROES were an attempt to go back to the touchstones, the things that initially created that spark in me to pursue music. In many ways I was coming full circle back to my solo Yorkville days. As a result there was a degree of uncertainty and lack of confidence. There weren't four other guys who were going to jump right in and say, "How about this or that." That kind of pressure was different from being in a band. I was at a point both in my professional and personal life where I was unsure of what I wanted or wanted to pursue. Now here I was attempting a solo album but as what? How did I see myself? What was I? A rocker with a band or a solo singer/songwriter/performer?

The cover tunes I chose were from very special records that I had really loved. Kicking them around with the band, they slowly took shape. We played all the tracks live and they were not over produced. Each instrument pulled its own weight in terms of a part that locked together with the other instruments. As *Guitar Player* magazine said in their review, "It is refreshing to find true surprises in this industry still." The idea of John Kay playing a dulcimer and singing *Bold Marauder* must have bowled them over because their expectation was *Born To Be Wild* and heavy guitars.

Bill Cooper: THE FORGOTTEN SONGS AND UNSUNG HEROES *album was a whole different animal than the Steppenwolf thing. There were things that worked and things he should not have done. Some of the songs really took the mystique away. Steppenwolf had an energy and a personality. Some of this stuff was too light. John was going out on a limb but it was something he definitely wanted to do. A lot of people didn't realize he had those roots. I think he had heard every blues record ever made. He borrowed from a lot of blues ideas in his writing in Steppenwolf, pumped it up, put it on electric guitar, and gave it a Steppenwolf sound. It was clever repackaging and people didn't see the roots. Now John wanted to stretch out and show intellectually that he was capable of a lot more, that he knew a lot more, and did have more of a background than just being lucky to be in a hit group.*

Many A Mile was a song written by Patrick Sky. We never met and all I know of him is that he was a Native American who had put out an album on Vanguard in the mid 1960s with the stereotypical folky photograph of him in a fleece-lined jacket, the kind I wore myself back then. I learned the song from Hamilton Camp back in 1965 at the New Gate of Cleve in Yorkville. Buffy Sainte-Marie had done it on her second album. It was one of those songs you knew you'd heard somewhere before but never knew where. I hadn't played it myself until the solo album. Despite its simplistic lyrics it remains one of the best songs written about the romantic folk singer image, a guy with a guitar on his back bumming around the country.

What influenced my decision to record Hank Williams' *You Win Again* was that it was one of the first songs I ever learned by him and it had always been one of my favorites. Probably because it struck me a little bit different with the breaks and the rising bridge. As a kid I had memorized all the Hank Williams' songs I could get my hands on. I had his song book that taught me my first guitar chords. By the time I was seventeen I had memorized over a hundred country and western songs. Hank Williams became one of the main people in my country and western sphere of influence, along with Hank Snow (*I'm Movin' On*), the Louvin Brothers, Johnny Horton, Lefty Frizzell, and some old Jimmie Rodgers records. Initially it took me awhile to get used to Hank's voice, to get past what is normally considered a lack of polish in his voice, and appreciate his roughness and honesty. I felt the same way about Dylan. I had all of Hank's albums, even his obscure alter ego album LUKE THE DRIFTER, and went through them all before deciding to record *You Win Again*. My favorite interpretation of the song was done by Jerry Lee Lewis.

Walk Beside Me was a song for my daughter Shawn. With the Wolf on hold, I had this great load off my chest and more time for my private life, more time for Shawn and Jutta — going to the beach, doing things we used to do — and those were the thoughts that came to me. I also had time to consider the world at large. Shawn was three years old, and although the song was for her, it was also about her generation which, certainly in the context of a large urban sprawling metropolis like Los Angeles, I feared had little or no link with nature or the natural world. How many of them had seen a real sunrise other than on television or in a movie?

Because of all the activity in the Wolf, Jutta and I had gone through the previous couple of years rather quickly. We were married, we had a beautiful child and a nice house. But things were changing. Were we as individuals feeling constrained? Were we infringing on each other? Would we feel better if we were separate? We talked about how we would handle the changes and contemplated briefly that we might want to separate. Out of this turmoil came *Two Of A Kind*, probably the most personal song I've ever written. It's a one-sided conversation with myself after having spoken with Jutta at length and gone in circles through the same subject matter repeatedly. We were both exhausted, so I just let it be and wrote a letter to her to communicate my thoughts clearly. I tried to get all of my feelings formulated in a presentable fashion.

I don't know what it is, you've got the same sweet kiss.
And though I love you more than I did before we lived as one,
I feel alone.
I know you feel the same, but there's no one to blame,
Because the joy we've known
Is more than our own lives should bring.

TWO OF A KIND, 1972

At that point in my life I had a hard time performing a song I'd written myself about things which were truly personal to me. To let the outside world hear my innermost thoughts and feelings seemed almost exhibitionistic and self-indulgent. Besides, my attitude toward writing very personal lyrics had always been, "Everybody's got their own problems. They're really looking to get away from their's not to get into yours. . . . deal with it." Ironically some of my favorite artists include Joni Mitchell, Bonnie Raitt, Rickie Lee Jones, Shawn Colvin and others whose music and lyrics are at times extremely personal. Although I've become far more comfortable with writing the like in recent years, at the time *Two Of A Kind* was very much an exception and something I did not do easily.

To Be Alive is my other side, my conscience, talking to me. I get furious with myself because I'm a lazy person by nature, self-centered, willful. I'm aware of my faults and I try to work on them. I'm impatient with myself when I get that way. It's a lifelong balancing act with the pendulum swinging back and forth. I usually permit myself to get too lethargic for awhile, then I get pissed off with myself and I go through an intense period of work. At times certain songs can be a catalyst, a motivational tool. *To Be Alive* was one of those. It came out of a period where I was becoming bogged down in self-pity but resolved to get rid of the negativity and get on with it.

The album received good reviews but sales were only around the 100,000 mark, modest compared to Steppenwolf product. *I'm Moving On* received considerable airplay and was a turntable hit when released as a single. On the one hand, the album found interest because it offered such a departure. A lot of people were saying, "Really? This is him?" Over the years I've found that many who bought my solo albums became real John Kay fans. On the other hand, the Steppenwolf fans were used to the in-your-face kick-ass stuff and didn't automatically support my solo work, and people who at that time bought albums by singer/songwriters like James Taylor naturally assumed that my solo album was merely an extension of Steppenwolf. There was a lack of proper PR to explain that FORGOTTEN SONGS AND UNSUNG HEROES was by John Kay *of* Steppenwolf who has his own musical persona as well. A reviewer in *Crawdaddy* got the point, though: "It must have come as a bit of irony to hear John Kay, who became famous as a growl mounted on a pair of leather thighs, pull off a Hank Williams ballad with style and true cool." Too bad not enough people did so. I think it still stands up as a good album, one that I am proud of. If the cards had fallen a little differently, it might have been the beginning of something altogether different for me.

The John Kay Band undertook a short promotional tour playing showcase gigs in Chicago, the Bitter End in New York, the Troubadour for a week in LA, and the Underground in Atlanta. We then went on tour as a special guest act with Deep Purple around the time they released *Smoke On The Water* and did a handful of dates with Cactus in Florida. I didn't play any of Steppenwolf's hits with the John Kay Band and audiences generally accepted that. We performed on *The Midnight Special* and Bill Russell's television show (with Ossie and Harriet as guests) as well as *Rollin' On The River* hosted by Kenny Rogers and the First Edition.

Hugh O'Sullivan's extraordinary drug intake became glaringly evident after the taping of *Rollin' On The River*. We were staying at the Four Seasons Hotel in Toronto and Jerry Sloan, our road manager, came to my room in a panic. "John, I don't know what to do. Come here." We went down the hall and there was Hugh's room with the door wide open. Jerry claimed that's how he had found it. In the room was an Afghan dog wandering about and every piece of bedding except the sheet laying on the floor. Hugh was out cold wrapped up in the lone bedsheet like a mummy in the fetal position. On the night table next to him was evidence of a night of ingesting a variety of chemicals with a couple of amphetamines lying there. Jerry shook Hugh, threw water on him, anything to get him to come around. All he got was a few groans. Meanwhile the girl who belonged to the Afghan showed up claiming he'd been unconscious for hours and she didn't know what to do. We had to catch a plane, so Jerry took the two amphetamines, put them in an ashtray, crushed them into powder, fashioned a tube out of a piece of paper, and blew them up each of Hugh's nostrils. We watched for awhile waiting for any kind of reaction. Sure enough, a few minutes went by and one eye opened partially. "Hugh, we've got a plane to catch!" Hugh grunted, "Alright, just a minute." He then proceeded to crawl on his hands and knees dragging the sheet behind him like Sweet Pea in Popeye, knocking open the door to the washroom. There he was on his knees on the floor of the washroom. He reached up to the vanity, grabbed a bottle, poured an undetermined number of pills into his hand and threw it all back with some water. Then we heard some shower activity and a few minutes later Hugh emerged, eyes wide open, saying, "Alright, let's roll!"

Jerry Sloan: *I'd never seen drug abuse like Hugh O'Sullivan did, and I had been around a lot of bands. He'd take like five black beauties just to shock his system into waking up. He liked speed. We were in London looking at a bunch of pills somebody had and we were asking what they all were. Hugh came over and said, "Let me see all those." He put them in his hand, threw them down his throat, and said, "We'll see."*

The John Kay Band kind of floated along but it seemed fairly obvious that the album wasn't going to catch fire. We were in my studio kicking around ideas for the next album when Burt Jacobs called me with an offer for a Steppenwolf tour in Europe for the fall of 1972. A European agent had a pile of signed contracts to back it up, good dates with good money. Burt told him that the band had broken up, but the money was so attractive that Burt pitched Jerry and me on the idea of a European farewell tour. I accepted on the condition that the John Kay Band go along as opening act in order to piggyback my solo career in Europe using the identification with Steppenwolf. Although it introduced me as a solo artist, it did not distinguish me enough as a separate identity from Steppenwolf.

Jerry Sloan: *John was singing with both bands and it looked weird. He'd come on with these very light tan shades on, a totally different look, no leathers. It looked like maybe his half-brother or something. Then he'd go backstage and put on his leathers and dark shades and come out with the Wolf and it was all* Born To Be Wild.

As we toured, it became evident that the John Kay Band had serious problems with Penti and Hugh. There were nights when the road and the fun part of it absolutely took everything that was left out of us. The shows were high energy so we were completely drained. George, Kent and I did double duty performing with both bands so it was hard on my pipes at times. The energy we had afterward was often artificial, taking a bennie or two. In Germany, Penti began drinking to excess and fell off his drum stool in Frankfurt. He took up with actress Christina Kaufman, recently divorced from Tony Curtis, and was living the life of a bon vivant, Christina on one arm, a fur coat and glass of champagne in the other. There was some friction growing between Jerry Edmonton and Kent Henry who was indulging pretty heavily and rapidly wearing out his welcome. Hugh became involved with a woman during the tour and went off the deep end as well. On one occasion we had to pry him out of bed, he was damn near comatose on whatever, and strap him into the seat for the flight from Manchester to London. On the way he passed out totally to the point that smelling salts could not revive him. When we got off, Hugh was taken away on a stretcher and spent an extra day in London in the hospital detoxing before flying on to join us.

We arrived in Munich not long after the terrorist massacre of several Israeli athletes during the Olympic games and police with machine guns were all over the airport checking everyone out. Here we were coming off a private plane and being processed by customs with a young German policeman about our age holding a machine gun watching us. Hugh O'Sullivan, in his normal 'I don't know where I am, I just carry on' mode reached into his shoulder bag and pulled out a hand grenade. He was a fanatical collector of war memorabilia. Hugh's idea of a good time was to spend the afternoon looking for bullet holes in old war ruins. He smoked and so he pulled out a cigarette and the grenade was a dummy with a lighter inside. Well, in about three seconds, fourteen different emotions swept across the face of the young guy with the machine gun: "What? Is it real? Do I shoot?" As Hugh brought the grenade up to his face he noticed the guy twenty feet away from him. Very nonchalantly he pointed to the cigarette and a flame went up. The German guy just went "Whew."

Ironically, most of the ex-Wolf people were getting along fine, the time away from each other obviously being just what the doctor ordered. Jerry and Goldy had some mutterings about what they had tried and failed to accomplish with their bands Seven and Manbeast. They still had some ideas kicking around and so did I for new Steppenwolf songs, so a couple of things were done fairly quickly: first, forget about the farewell thing, it's a Steppenwolf tour from now on; and second, when we get back let's see what we've got in the way of material and whether we want to reform Steppenwolf.

By the end of the tour the guys in the John Kay Band sensed that their days were numbered after observing the rather obvious comraderie between the former Steppenwolf members. I had already begun recording a second solo album, MY SPORTIN' LIFE, prior to the European tour, but the Kay band only appeared on one track, *Sing With The Children*, a leftover from the first album that we had been performing in our concerts. Following the tour I went back to finishing the SPORTIN' LIFE album, working with some of LA's best session musicians — Mike Utley, Danny Kortchmar, Lee Sklar, Larry Knechtel, Russ Kunkel, all fine players. I enjoyed making that album because it had a different flavor than the first one. The first was roots-oriented while the second was a bit more polished and sophisticated, though some aspects of that album were a bit overproduced. Perhaps Richard Podolor's pop sensibilities got a little bit in the way, but at the time I was too close to notice. With hindsight, I would have kept it a little more raw and basic.

The title song, *My Sportin' Life*, was a recollection of my travels as a solo performer in the early days playing on both coasts as well as Toronto, in the coffeehouses, bars and basket joints. Then I met Jutta and found a new focus in my life. For the first time, someone came into my life who meant enough to me that I was willing to consider altering my lifestyle in order to remain with this person. *Nobody Lives Here Anymore* was the story of my departing LA in 1965 after the Marsha incident, heading back to the Buffalo folk music scene only to discover to my disappointment that it had dissipated during my absence.

One of the more enjoyable moments of working on the album was singing with Gloria Jones who later married Marc Bolan from T Rex. She and I did a duet on *Easy Evil*. That woman had one of the sexiest voices I ever heard. She reminded me of Mavis Staples. *Moonshine* came from Les Emmerson of the Five Man Electrical Band, a bunch of Ottawa, Ontario guys who had been The Staccatos back in the Sixties gigging the same Ontario circuit as The Sparrow.

ABC Dunhill let the SPORTIN' LIFE album twist in the wind. I suspect that they had already heard the rumors via management that the Wolf was considering getting back together again and therefore purposely let it die stillborn, dead on arrival. It received even less promotion than FORGOTTEN SONGS. If that second solo album had been a modest hit, the Wolf reunion most likely would not have happened.

Drift Away was ready to go as a single three months before Dobie Gray released it as a hit, but the label decided to wait to hear the whole album before selecting a single. But completing the album was not easy. I was waiting behind Three Dog Night who were putting together their LIVE AT THE FORUM album, same studio, same engineer, same producer, and taking forever to wade through a mountain of live tape. So I sat twiddling my thumbs for six or seven weeks waiting to complete my album. In the interim, despite the publisher's agreement to put a freeze on anyone else covering *Drift Away*, the writer of the song, Mentor Williams, produced Dobie Gray's hit version. With the one sure hit already gone I told

ABC Dunhill to run with *Easy Evil*. But again they stalled. There were always excuses. *Moonshine* wasn't as strong as those two and died. In the end, the album sold about half as many copies as FORGOTTEN SONGS AND UNSUNG HEROES. When it died, I told the guys in the Wolf that if we get together again, I didn't want to record on ABC Dunhill. They agreed. If Jay Lasker thought he could have the Wolf back by torpedoing my solo career, he was mistaken.

Money was a major inducement to Steppenwolf reuniting in early 1974. The band was a known commodity, a marketable product with an already existing audience base, whereas Seven, Manbeast, and the John Kay Band weren't. But more than that, there was a renewed optimism, freshness, and energy among us. In the intervening time, we had gotten various things out of our systems and discovered that the parts were not greater than the sum. Everybody came to the table with ideas, even Goldy initially, and we encouraged George to start writing more. We all agreed that Kent Henry was out of the question, and in his place we hired Bobby Cochran from a band called Kindred. Bobby was the nephew of rock 'n' roll legend Eddie Cochran and proved to be a creative element — good in the studio, worked fast, full of ideas, and a hot player.

Bobby Cochran: *It hadn't worked out with Kent, so they were looking for the right guitarist when they called me. Kent and I were old friends from the clubs on the Sunset Strip in the Sixties. I was in a group called Kindred that was being produced by Chuck Negron of Three Dog Night. We all shared the same management and would see one another at various company functions. Kindred was the next thing they were trying to break but we split up. When I was first approached about joining by Jerry, I didn't know the guys personally, so I figured I'd better find out if they were on the up and up and whether they were all drug freaks or not. So I phoned Kent to ask him about the guys in Steppenwolf, and it turned out he didn't know yet that he wasn't going to be in the new band.*

I got together with Jerry, Goldy, and George to jam and everything went great. John was still involved with his solo career, but the idea of a Steppenwolf reunion was already in the works. We were learning some of the stuff that later showed up on SLOW FLUX. Some of it was ideas left over from Manbeast. Jerry was really calling the shots before John joined the rehearsals.

But my first practice with John was strange, the tensions and dynamics that were there between all of them that had developed over the years. John was seated directly in my view and Goldy was behind him. Now John likes to explain everything very methodically, step by step, chord by chord. He likes structure and to know precisely where everyone is going. Because his eyesight isn't great he does this usually looking down, not directly at you. I'm listening to John go on and on and on, but I can see Goldy directly behind him making all these ridiculous faces with everything John's saying. I was trying not to laugh but I thought to myself, "There's some weird vibes going down here."

I came from a pretty humble background and I was impressed with John. He's so intelligent, articulate, and a powerful speaker. I remember we were doing an interview and in response to a question, John used the word "antithesis" and I thought to myself "Antithesis?" I had to go home and looked it up in a dictionary.

One thing we were all agreed on from the outset was the need for a clean break — new management, new public relations firm, and a new label. Don Sterling, our business manager, was friends with Bobby Roberts who had been one of the three principals originally forming Dunhill Records and had been the manager for The Mamas and The Papas. Bobby had sold his interest in Dunhill and was looking for something new. He and Don met to discuss a possible management arrangement and both sides liked the idea. Bobby became our manager.

The first thing we insisted was that Bobby arrange our release from ABC Dunhill. In order to obtain a release, we were forced to give back the masters of our recordings. The advice we received from various sources assured us that giving up the masters was no big deal. "After all," our legal eagles told us, "they're just old songs that won't have much shelf life, and thus royalties, anyway." Since the Wolf had split up, Jay Lasker had already saturated the market with repackaged product on REST IN PEACE and SIXTEEN GREATEST HITS. With the advent of CDs, movie soundtracks, and Classic Rock radio formats, our decision to return the masters turned out to be ill-advised. I still receive royalties on all those records, but if we controlled the masters I'd own three thousand acres instead of sixty.

While scouting new labels, we met with Mo Ostin at Warner Brothers. Mo was a very pleasant man, very courteous, whom I always thought the world of because of the way he supported acts like Bonnie Raitt, Randy Newman, and Ry Cooder, all acts I liked tremendously. They were definitely a music oriented label. The idea of being on the Warners label was attractive, but Bobby was looking for a deal. Warner made a decent offer, not unacceptable but by no means overwhelming, based on a realistic assessment of our marketability at that time. Bobby turned it down along with offers from Capitol and others. Eventually Bobby took off his manager's hat and donned his record executive hat to make us the offer he had been after. With his partner Hal Landers, Bobby owned MUMS Records, an independent label distributed by Epic/CBS, which had scored a huge hit with Albert Hammond's *It Never Rains In Southern California*. The offer: four albums, an impressive royalty rate, with a six figure guarantee on delivery of each album. We could hardly argue with that; it was the kind of deal only a manager would write.

After spending some time trying out new material at my studio, we decided to record our reunion album there. The studio had been converted from eight to sixteen tracks by Ed Bannon who worked as engineer on the album. SLOW FLUX, recorded during the spring of 1974, became the first self-produced Steppenwolf album and featured people like Tom Scott and Don Ellis on sax and horns with writing contributions from everyone, including Goldy. Jerry wrote *Straight Shootin' Woman*, a strong tune with a bluesy upbeat shuffle feel and a horn arrangement. Kim Fowley had begun a song called *Gang War Blues* that Jerry, Goldy, and I completed. We picked up *Smokey Factory Blues* from Albert Hammond. I brought in *Fishin' In The Dark, Justice Don't Be Slow* (about the Watergate hearings going on at the time), and *Children Of The Night*.

> *Oh, the dream was born in the summer of love,*
> *And it died with the Woodstock Nation.*
> *But what has it left for the carpenter's son,*
> *And the new coming generation?*
> *We all believed we knew the way,*
> *But fate did not agree.*

Now we're tired of asking who we are,
And what we ought to be.
Children of the night, howling at the gates.
Here to claim forgotten dreams.
Too late, too late.

CHILDREN OF THE NIGHT, 1974

By 1974 the utopian pursuits of the late 1960s of peace, love, and brotherhood were being replaced by aggression, hostility, greed, bitterness, disenchantment. The Woodstock Nation had turned into Altamont and Nixon was in the White House. I'm not a visionary but when I look back at some of the things I've written that predate many issues, like the environment in *The Ostrich* and the disillusionment of *Children Of The Night*, they're almost prophetic.

We released *Straight Shootin' Woman* as a single and it got us up there again into the Top 20. We landed appearances on Don Kirschner's *Rock Concert* and hosted *The Midnight Special* to push the album into the Top Forty, nothing to sneeze at considering our last release, FOR LADIES ONLY, failed to perform as well.

With the album out, off we went on the road again. Jerry took an active hand in the visual presentation of the band, including the cover concept of metals melting together in a 'slow flux' and a new Wolf logo. The world of rock performance had changed dramatically in the intervening two years and audiences had started to expect more than just five guys standing there in front of a pile of amps. David Bowie and Alice Cooper had brought sets, costumes, and theatrics to the rock stage. We put together a production team employing elaborate lighting and sound as well as sets. I had the idea to have no amplifiers visible on stage, and we had a Hollywood motion picture set designer build us some break-down staging forty feet wide with a drum riser and a set of black curtains behind it to hide the amplifiers. On the curtains hung a huge Wolf logo. Along the sides of this setup were aluminum wings that covered the remainder of the speakers. The whole thing presented a very clean appearance in black and silver that had a focal point, the drums in the center with the large Wolf logo behind. We were one of the first bands to use wireless guitars and mikes to continue the clean stage look. All this became *de rigeur* for bands a year or so later. We even rehearsed the whole show on an old Hollywood sound stage later taken over by Studio Instrument Rentals with people like Alice Cooper rehearsing their entire elaborate theatrical productions there.

Another change was that we went in for elaborate costuming that had me in studs and breast plates, beaded chain mail and armored accessories looking like Ming the Merciless ("a cruel man but fair"). The staging was one thing but we went overboard on the costuming. We looked like visitors from Mars. We were trying too hard to draw attention to ourselves since we had been away from the scene for a couple of years. We kept the staging but soon got rid of the costumes.

We went on tour carrying our own sound and lights operated by Pirate Sound, a company out of LA run by some ex-bikers. They had good gear but they were a little bit rough at times. We had to let them go some time later after one of them chased someone through the hallways of the Westward Ho Hotel in Anchorage, Alaska. It seems this guy's wife had run down the hall nude with someone else in pursuit. The biker lifestyle would come through once in awhile and we needed people who were a little more conciliatory. KISS were just starting to take off and opened for us once on the tour. Our road crew gave them a pretty rough time over their staging. These ex-bikers didn't quite warm to all the make-up and smoke bombs. We were playing the Ambassador Theater in St. Louis, a nice venue but with a small stage. We required a lot of stage room for our backdrops and when KISS demanded that we move our setup to accommodate their staging, we said no way. There wasn't enough time to set our stuff up after their opening set. They refused to go on with anything less so we had to leave them off the show. Only a couple of people demanded refunds.

On another occasion, we were slated to play at the Orange Stadium in Miami but the show was cancelled due to rain. There was no alternate rain date in the contract so we sat around at the Newporter Hotel before deciding to head down to the showroom to check out R 'n' B lounge legend Wayne Cochran and the C.C. Riders. We had all heard of them but had never witnessed a performance. And what a performance it was! The band, horns and the whole soul revue routine, came out and did a few tunes on their own before introducing Wayne with his enormous white pompadour. As he proceeded to really get the crowd cooking, it was fairly obvious that his voice was giving him some trouble that night. Perhaps in an effort to divert attention from his strained voice, Wayne went to the back bar and, while the band kept up the groove on stage, he pulled out two bottles, one vodka, one whiskey. He then sashayed through the audience, table to table, pouring these bottles left and right into every glass regardless what had been in them, shouting, "Hey, everybody have a good time." I had never seen anything like this before. I was drinking pretty hard myself because I had the night off and didn't have a gig the next day. Finally, I got up from the table and realized I might have had a bit too much to drink. When I returned to my room, I managed to get it to stop revolving long enough to crash. Some hours later I was awakened by a phone call from the promoter to say that the concert had been rescheduled for two o'clock. They'd been hyping the concert all morning on the radio. That was the one time I performed under less than ideal circumstances. A review in one of the local papers the next day noted that "Mr. Kay seemed to be unusually inanimate during the performance."

Following the release of the SLOW FLUX album, the entire band was invited to the CBS head office in New York for dinner with the chief executives. Everyone was pumping the flesh and talking the talk but I had mixed feelings. On the one hand, if these people got to know us as faces and liked what we brought them we might get the attention it took to push a project through. That was important because MUMS was a custom label, not the same as being signed directly to Columbia or Epic whose artists get the first line of attention. But by the same token, I wasn't digging what I was seeing: too many suits, too much power-based 'protecting my own turf' kind of thing. The feeling was too corporate, too New York, and far removed from the way we were out in LA. They were going through the formalities but their commitment seemed tentative.

Bobby Roberts' company was also into films and had been heavily involved in the first *Death Wish* movie. When that took off in a big way, Bobby and Hal Landers went into the motion picture business full time. All this came down around the time we were recording the second album, HOUR OF THE WOLF. They collapsed

MUMS, shunting their acts to Epic. Don Sterling and I flew to New York to meet with the Epic executives to discuss a promotional tour for the next album. At that meeting we were told that the reason SLOW FLUX had not built further was that we were not playing in the markets where the record was breaking; we were always in the wrong place at the wrong time. We therefore asked Epic to help with a promotional tour for the next album in the key markets, but we left with the feeling that they weren't behind us, and our suspicions were later proven correct. Epic never came through with any support or adequate promotion for HOUR OF THE WOLF.

Between SLOW FLUX and HOUR OF THE WOLF, Goldy was fired. Both his musical contributions and personal behavior had become far too erratic. From about the SEVEN album on, his contributions and capacity had greatly diminished, except for flashes of brilliance on FOR LADIES ONLY. It was a regrettable situation but necessary. He was told of his fate at a meeting that quickly turned confrontational with accusations flying back and forth. He refused to believe that Gabriel Mekler had covered for him in the studio at times. Andy Chapin was brought in by George Biondi as Goldy's replacement. He was a talented guy and good player, though not as aggressive as Goldy had been in his early years.

Bobby Cochran: *Goldy was the kind of guy who had this outer facade but at any moment he could sit down with you and be in tears about how unhappy he was. He was a very heartfelt kind of guy, his experiences were very gut wrenching. But the problem with Goldy was that he would get messed up on drugs and embarrass everyone in public. We'd be in the hotel lobby having just stepped out of our limos, fancy clothes, the whole trip and a fancy couple would glide through the lobby, the woman in mink and expensive dress, the guy in a tux and Goldy would say loud enough for everyone to hear: "He bitch, wanna give me some head?" John and Jerry were classy guys and this kind of behavior was really embarrassing to them and the band.*

Jerry Edmonton: *Goldy was burnt out by then. He had gone over the hill. He was really stoned all the time and doing weird things, hurting people, threatening people, he threatened to kill John and*

*me when we fired him. A lot of weird stuff went down. He was
becoming unpredictable and dislikable. When he would get stoned
on acid he couldn't keep it together. We had an outdoor photo
session in a suburban community and Goldy had taken acid. We
later heard he had been arrested for leaping and diving and laying
on someone's well-healed lawn.*

*We were all invited to some public relations event but only Goldy
decided to show up. Mick Jagger was there and Goldy went up to him
and said something like, "So did you push Brian Jones into the pool
or did he jump?" Jagger just put down his plate and said, "I think
you had better leave." Our management phoned us up the next day
and had a fit about how embarrassing Goldy's behavior had been for
the band and to never allow him go to these events again. We sent
the Rolling Stones a letter of apology for Goldy's actions.*

*The band had decided to do a live recording and Richard and
Bill came down with a remote and recorded a performance. But
when we listened to it afterward we knew it wasn't a good show.
Goldy just didn't know where his fingers were. The rest of the band
was pretty good but Goldy was gone, he was so out of it. We
couldn't erase him because there was too much leakage to other
mikes. So we just scrapped the tapes. That led up to Goldy being let
go, a combination of bad playing, threats and bad behavior.*

We felt fairly optimistic about the HOUR OF THE WOLF album. Mars
Bonfire had come up with one of his best tunes in a long time,
Caroline, featuring Tom Scott playing his sax through a Leslie
speaker. *Mr. Penny Pincher* was an interesting tune, and there was
some decent material contributed by band members, notably Jerry
and Bobby Cochran. We recorded again at my studio with Ed
Bannon engineering. Jerry handled the art direction, and Roy
Halee, an old friend from The Sparrow sessions in New York, mixed
the album. I liked the overall sound of that album better than
SLOW FLUX.

By the time we completed the HOUR OF THE WOLF album, I
was already starting to step back. The whole rock 'n' roll routine
was rearing its ugly head, and I was once again resenting the time
away from things I wanted to do. Since we had no manager, I was
spending too much time having to deal with business. Morning,

noon, and night it was Wolf business. I was watching the world go by sitting at the phone. Shawn was now seven years old and my private life was again taking a back seat to my professional life. I wanted to be John Kay the private citizen for awhile. As a result, my writing credits on the album were rather slim.

Because Epic failed to back the album, we were all disheartened. I announced to the others that I wanted some time to be off on my own, sort out my life, and decide what the next move would be. The problem was we had another two albums to deliver and a lot of money at stake.

Bobby Cochran did his best to keep the Wolf alive. He and George needed the cash more than Jerry and I because they didn't have our financial reserves. Bobby was a hard worker. He was writing to fill the void, contributing songs that he believed would fit into the Steppenwolf mold, perhaps catering a little too much to the stereotyped image. I didn't really dig all the material but my well had run dry. We recorded SKULLDUGGERY fairly soon after the second album to fulfill our contractual obligations. The album lacked enthusiasm and conviction. We might have been saying something on SLOW FLUX and HOUR OF THE WOLF but on SKULL-DUGGERY it was watered down. Andy Chapin's reluctance to go on the road hastened his departure and Wayne Cook was brought in to complete the album. I had a co-writing credit on one song and the rest of the cuts were either covers or tunes from Bobby and George.

Bobby Cochran: *The* SKULLDUGGERY *album cover was originally Jerry's idea for the* HOUR OF THE WOLF *album but it didn't fit the material on that record. In the end it worked out better because we needed a cover fast for the third album which was a real rush to get out because of contractual obligations. We had a depressing meeting where we were told that we had to get his album out or lose a lot of money, so I went home and wrote the song* Skullduggery. *The lyrics are about some of the stories John and Jerry used to tell me about their earlier experiences as well as the way the label was treating us — which was really underhanded skullduggery.*

We delivered the album to Epic with the knowledge that they would do nothing with it other than give us the guarantee according to the contract. When we presented it to them we asked when they wanted the final album. We fully intended to honor the contract. Epic offered to settle the contract, cut their losses and be done with us. They contacted Don and a settlement was worked out for the remaining amount. In the end we received payment for a final album that was never recorded.

We did a few more gigs to fulfill contracts but there wasn't much spirit left. By that point I'd had enough and told Jerry I was quitting. The band just wasn't what it had been before or what we had hoped it might have become when we got back together. Unlike in 1972 when we left on a high, the reunited Steppenwolf died a quiet death.

The John Kay Band recorded the album
FORGOTTEN SONGS AND UNSUNG HEROES
*(left to right: Kent Henry, John Kay, George
Biondo, Hugh O'Sullivan, and Penti Glan.*

*Sunset Strip billboard announcing the return
of the Wolf and introducing the band's new
logo, 1974.*

301

*Performing at the Ambassador Theater,
St. Louis, 1975.*

*Photo session for release of the album
HOUR OF THE WOLF (left to right:*   *John Kay, Andy Chapin, George Biondo,
Jerry Edmonton, and Bobby Cochran).*

TWELVE

NEVER GIVE UP, NEVER GIVE IN'

A rough night in the daily jungle
And it's tough times on the nightly news
Somehow you ignore the rumble
Of the heart that's shakin' in your shoes
Someday, you just keep on saying
Someday, I will find a way to live my dream
But there's no guarantee
Still, you've got hope and your fantasy
Hold on, never give up, never give in
Stay young, and believe in your chance to win
Hold on, never give up, never give in
Stay young, and don't ever betray your dream

HOLD ON, 1987

In 1976, I said goodbye to the Wolf for the second time and hello to my family. My relationship with Jutta and Shawn was suffering as a result of my discontentment with the band, the record label's indifference, and the showbiz lifestyle. The same problems that had plagued me in 1971 were rearing their heads again in 1976. I needed the time away to re-establish my priorities. Jutta, Shawn, and I really got to know each other again. During this period we experienced things together as a family by getting out of the house, going on vacations to Hawaii, camping trips to Arizona and Northern California, seeing some of the natural wonders together, singing silly songs in the van, cooking over the barbecue, sleeping in camp grounds. All of these things were just what the doctor ordered, not only for family reasons but to replenish my depleted energy when at some point down the line picking up a guitar again held a promise of excitement rather than drudgery.

Despite my frequent absences over the years, Shawn had a normal, happy childhood. The three of us shared a warm and cozy home where Shawn grew up playing with her pets and toys, doing what children like to do. Jutta was always there when I wasn't and my mother and stepfather who lived in Los Angeles providing her with a sense of extended family. There weren't many kids her age where we lived in the canyons so we enrolled her in a pre-school daycare center that she took to like a duck to water. She was a very sociable child and liked to be around other kids, the more the merrier. We also had live-in maids who looked after her at times. Jutta and I have always been affectionate with one another and no doubt Shawn was affected by our loving relationship. Once she started school, she discovered many of her classmates had a far less solid family situation. In the entertainment world, having both natural parents together was the exception rather than the rule, and consequently she was envied by some of her friends. She never felt that disruptive 'doesn't anybody want me . . . where do I belong' feeling.

Both Jutta and I knew what it was like to grow up without our fathers; our mothers did a pretty decent job of raising us. With two parents, Shawn was ahead of the game.

Shawn Kay: *My father was on the road during the majority of my childhood, so for that reason my mother takes credit for raising me.*

*She made all the decisions pertaining to my life on a daily basis —
curfew, sleep overs, homework and all that. My father was more
concerned with my education. He was responsible for lecturing me
when I received poor grades in school. That's when he was a
disciplinarian. Education was important to him. My Dad wanted
me to attend a Waldorf School because of what it had done for
him, so I went to Highland Hall in Northridge, a Waldorf School. It
was a strange institution, very European and traditional, but I have
fond memories of my three years there and I had some wonderful
teachers. We had gardening classes, painting, knitting, Bible
studies, mythology, which were not in the other schools. It was a lot
more individualized with smaller classes. But it was from a
different time and I couldn't relate to it. I left to go to Oakwood
School because my friends went there. I kept pushing and pushing
my parents until they agreed to let me go.*

*Most of the children I went to school with were musician's kids
as well. My best friend was Carney Wilson. Among others were her
sister Wendy, Chynna Phillips, Moon Unit and Dweezil Zappa,
Ethan Browne (Jackson Browne's son), and Dante Spector (Phil
Spector's son). We all shared a similar lifestyle, so my upbringing
appeared quite normal to me. I remember being quite young and
hanging out with my parents at clubs like the Troubadour and the
Roxy. I was usually the only kid there but everybody knew me and I
felt very comfortable. I know I had a very liberal upbringing
compared with most children, but I think my parents instilled in
me certain morals and values that many people my age don't seem
to have anymore. I had a lot of freedom as a child, but I could
always talk to my parents about anything. They always trusted me.
I think I was a fairly responsible kid as a result.*

*When my father came home from touring he was a very private
person. We called him a hermit. Around the house he liked it quiet,
so I spent a lot of time at friends' houses. I was intimidated by him
when I was small. He was, at times, impatient and intolerant, but
he was also very busy, and I never wanted to bother him. I think we
both tried to avoid each other. But it wasn't always that way. I also
remember fun times with him in the summer playing in the pool
together.*

Dad was always home for Christmas. Being German, we

followed the tradition of opening our presents on Christmas Eve rather than Christmas Day. I have very fond memories of Christmases. Grandma and Grandpa would come over the day before or the day after. Christmas was very important to Dad. I wasn't brought up on any religion and I don't recall ever being in a church; however, on Christmas Dad would take out the Bible and read from it. I could tell that it meant a lot to him. He would put that old Santa ornament he brought with him from East Germany on our tree every year, and still does to this day.

My Grandma was strict, more so than my parents were at that time. She was a strong, loud, outgoing woman with a tendency to talk a lot and interrupt people. But she was very patient with my Dad and he's very sweet with her. They would talk on the phone a lot and when they did, they talked in German. She was always very interested in what he was doing and his success. She wasn't crazy about the way my parents were raising me, though. I was this little hippie kid. Mom used to dress me up in jeans and little jean jackets. She'd put little studs, beads, and patches on my clothes. My grandmother would take me for the weekend and in the car before we even left the house, she would change my clothes and put me into frilly pink dresses with ribbons and bows in my hair. Mom saw that once and was angry.

My parents had a van, and in the Seventies we used to take trips in the summers. These were very special times. The special times in my childhood were when it was just the three of us. I think my Dad liked it too.

By the mid-1970s, Jutta and I finally realized that our use of cocaine was altering our lives in a negative way. It got to the point where I hated it, didn't like to see it, smell it, and disliked the way I felt when I was on it. I had given up uppers and acid some years earlier though grass hung around a little longer. Quitting blow was easy for me, but Jutta had a tougher time because she took to it more. The grass too soon subsided. I realized one day that I hadn't touched a joint in over a year because I had been too busy with other things and felt the use of it would interfere. Don't get me wrong, I still like marijuana. But I can't remember the last time I smoked it, nor do I think about it. Where I live now is very peaceful; I don't feel stressed out enough to need something chemical to relax. I'll have some beer or wine once in awhile when I'm at home but I don't touch alcohol at all when I'm on the road. The buzz I get from it doesn't compensate for the miserable feeling that results from not being able to sing well the next night on stage. I need lubrication on my pipes and alcohol dries me out.

Jutta and I started practicing transcendental meditation which gave us the impetus to leave the drugs behind, including cigarettes. With the meditating, the urge to smoke just seemed to go. Like coke, giving up cigarettes took longer for Jutta, but she did eventually quit.

My infidelities came to an end around this time as well. When Jutta finally confronted me, we addressed the issue squarely. I couldn't look her in the eye any longer and lie, so I came clean. Maturity had a lot to do with it; I had drifted out of that rock-star mind set. We had always viewed being together as the most important thing in our lives. More than my lover and wife, Jutta is my soul mate, my buddy and true friend. She knows me better than anyone.

Jutta Maue-Kay: *We both stopped the coke cold turkey after we turned thirty. John stopped a little sooner than I did. I started hiding the stuff and I had a few experiences that were really bad so I knew I had to stop. And I did.*

When the herpes scare started, I confronted John and he admitted his activities and promised it had stopped. But by then he was a lot more grown up and had played the rock star image long enough. I used to have dreams about what he was up to on the road, but after that those visions stopped and never came back again. Being away from each other in the early years made us keenly aware of how precious our time together was and we tried to minimize any friction between us.

Since the late sixties Jutta and I had spent pretty freely. Not overly extravagant with the exception of that damn Lagonda, but if we wanted something we simply bought it and sent the bill to Don Sterling. We had only a rough idea of our financial situation and had been living that way for ten years when one day Don came over and informed us, "You've been kids all your lives. From the time you have been old enough to make money, you've turned it over to other people to handle it for you. You don't even know how much you're making or spending. It's time you became familiar with your responsibilities and obligations." The royalties were no longer accumulating, and with me off the road, there were no concert revenues. ABC Dunhill was in steep decline so they weren't pushing the back catalog. This was before MCA bought out ABC Dunhill and restored our entire catalog. There was no classic rock, just old rock, and no one could have predicted CDs and the Sixties revival that would stimulate our record sales. The reality was that by the late 1970s we were almost tapped out.

Some of our investments and retirement funds that had been built up in the late 1960s to mid 1970s were being depleted rapidly in the years between 1976 and 1980. These reserves had seemed substantial, so much so that I felt there would always be some money there for our future. But that was viewed through the distorted vision of someone who let someone else take care of his finances and just occasionally looked over his shoulder.

We suffered a couple of serious financial mishaps along the way as well. Nobody took our money and ran off to Ecuador, but a substantial investment went bad involving a Homestake secondary oil drilling deal out of Oklahoma. A lot of people in Hollywood got sucked into this scheme thinking that it was wonderful because of the tax write-off. The investment appeared solid until our business advisor told us there was a big problem: the principals involved in the deal had apparently vanished taking a lot of money with them, and the IRS was disallowing the tax write-offs. The government had determined that it wasn't a legitimate investment in the first place. Our advisor had heard some rumors prior to all this coming down and had flown out to Oklahoma to see for himself. He came back and urged us to find a charity that we believed in and donate the entire investment. Despite some warning signs, there were a variety of reasons offered as to how this would work us out of our jam. Following that advise, Jerry and I contributed a considerable sum to the American Civil Liberties Union. The ACLU held a fund raising banquet at Hugh Hefner's Playboy West mansion in Holmby Hills, a real Hollywood soiree with celebrities like Kirk Douglas and Burt Lancaster, that we were invited to in appreciation of our contribution. Then, a year later we found ourselves in tax court.

The IRS initially wouldn't allow one single dollar of the donation as tax deductible, but they finally settled for about fifty cents on the dollar. That was still quite a substantial figure, and in order to keep from liquidating certain fund contributions that held substantial tax penalties for premature withdrawal, Jutta and I were forced to refinance our house, even though we had bought it cheap in 1968 and by the late 1970s the mortgage payments were laughable, even less than the power bill. Doing that, however, allowed us at least to write-off the interest on the mortgage while we used the refinancing to pay off Uncle Sam. Then as soon as Uncle Sam was done with us, the State of California lined up to get its piece. We managed to preserve some of the retirement money but eventually that too had to go.

In the years between 1976 and 1980 we were living off of our reserves. We weren't totally broke by any means, but it didn't take a rocket scientist to figure out that at the current rate of depletion, our money wasn't going to last more than a few years. So what was I going to do? I wasn't ready to retire at the age of thirty-four. This situation caused a considerable amount of anxiety and some sleepless nights. I didn't need mansions and art collections. I know some people who believe that money is their source of identity; what they possess is who they are. But how much was enough for us? I wanted some privacy and to be able to do what I wanted, how I wanted, when I wanted. It sounds like the temper tantrum of a little child, but that's really what it all came down to. When one is lucky enough to have actually lived that way, you're an idiot for pissing it away. How many people can say they can do what they like and make a good living at it?

We needed the money if we weren't going to make serious adjustments to our lifestyle. Jutta and I both agreed that we could scale things down without much effort. Our house wasn't a Bel Air mansion, so we didn't need domestic staff, a pool man, maids, or a gardener. The two of us weren't afraid of work. When the time came to cut down, we let the pool man and gardener go and Jutta took care of the house and the garden. She also became our accountant, looking after the books, learning about computers and how to run an efficient office. I'm sure she never dreamed she'd become a business person, but with all this came a certain degree of self-reliance, pride of accomplishment, self-esteem, discovering abilities we didn't suspect we had, especially for Jutta. By the mid-1980s, once those hard years were behind us, we found we had matured. We were more confident and could handle our needs and affairs much better. We learned to live in the real world. But the down side was that the three of us did not have as much time with one another compared to the previous years.

After a couple of years of family time away from the music, I started getting itchy to get back to writing and recording. I had kept in touch with Jerry Edmonton, so we brought in Bobby Cochran, Wayne Cook, Mars Bonfire, and Jack Ryland, a bass player we knew who had been in Three Dog Night before they broke up, to try out some ideas. Under Morgan Cavett's supervision, we recorded some new songs at Heritage Studios where Morgan worked as a producer/engineer. But in the end I wasn't that pleased with the results. Morgan and I then talked about doing a solo John Kay recording on speculation, then hustling it to a label.

Back in the early 1970s, Jerry Sloan had introduced us to Steve Palmer who came to work for the band as part of our road crew. Steve was a drummer originally from Utah who had his own band, Tall Water, with his brother Michael on guitar and Kenny Blanchett on bass. Steve went on to work for us during the reunion period while attempting to launch Tall Water. They managed to record an album produced by Jerry Edmonton that didn't get off the ground. By 1977 the band was in limbo. I contacted Steve and enlisted Tall Water along with Wayne Cook for a John Kay solo session with Morgan and myself producing. The songs I had written rocked a little more than my previous solo albums but were still lighter than Steppenwolf, songs like *Business Is Business*, *Live Your Life*, and a few others. Various session people were called in, such as the Tower of Power horns, Nicky Hopkins, Little Feat keyboard player Bill Payne. Morgan suggested that *Live Your Life* would be perfect for slide guitarist Lowell George. Morgan and Lowell had gone to school together at Hollywood High, and I really admired Little Feat's work and Lowell's playing. Morgan called him and he agreed to come down and do the session. At that point he was quite heavy and drinking pretty seriously, but he played well on the track. He had that touch. That was the last time I ever saw him. Sadly, he died in 1979.

Morgan Cavett: *John was one of the first people around here ever to play slide guitar in a rock 'n' roll context with The Sparrow. Back in 1966, Lowell used to be at the Whisky watching John playing slide, gleaning licks from him. I asked Lowell to do the session and he said, "I get triple scale." I told him that was okay, it was about $300. Then he came back with, "Well, I really don't want to," and he hemmed and hawed until finally saying, "Get me three grams of coke and I'll be there."*

Cocaine was about a hundred bucks a gram, so I got some coke and Lowell came in and did the session. He walked in while we were getting the studio ready, moving mikes and stuff around. He was very fat at the time, wearing overalls and looking like a workman. John couldn't see very well and didn't recognize him, so when he saw this guy walk in looking like a maintenance man John got very uptight. Joking around, Lowell said, "Is this the room that has to be painted?" John just glared at me like, "You asshole, we're in the middle of a session. Can't you get your maintenance schedule arranged so as not to conflict with our recording session?" John can be a real bear to work with, especially in later years, but he definitely likes to be in charge in the studio.

We recorded an album's worth of material that I felt pretty good about then Lucy, an old friend from the New Balladeer days who had kept in touch with Morgan over the years, introduced me to Ron Stone. Ron was working with Elliot Roberts (who handled Joni Mitchell and Neil Young, among others) and managed Bonnie Raitt. Ron listened to the tapes and liked what he heard. He then shopped the tapes around to the labels with little interest. Somehow parts of the album became a demo that was played for Terry Woodford and Clayton Ivy down at Wishbone Studio in Muscle Shoals, Alabama, and they suggested that the songs would sound great with their studio musicians. Through Lon Harriman, a former Steppenwolf agent, I eventually secured a deal with Mercury Records to record a new album in Muscle Shoals. A few weeks later I flew to Alabama to cut what became the ALL IN GOOD TIME album.

Recording that album reunited me with Larry Byrom. Following his departure from the Wolf, Larry had formed a band called Ratchell, recording a couple of albums to limited success before returning to the south as a studio musician. He had become an in-demand player on the studio scene and a regular at Wishbone Recording Studios. Larry contributed to several of the arrangements on the album and played some tasty guitar. There was a nice groove to many of the tracks. Some of my favorite songs from my post-Steppenwolf period were on that album, such as *Give Me Some News I Can Use, Business Is Business, That's When I Think Of You,* and *Ain't Nothing Like It Used To Be.* Unfortunately, Mercury did very little to promote the album, probably because the A & R man who had signed me was no longer at the label. Still, the album did serve notice that I was still in the game.

When the ALL IN GOOD TIME album was released in 1978 I had no band with which I could tour and promote the record. Then, out of the blue, Steve Palmer called me up.

Steve Palmer: *I was building studios with Ed Bannon to make ends meet and playing fusion jazz-rock stuff with my brother Michael and people like Tom Scott. I had not heard back from John since the sessions with Morgan, so I phoned him up and said, "You've got a new album out, a bunch of new songs, why don't you come down here. We've got a whole band together, so let's just kick a few things around." He was depressed at that time because of the lack of interest from Mercury and lack of publicity. It was a good enough album to stand on its own and put an act together and tour. So we did and that became the John Kay Band. We got a set together and played a few gigs like the Roxy and the Palomino, just clubs in town.*

This new version of the John Kay Band with the Palmer Brothers was a fairly loose arrangement; we played a few showcase gigs around LA and southern California, nothing too far or for too long. It gave me the opportunity to ease back into gigging without the full blown lengthy tours. The guys were young and enthusiastic, so there was an energy there that made the gigs fun. Gradually, we worked it up to going out on the road. Somebody arranged a small tour in Texas, eight dates in a row. We drove out in two vans, Steve's van, dubbed 'the crippler,' for the gear, and my Dodge van, outfitted like a motor home. It was a real low-key, compact little organization. We did this on and off until late 1979. Then all hell broke loose for me. I was about to discover that my insulated, private, little world would never be quite the same again.

Back in 1976, Jerry and I had agreed to lay the Steppenwolf name to rest. Neither of us had any intentions of touring as Steppenwolf and, as far as we were concerned as the two sole shareholders of Steppenwolf Productions Incorporated, no one had the right to use the Steppenwolf name without our express permission. That was that. However, with the name out of action but a demand still out there for Steppenwolf, a few unscrupulous individuals decided to take it upon themselves to fill that void and in doing so line their pockets. A character named Steve Green made a pitch to Goldy and Nick: allow your names to be part of a "new" Steppenwolf and receive $1500 a week each to go on the road. Apparently, Green made his living finding former members of defunct name bands, having them assemble a band by filling in the vacant slots with unknown players, and sending them out posing as the real thing. For Goldy and Nick, the promise of steady money must have been enticement enough since they didn't leave the Wolf with any substantial reserves. Further inducement likely came in the form of revenge. Both had been turfed on less than amicable terms and resented what they considered unfair treatment from Jerry and me. Greed and revenge can be a potent combination. Kent Henry was also lured into the sordid affair at one point.

When I first got wind of this whole mess I was livid. I said to myself, "How dare those sons of bitches!" Thinking about it now, they're both lucky to be alive today after what they did. I knew people who in turn knew people who, for a price, would put a serious hurt on someone with no questions asked. And I must admit I fleetingly considered it. Steppenwolf was a very personal thing to me. I realize that the rest of the guys will never see it from my perspective. Having been the lead singer, spokesperson, and main writer, Steppenwolf was an outlet for my own personal feelings, point of view, beliefs, and sound. All of a sudden, there was another version of Steppenwolf out there, presumably some starving bar band which had nothing to lose and which at varying times was fronted by one or more of the three principal offenders, all of whom I had brought into the original Wolf in the first place.

Goldy and Nick should have known better. Back in 1970 the

five members of Steppenwolf agreed that no one removed from the band by a four member to one vote would have any further rights to the name. Although this 'four against one' arrangement had been agreed upon at a corporate meeting attended by all of us, no record was kept of that meeting. Our legal advisers at the time were probably too busy talking showbiz deals to note it. When the bogus Wolf popped up, Jerry and I immediately thought we had this covered, but in subsequent searches of corporate minutes, we discovered to our dismay that it wasn't there.

After much gnashing of teeth, we listened to our legal advisers who told us we would have a hard time getting an injunction against these people because of the deficiencies in our corporate records. They said we would be well served by listening to what the other side wanted, which was to use the name and to be left alone. Acquiescing to legal opinion, we reluctantly allowed Goldy and Nick to lease the use of the name from us for a percentage of their gross earnings payable at regular intervals. Steve Green had apparently convinced Nick and Goldy that they were going to make millions. It was a small price to pay, they figured.

When our attorneys were drawing up the agreement, they suggested to us to demand not only that Nick and Goldy pay a percentage of the gross but that they also relinquish their Steppenwolf royalties. Jerry and I doubted they would agree to do that. Rule number one we all learned when we got into this business: never give up your royalties. Imagine if Mars Bonfire had given up his royalties on *Born To Be Wild*? That one song set him up for life. But they agreed to those terms. Still, the very idea of permitting Nick and Goldy to use the name in this manner was intolerable. I kept thinking about how we could use the newly proposed agreement to accomplish what our old corporate records should have done, namely to bar Nick and Goldy from rights to the name in perpetuity. Slowly the following plan unfolded.

Jerry and I, along with our advisors, assumed correctly that Nick, Goldy, and Steve Green would inevitably have a falling out. There were certain people involved in this scam who by reputation were questionable at best. At some point cracks would show, and when that occurred, they would be in default. Then we would have them by the balls. Failure to live up to the conditions of the agreement would result in complete forfeiture of the name forever and continued use would be illegal. They knew what they were signing. We gambled that they would default; sooner or later they would turn on each other. They did not disappoint us.

Nick St. Nicholas: *I had a new band, Pacific Coast Highway, an Eagles kind of thing. Then one day, Goldy came over and said, "Want to go back out as Steppenwolf?" He said, "Nick, it's all worked out. You've got to listen to this guy Steve Green. I'm gonna have him call you." He was an agent out of Phoenix or somewhere. I got this flurry of calls from Steve Green, promoters, two attorneys, saying, "Nick, you gotta do this thing, it's legit. We're in contact with Jerry, John and all the rest of the guys and everything's legit so what are you waiting for?" Steve Green's a smooth talking devil. He ended up in jail. That was my fault for listening to him.*

Steve Green and his buddies basically wanted the name. They were the ones running it. They had three or four Steppenwolfs out there. I was just used as a scapegoat and the blame fell on my shoulders. Steve Green was the main instigator. They wanted to call it the New Steppenwolf. I always felt that I was unjustly thrown out of the original band, so there was no love lost between John and me. I knew John had something to do with me being thrown out, he threw everybody else out. But with me it was different, at least I could fight back. I figured I did that much work for the band, therefore I was entitled to something.

The first group we got together was awful. Kent Henry would be so drunk and Goldy would be on drugs and the band didn't sound right. Then they started not paying me what they promised. I figured that maybe with some really good players at least we could be better impostors than the first bunch of impostors.

The guys behind this whole thing were heavy duty. They screwed me so hard and so fast that I didn't know where I was coming from. I ended up selling everything I had left and moving to Minneapolis. I'd had enough of Hollywood. But once I signed off the whole thing, I thought I would get my royalties back.

Nick always believed that his departure from Steppenwolf in 1970 was going to be a detriment to the band because he had his own little following. In his mind he remains convinced that he is an original member of the band because The Sparrow preceded Steppenwolf. Years later he called up Jerry with an offer from a promoter to put the original Steppenwolf back together. "Just the five of us original guys." Jerry replied rather acerbically, "Well, how are we gonna do that? Rushton's dead."

In the beginning, we received small amounts of money according to the terms of the agreement, then the payments stopped. But the bogus band continued touring and getting terrible feedback from promoters phoning to complain, "What the fuck is this? I hired Steppenwolf and a bunch of other guys show up. Where's John Kay? This isn't Steppenwolf." Kent was kicked out; the band regrouped; then Goldy and Nick fell out with each other. Jerry and I feared that the good name of Steppenwolf was going to be totally ruined, so we proceeded to terminate the agreement. We sent out the required written notification that they had x number of days to cure the breach, and when they didn't respond, we launched a lawsuit against them, got an injunction to halt their activities, and even ran ads in trade magazines warning promoters that there was a band out there touring as "Steppenwolf" under false pretenses.

Steve Palmer: *They had John Kay lookalikes going out impersonating John with the sunglasses and everything. It was almost like Elvis sightings. I remember seeing a photograph of one of the bogus bands with a John Kay lookalike. I thought it was John. This asshole had the same Snidely Whiplash moustache, the exact sunglasses, the exact clothes. They'd take deposits on gigs, then not show up. It was really upsetting for John.*

With the uncertainty over my personal financial situation combined with the bogus band fiasco, it was almost like I had a cause that pulled me out of the mire. All of a sudden I had a goal, something to focus on. Once I locked onto it, I was like a bulldog. Being an Aries, I can be very stubborn.

I had had enough of waiting and doing nothing. The best way to knock the legs out from under them, I surmised, was to get out there myself and compete with them on the road. I told our legal advisor Jay Kenoff, "You handle the legal stuff and nail this sucker down, meanwhile I'm going out as John Kay and Steppenwolf and cut them off at the pass." In January of 1980, the John Kay Band quickly transformed into John Kay and Steppenwolf and went out nationwide. There was no question that the single most powerful emotion that kept me going for four years was hate. It was a battle of nerves and will between me and those who were trashing the name. It was a war, city by city, region by region, to drive those bastards right off the map.

We retained what we were doing as the John Kay Band in that we continued to have a significant amount of new material interspersed with the old. My approach was and remains: give 'em enough of the old and we'll buy enough of their tolerance for the new. And if they get used to the idea, maybe we can get to a point where they'll want to hear the new. From the get-go in 1980 I told the guys in the band that we would use Steppenwolf's past as a means of bankrolling a future for us. I made no bones about that. When people looked up at the stage they saw John Kay as the only recognizable face, but that didn't seem to stop them from coming.

When all was said and done, the bogus band had all but destroyed the earning capability of the name through their dismal performances. We were like hurricane victims who once had a house and now are left with rubble. We had to rebuild from the ground up, starting with nothing. We had a name and a reputation when we quit in 1976. We could fill decent sized theaters and small arenas. When I picked the name out of the gutter in 1980, it had been left in blue collar beer bars on the outskirts of Anywhere, USA. In return for this devalued name, Jerry and I had Nick and Goldy's royalties in perpetuity — which in the 1980s turned out to be substantial enough. I feel at least somewhat compensated.

Why didn't I invite Jerry Edmonton to join a reconstituted Steppenwolf? I know it's a bit of a sore point between us, but there were a number of reasons. When I decided to rescue the name, its street market value was extremely low. We played shit holes and got paid accordingly. The Palmer boys were hungry and willing to go out there and put themselves through this whole fight because it might eventually go somewhere. They were as committed as I was. I didn't have a lot of money to offer them, just a lot of work and the possibility that we might be able to dig ourselves out of this mess. We had already been playing together as the John Kay Band for at least eighteen months, so we were able to make a very quick turnaround, add twelve songs, change the name, go out as Steppenwolf, and drive the bogus act out of business. If I would have asked Jerry in, it would have altered the financial end to the point that it would not have been worth it for either of us. If I was going to throw myself one hundred percent into this effort, then I wanted it to compensate me adequately.

In order for Jerry to join, Steve would have to leave and I don't think Mike Palmer would have stayed on without his brother. The rest of the guys were extensions of the Palmer brothers and probably would have left as well. Finally there was this to be considered: I had gone from the inception of Steppenwolf until the ALL IN GOOD TIME album in this on again/off again, Steppenwolf-John Kay, Steppenwolf-John Kay pattern. I didn't want to be in that either/or quandary anymore. As John Kay *and* Steppenwolf it could sound the way I wanted it to sound.

At that point in my life, I knew from experience what worked for me. What didn't work was a perpetual tug of war in which I had to justify my preferences or wishes to someone else. I wanted to find people who liked what we were trying to do musically and who could contribute and enjoy the work. If major differences arose, I could find somebody else to take their place and get on with my life. For all these reasons, I decided not to ask Jerry to join.

Jerry Edmonton: *I think John looked at it and concluded that he wasn't making much money as the John Kay Band so he would like to use the name Steppenwolf. That's when I heard from him and he wanted to know what I thought about that. That's when it became clear to me that John had no intentions of putting together a Steppenwolf from any of the members from the past. He just wanted to go out and use the name because his booking agent told him, "This is the best we can do as the John Kay Band. Now, if you were John Kay and Steppenwolf, hey, that's a different story," because the name John Kay is quite synonymous with Steppenwolf, like Mick Jagger and the Rolling Stones. I told him I thought it would be nice to put some of the old guys together, but I could just tell by his voice that he didn't want that and had no intention of* *asking me. I didn't push it because I didn't want to break up our friendship. I figured I wasn't going to use the name on my own but the name was there, it's an asset. I could have said, "No, I'm not granting you permission," and it would just sit there not making any money. Or John could have permission to use it, he makes some money and I make some money. I'd rather have John using it because he's the voice. So he pays me a commission and if he's in breach, I get the name. The agreement is really simple and easy and we don't mess with it.*

The decision wasn't meant to slight Jerry or deny him anything. Seen from my perspective, circumstances were such that the course of action I chose made the most obvious sense. I had no doubts about using the Steppenwolf name to my advantage. Here I was with the John Kay Band playing clubs and deliberately not doing the Wolf tunes, while somebody else was out there pretending to be me singing Steppenwolf songs, many of which I'd written and all of which I had sung originally on our records.

Richard Halem at Variety Artists took us on and booked the hell out of us. With a few exceptions, most of the gigs were places you wouldn't want to go into without a whip and a chair. But the first time through, that's where we had to start. At one point I looked around and thought "Jesus, a few short years ago we were headlining at the Forum and now I'm playing here. How badly do I want this?" Maybe the place didn't hold more than eight hundred people but it was packed, they loved it, and went home happy. The word of mouth was good. The agents were happy and the money went up the next time through, so it appeared that we were on the right track.

Steve Palmer: *We played the worst places you've ever seen in your life. We traveled in the two vans, did our own set up and tear down at first until we could afford a crew. But we started to get tight because we were energetic players and getting a charge from the feedback we received from audiences when they realized this was not some bogus act. We started to take back cities that the bogus bands had been through and damaged the reputation. John started phoning local radio stations and doing interviews warning people*

*against the bogus bands. People would come to gigs just to see if he
was the real John Kay.*

*Sometimes we'd come into a city just after the bogus band had
been there or they'd follow us in and have to cancel. Steve Green
was stupid. He'd book them within 150 miles of where we were
playing, take huge deposits, and not show up. He had splinter
groups out there as Steppenwolf who had nobody from the original
band. What kept us going was hearing what was happening to
them or the situations they'd be in and we'd constantly be laughing
about it. We'd see articles in the papers or hear horror stories from
disc jockeys about how their gigs went, how they'd play two songs
and leave, or one guy wouldn't show up. The guys in the bogus
bands were heavily drugged.*

*We toured the USA and Canada constantly, working it up from
the beer bars to small theaters like the Agora, and opening for
larger acts. The confidence was there. When we first started out,
John had so many people tell him he was finished, dead. He really
wanted to prove to everyone that he could do it again. There was a
guy who wrote an article in London, Ontario stating, "John Kay
will be playing Holiday Inn lounges someday doing the same act."
That really hurt him and he determined to prove that guy wrong.
And he did.*

*John was excited about the band because we were getting better
with every gig. We started looking forward to sound checks to throw
around new ideas, and that's where John and Michael linked up
and started writing together. Mike was the king of riffs. We'd record
some of it and John would take it home and write lyrics to it.*

*It was the invasion of John's territory that gave him the drive
and a new lease on life to go 100% full out to make this act work.
That drive to take back territory was the fuel that kept us burning.
The name was more attractive to agents and management
companies and would give us better hopes of getting a record deal.
John viewed it as a necessary means to an end, but he never
abandoned the drive to create new music and get a record deal.*

*Nick St. Nicholas showed up at a gig in Minneapolis and came
into the dressing room wanting to make peace. John wouldn't talk
to him. He had not one word to say to him.*

There were times when I would wake up at three in the morning in a cold sweat. There was so much to be done — all of it basically unpleasant and stressful tasks. We had no record company, no PR firm, no management, just Steve Palmer and me. Resuscitating the Steppenwolf reputation required a constant battering ram of touring, touring, touring, four years of grinding it out on the road. I found out what character strength I really had when I had to kick, scratch, and rebuild the name.

We were playing in a club in Minneapolis during that first year of rebuilding when a kid came up to me and said right to my face, "You're not John Kay because he wouldn't play a shit hole like this." That completely knocked me for a loop. I asked myself if my ego was too bruised to play here because we used to headline and sell out venues all over the world. Could I not find it within myself to stand up on this stage and play for eight hundred people in this club? Was I still in touch with what got me into this profession in the first place, namely that I liked making music? If that was the case, should I take the position that I'm superior to those who paid their money, set their evening aside, and are still interested in hearing what we have to say in spite of all the damage done by the bogus Wolf? "Yes, it is a shit hole," I told myself, "but these people are not above being here tonight. They paid good money to see you play. They don't think of it as a shit hole. It doesn't really matter to them. Why is it a shit hole anyway? This is a place you would have killed to play in as The Sparrow but you now view it as a shit hole because you'd once played arenas and festivals. It's smokey and it's a bar and everybody's kind of juiced but the music still rocks and the people rock with you. So, this is what you do. You make music as a living. Now it's up to you to see to it that you conduct it in such a way that on the one hand you are successful enough to take care of your family and at the same time you still have enough energy and time left to make some new music. That is really your lifeblood and psychologically what keeps you from viewing yourself the way some people view groups of this ilk, because the majority of them only do retreads and are viewed as such. Now go out there and kick their asses and do it often enough until the word gets around and maybe there is a way out of this."

It was a harrowing, endless four-year cycle of nonstop touring, with the exception of Christmas breaks, across North America, Europe, and Australia, finding ourselves stranded in Europe with no money, driving day and night at the risk of life and limb in order to make leapfrogs from here to there, selling out and slowly rising to bigger clubs then theaters and county fairs. I went through a character building period of enlightenment that I hope I never have to go through again. Once, after a particularly hectic pre-tour preparation period of working sixteen hours a day, weeks on end, I found myself exhausted on an early morning flight to meet the band and crew somewhere back East. The plane took off from LAX, and I could hear the engines laboring, the running gear noisily retracting, and saw passengers nervously looking around the cabin. An unusual calm came over me at that moment and I heard my inner voice say, "I don't care if it goes down. If it's time to go, I'm ready. I'll miss Jutta and Shawn but at least I've provided for them if I go." I sat there numb, quiet, tears rolling down my cheeks. For the first time in my life I had ceased to care about living. A few moments later I resolved to make a change in my life, that nothing was worth the sacrifice of your spirit and joy of living.

During those years, Jutta proved to be my real partner. She was always there. When I'd call her from the road to tell her my problems, she told me to keep hanging in there. From 1980 to 1984 were the toughest, the roughest, the leanest years of our lives. Because I was gone so much, Jutta had to run our business affairs. There was also a daughter to be raised, a household to run, and a lot of times she had to be my psychiatrist. She held up the whole support system at home while I was out on the road. All this drew us a lot closer. We became like old army buddies. "Remember when we. . . ." We shared experiences. A team for life. Everything else is built on that.

Jutta Maue-Kay: *It was hard for John to see the name dragged around. It's something he was and is very proud of. The whole thing, the bogus act and the rebuilding, made him very bitter, cynical, and down on the music business. He was angry alright. As anyone who knows him will attest, John is very fair and he expects the same from others. He likes justice to be done.*

It was a time of positive growth for me. It was good for me to be more involved in the business, to see where the money was going and what was involved because it was our business, our life.

It was hard too because he would be on the road so much and when he was home he was always taking care of the business or getting ready to go back on the road. So there really wasn't any time for us to be together, which is almost harder than if you are apart.

Shawn Kay: *Dad and I never discussed business. Many times I remember him leaving for a tour and not even knowing Dad had left. I knew from Mom telling me that it was a very bad time for him. From the age of thirteen to sixteen he wasn't around much, and when he was around, there was a certain amount of tension in the air. I'd hear from Mom how he was struggling on the road. When he was home, he'd be on the phone trying to get business taken care of. It seemed like he'd be on the phone all the time. That was when the family vacations stopped. One summer Mom and I went to Germany but Dad couldn't come.*

I had missed a lot of Shawn's early years because of the touring, writing, and recording routine from the time she was born until the breakup of the band in 1971. Then I did the two solo albums and the reunion and I was at home a little more often. I saw Shawn fairly regularly during the week when we used to fly out and tour only on weekends and the reunion albums were recorded in my home studio. So from about 1970 on, I was in and out of Shawn's life on at least a regular basis. From 1976 to 1980, that was the period where there were a lot more family outings and trips. By the early 1980s I had gotten a number of years of family life under my belt, and Shawn was by then a young girl who no longer needed her parents and their friends for socializing. She was a teenager and started the normal process of separating herself from her parents. She still thought we were cool but now had her own social life and circle of friends. But everybody made family adjustments, compromises, and concessions to my being out on the road so much.

By the early 1980s we had boxed Steve Green, Nick, and Goldy into a corner. The legal maneuvers had worked, and John Kay And Steppenwolf had cut off their ability to book venues. We had a federal injunction against Steve Green and Goldy signed off as well. Steve Green was eventually convicted on an unrelated matter, I believe it was interstate wire fraud, and was sentenced to a term in the penitentiary. Nick finally agreed to bow out if we would pay an insignificant sum that he owed to his lawyer. In return, Nick agreed that he had no right to use the name Steppenwolf, nor could he refer to himself in the future as "formerly of Steppenwolf."

Of all the people involved in this bogus debacle, Goldy was the one guy that I could have perhaps forgiven for what he did, more so than Nick. Nick was not in the original Steppenwolf to begin with. He had been hired by us more or less for old times sake and he then rewarded us by going off the deep end to the point where we had to fire him. He then had the audacity to claim he had a right to the Steppenwolf name.

I bear Nick and Goldy no further ill will. It's taken many years but I've come to terms with what happened. I stay out of their lives, they stay out of mine. But if they were ever to stir things up again, I would not hesitate for a moment to lower the boom on them with everything at my disposal. Those two have done enough to affect my life that I feel little sympathy for what they have gone through since then.

John Kay And Steppenwolf undertook a European Tour in 1980 arranged by an ex-Steppenwolf manager living in England. But when we arrived we discovered it was totally mismanaged. We returned from Europe after the tour in the hole and I fired my manager.

Steve Palmer: *The band went over well in Greece. We had a German tour manager, playing on some band from Yugoslavia or Turkey's equipment, the sound company was from Italy, so there were all these major language barriers. We arrived at the hall, about 9,000 seating and it had been oversold by 2,000. At the venue we started to hear bricks and windows breaking, panes of glass getting rocked out. We didn't know what was happening. So we did the show and people loved it. They sang the lyrics to the songs so loud that you could hear it over the PA and they didn't speak English. It was an amazing gig. We finished and went outside to the red Mercedes that the promoter had rented for us and it looked like it had been in a demolition derby. They had smashed everything around the place. A giant riot had broken out that made all the papers the next day. So we were major news over there.*

We played Athens two days later and they had the water cannon trucks around the venue, riot control guys all around with helmets and guns, and had closed a whole city block around the venue. Our cab driver stopped a block and a half away from the gig to let us out because he couldn't get any further. The police took mug shots of us in one of those little photomat booths like they have at shopping malls. The guy put a drachma in and got our mug shots. We had to pay off a whole lot of people to get the equipment through. It was crazy but the gig was great.

In Germany we had to go through the DMZ on the train in the middle of the night. The East German police stopped the train and boarded it. We got stuck in the ribs by the end of a gun and told to get up and show our papers. It was a total shakedown and very uncomfortable, especially for John.

On the last night of that European tour, we recorded the gig at the Lyceum in London for an album that Phonogram released later only in Australia entitled JOHN KAY AND STEPPENWOLF LIVE IN LONDON. It was the first gig I had done in London in eight years, and although it was raw, it offered a cross section of old hits and more recent material, including *Hot Night In A Cold Town* which we later re-recorded and released as a single and video. John Cougar Mellencamp released a version of this song after hearing a demo tape of our version on a San Jose radio station. The album was produced by me and engineered by Kevin Kern.

The live album led to a unique Australian pub tour later that year. Many of the old hotels in the cities were on the decline but still had large ballrooms which had become regional rock venues. There were so many that we played Sydney for two weeks at a different ballroom each night. We stayed at a hotel on Bondi Beach, leaving every afternoon in a minibus for a different venue. We repeated this all over Australia — Melbourne, Adelaide, Perth, Canberra, Brisbane, Lismore, and the Gold Coast. I had brought along my film equipment and was busy visiting wildlife preserves making movies. I had editing equipment and would get the film processed and edit it back at the hotel.

The guys in the band would carry on ferociously at the infamous Manzel Room, the place for rock 'n' roll musicians to hang out in Sydney at the time. I had curbed my partying by then, so I had no interest in joining their antics. As I would be leaving the hotel in the morning with my camera gear en route to grab a train out to the outskirts to film some more wildlife, our own wildlife was clawing its way along the curb into the lobby of the hotel after a night of carousing. They had a phenomenal time but were ready for the sanitarium when we got home again. For quite different reasons, we all loved Australia.

Steve Palmer: *John had cleaned up by the* ALL IN GOOD TIME *album. In the old days of the original Wolf, those guys used to pack heavily. John had his little road case, an anvil case, with a bottle of Kahlua on one side and a bottle of Vodka on the other. You'd lift the false bottom up and there'd be bennies, downers. The tour manager used to carry a scale. John had a lot of edge to him back then. When he cleaned up it lightened his attitude quite a bit. With us, he'd maybe have a beer or two but that was about it. Then he stopped that too because he was worried about abusing his voice on the road. Drugs make you aggressive or depressed, on edge and on guard. John had a hell of a temper when he was doing drugs, and mood wise, you'd either talk to him or you wouldn't. But he became real consistent and ready to deal with the rest of life once he stopped doing the drugs. You could always count on him.*

In 1981, Ron Rainey, who had been our agent at Magna Artists, took on management of the act. Between the two of us, with Jutta running the home front and Steve Palmer as my right hand man on the road, we built our little team. Since then, we've turned a profit on the road every year.

Ron Rainey: *The name had been beaten up so badly that it put John in a difficult situation when he decided to go back out. We were at a low price starting out in small venues that made it hard to raise the profile. The early gigs ranged from $2000 to $3500 per night. A few years earlier they had been pulling in ten times that.*

We started putting them into large clubs and small theaters and they were selling out every show for a percentage of the gate. By January of 1981 we had turned a corner and really started to do business and were getting publicity. They were selling out almost everywhere they went. We kept them on the move and didn't saturate the markets. All this was with no record label deal. Record companies were looking for the next big thing rather than recycling something old.

By then we had gone through several personnel changes. Our bassist, Chad Peery, was replaced by Gary Link, and Danny Ironstone, who went with us on the 1980 European tour, was replaced in short order by Brett Tuggle. Brett later left to join Rick Springfield's band, but he did more than redeem himself by suggesting Michael Wilk as his replacement. Michael has been with us ever since and has become the backbone of this band. The nucleus of Steppenwolf for the next few years was the Palmer brothers, Michael Wilk, and Gary Link.

We continued to crisscross North America month after month. Steve's old crippler was put out to pasture and we picked up a decent sized Ford cube van because the equipment was starting to grow. Our old family van was retired, and we bought an Airstream motor home which we equipped with additional bunks for the band. We hired a driver for the bus who also handled the merchandising. Everybody took turns doing double duty because we couldn't afford additional people — the driver sold merchandise, the crew took turns driving the equipment truck. Once, in Wyoming, the Airstream fuel pump went out on the highway, so we all had to ride in the crew van to the gig, then go back afterwards and replace the fuel pump ourselves. Then it was off to the next gig.

One winter in the early 1980s, the band and crew were en route to Toronto for two sold out shows at the El Mocombo, line-ups around the block. Somewhere near Sydney, Ohio they hit a snowstorm, a real January blizzard. I had flown up to Toronto earlier and received a call from Steve Palmer who was phoning from a hospital. He had been driving the van and had passed a semi-trailer truck in the fast lane. He then got on the CB to tell our truck driver and sound engineer, Logan Davis, to come on around and also pass the truck. As Logan was coming around from behind the semi, he passed a break in the median strip for emergency access to the other right of way. A snow plow going about fifteen miles an hour in the opposite direction decided to make a U-turn from the other side of the median into Logan's fast lane. Logan nailed the back of the snow plow and the front of our van was pushed right into the cab. Two of Logan's fingers were severed, his eye was nearly punctured, and he had the engine lodged between his legs. The truck was totally wrecked. Someone found his severed fingers and got him to the hospital where they grafted them back on. That was the last time we ever toured in winter.

We played Harrah's in Reno and Tahoe, the first heavy rock band to play those venues. Some nights we had a dozen people in the audience, and some of those people were so drunk they don't even know their own name. But we always gave it all we had, even if there were only a handful of people.

I had been approached by a couple from Hoodsport, Washington who offered to make some silk screened t-shirts to merchandise at our shows. This proved to be so successful that they couldn't keep up with the demand. We set up a separate company, Wolf Wares, and went full blown into merchandising, adding caps, badges, buttons, pictures. The additional income enabled us to tour in greater comfort.

A German promoter came over to see us in Minneapolis and got so excited that he offered us a German tour, handing us a check for the deposit right on the spot. We deposited the check at the Bank of Beverly Hills where we had our accounts. They declared it okay, so we accepted the offer. The tour turned into a disaster because the promoter ran out of money. One night Jutta called me in Germany to say the bank had phoned to notify her that the check it had previously approved was in fact no good. We couldn't take a financial blow like that without folding. The bank denied it had done anything wrong, but after we launched a lawsuit against them they settled out of court.

We were playing in Copenhagen and had to get to Luxembourg by nine o'clock the next morning to do two songs on Luxembourg television. We hadn't gone on stage until midnight, then we had to tear down and race across Europe in two Opel station wagons. The little four cylinder engines of those cars were screaming for mercy; four in the morning, no speed limit on the Autobahn, the pedal to the firewall, flying a hundred miles an hour, going so fast that no one could sleep. I was just happy to get there alive. We pulled into the television station parking lot and left those cars mere smoking hulks.

But there were also nights of phenomenal satisfaction, playing a town for the first or second time and selling out. In Toronto, we played the El Mocombo the first time through, next time a theater on Yonge, then two or three times at Massey Hall, finally graduating to the band shell at the CNE. Each time it was like Sally Field, "Hey, they really like us!" There was at least the feeling that it was getting better.

Ron Rainey and I bought a full page ad in *Billboard* identifying our agent, management, and a blank space for a record label saying — "Space available" — overlayed onto our touring schedule for the year. That list was phenomenal. After seeing that ad some bands phoned their agents demanding to know why they weren't playing all those venues. Throughout this time, we were writing new songs but we couldn't nail down a recording contract. I needed to get certain things out of my system as a release valve for all the frustrations, and the band needed an affirmation that we weren't just spinning our wheels. In March of 1982, Ron and I bankrolled a recording session at Ocean Way Studios in Hollywood. It had to be quick, cheap, and good. Tom Scott, another act Ron managed at the time, had just recorded a direct-to-two track album at Ocean Way, no overdubs, just played live in the studio, all instruments, vocals, background vocals mixed right on the spot. We decided to give it a try, once again with me producing and Kevin Kern engineering for Ron's and my production company, Wolf Records.

The resulting album, WOLFTRACKS, was released on the Attic label in Canada with an audiophile version for CD on Nautilus Records in the US. I was somewhat disappointed with the results. The sound overall was not as ballsy as I would have preferred and the mixes weren't quite as smooth. Though it wasn't as punchy or rock 'n' roll as I had hoped it would be, it nonetheless served the purpose of getting some new material out. It was a statement to all those who came to see us every night that, yes, we'll play the old stuff but we're also moving on with new material.

In 1984 we recorded another album, PARADOX, produced and engineered on spec by our old friends Richard Podolor and Bill Cooper. That album came out more satisfying than WOLFTRACKS and included remakes of two tracks from ALL IN GOOD TIME, *Ain't Nothing Like It Used To Be* and *Give Me Some News I Can Use*. It also featured cover photography by Randee St. Nicholas who, since divorcing Nick, had become one of the top photographers in the business. The Palmer brothers inclination towards fusion rock found a bit more space throughout the album, though the highlights for me were the softer, more personal songs that I had been writing, such as *Slender Thread Of Hope*. Again the album was released by Attic in Canada. We just couldn't scare up a decent US deal.

Steve Palmer: *Record companies didn't want to participate and even when they did, it was through another company in Canada. If we'd have had a major label behind us, the act would have been successful. With no album out in the US, there was no point in touring. With no income, we broke up the band in December of 1984.*

Throughout those grueling years, the support of the fans sustained me. For their letters and comments following the shows, I am eternally grateful. There were times when I would literally break down reading those letters.

> *Last night, got no sleep at all,*
> *Kept on thinkin' 'bout your letter, yeah, yeah.*
> *Don't you know it was so good, just to know that our song,*
> *Made you feel a little bit better, yes it did.*
> *Had you singing along,*
> *That's why this song is just for you,*
> *For all the times you stood and cheered,*
> *When we passed through.*
> *Sometimes I get down and blue.*
> *Oh, the road goes on forever, you know it does.*
> *Got me crazy again, somehow nothin's goin' right.*
> *And I wonder will it ever get any better.*
> *When I'm starting to feel as though our song was never heard,*
> *I see you there, singin' along with every word.*
> *And you're singin'*
> *Keep rockin' 'til the early morning,*
> *Keep rollin' 'til the break of day*

For the words that keep me goin'
For the time you shook my hand,
When you seemed to understand.

KEEP ROCKIN', 1989

We were somewhere in Missouri when a Vietnam War veteran approached me following our show. He came right up to me and said, "You guys saved my life." I was somewhat taken aback by this declaration. "Hey man, I don't want that kind of responsibility. What are you talking about?" He proceeded to relate his story. "We were in Vietnam in the bush and we had a little single speaker cassette player. We would get high and listen to Hendrix and Steppenwolf and so forth. One time we were ambushed by the Viet Cong while we were hunkered down and they were cutting our buddies to ribbons. We were off to the side, these two other buddies of mine and me, and we had the Steppenwolf tape. So we put it in the player, cranked it up loud and threw it as far as we could away from us. It diverted some fire and we got out of there. We're alive today because of that." Uneasily, I replied, "That's too much responsibility for me to deal with. It could have been anybody's tape, any band's music." "No, you don't understand," he insisted. "I will always know it was your music that saved my life." He then broke down crying in my arms and I could not find a single word to say.

The people who felt something in our music that helped them through some rough time in their lives, and told us so in person or through letters, were the people we kept doing it for. At a time when we had been rejected three times by the same cycle of record labels, while some of our contemporaries from the sixties and seventies were signing contracts and releasing new records, those words of encouragement kept me going.

By the mid-1980s, I felt a tremendous sense of accomplishment. Our touring situation had improved, we could hold our heads up around town, and we had managed to rebuild Steppenwolf's reputation as a solid rock band. When The Sparrow broke up in LA in 1967, record labels were signing almost anything with long hair with the idea that if nine out of ten of these acts don't pan out, the tenth would and it would pay for the other failures. The climate was far more open to taking chances. Steppenwolf came about at the right time. Timing and good fortune. But what we have managed to accomplish since since 1980 is far more rewarding to me personally because we did it by ourselves against the odds.

Trading licks with Michael Palmer at the Lyceum, London, 1980.

The John Kay & Steppenwolf band, 1980 (left to right: John Kay, Steve Palmer, Mike Palmer, Brett Tuggle, and Chad Perry.

From the video for the single Hot Nite In A Cold Town
released off the WOLFTRACKS *CD, shot near San
Bernadino, 1982, and broadcast on MTV to a new age of
Steppenwolf fans.*

From the PARADOX *album photo session, taken by our old friend Randee St. Nicholas, 1984.*

THIRTEEN

RISE AND SHINE

It used to be when things weren't right
I'd do my share and join the fight
And would surely stand and speak my mind
Then I got lost along the way
I spent my time chasing my tail
But I am here to say: I'm back to stay
For I've been searching for the man I used to be
I found him waiting alive and well
And he was screaming back at me
Rise and shine, show your color
Now's the time, raise your hand
Rise and shine, join your brother
Draw the line, take a stand

RISE AND SHINE, 1989

By the fall of 1984 we had reached the end of the dead end street known as the club circuit. Together with the lack of commercial success of the WOLFTRACKS and PARADOX albums, I felt the need to re-assess our goals. The Palmer Brothers were also frustrated and drained from the label rejections and road grind. We decided to dissolve the band. During the winter and spring of 1985, Michael Wilk and I started to hatch a new plan. We would find two new players, a drummer and guitarist, and Michael would assume the duties of bassist in addition to being the keyboard player. He had learned to play bass pedals earlier in his musical training, had a keen ear for bass patterns, and using some of the new technology of the day, he created various bass parts on a sequencer using recorded bass samples. Doing this gave us some financial breathing room, for we would now be four instead of five musicians.

With renewed energy we went in search of new Wolf members. First to join on drums was Ron Hurst from Holyoke, Massachusetts, a friend of Michael's who was raised in nearby Chickopee. Ron immediately fit in. The word was out that we were looking for a guitarist when we heard from the ubiquitous Brett Tuggle who highly praised Rocket Ritchotte. Richard Podolor was kind enough to allow us the use of his American Recording Studio to hold auditions, and a few days later we played with Rocket for the first time. Not only was he an excellent guitarist, he proved to be a very good singer with writing and recording experience. Michael and I knew we had our man.

With the new band we were ready to go back on the road, but we needed to break out of the continual club circuit grind and step up in some way. Ron Rainey had been busy trying to devise a means to achieve that next platform of success when we received an offer to tour jointly with the Guess Who, a reconstituted line-up fronted by their original bass player, to play a handful of dates in small theaters. The shows were heavily advertised on radio using snippets of both bands' hits. We found there were a lot of fans out there who were too young to have seen us in the clubs in the early 1980s but who had our records or had heard *Born To Be Wild*. They had never had the opportunity to see us play live, though. The mini-tour turned out to be a sell out at almost every stop, so both acts agreed to extend it, resulting in an eighteen month string of highly successful dates. That tour elevated our profile, got us out of the clubs, and became a major turning point in our fortunes.

During the summer of 1986 portion of this joint tour with the Guess Who, we received an invitation to perform as part of Farm Aid II on the Fourth of July in Austin, Texas. I had seen parts of Farm Aid I on television the previous year and felt it was a worthwhile cause. As the grandson of farming families on both my mother's and father's side, I had always respected that way of life. I gladly consented to participate and looked forward to seeing some of the other artists on the bill whose work I admired. Getting there was another story.

We played Mud Island in Memphis the night before. Next morning we flew to Fort Smith, Arkansas, then by ground to Dogpatch (yes there really is such a place replete with Daisy Mae and more). We played our regular show there in the afternoon, jumped into waiting vans, dashed off to a nearby airstrip, boarded two chartered planes, and flew to Dallas. We landed, pulled up next to a commercial jet, and ran up the boarding steps just in time for takeoff to Austin and made it on stage by 10:30 p.m. Our ex-bassist Gary Link was there as part of Rita Coolidge's band and agreed to play with us. A quick tune up and it was our turn. The Texas audience were into it from the first downbeat. Our fifteen minutes went by in a flash of goose bumps. It was another one of those nights that reminds you why you decided to do this in the first place.

All the feelings of frustration I had been experiencing over the six years or so that John Kay and Steppenwolf had been back on the road, along with all the support from the fans, laid the ground work for the writing on the ROCK & ROLL REBELS album. The record was about persevering and surviving, not letting the bastards get you down. Throughout much of that period I often felt at my lowest ebb. As a result, my writing took on a far more human touch than the pontificating that I was sometimes prone to in earlier years. On the two previous albums, WOLFTRACKS and PARADOX, I had avoided dealing squarely with those feelings during the years of slogging it out. But by 1987, with the new band kicking things into a higher gear, I was ready to exorcise those demons once and for all. The ROCK & ROLL REBELS album became my outlet to say, "Hell no, we're not gonna give in. We're gonna make it!" Songs like *Hold On (Never Give Up, Never Give In), Man On A Mission, Rock Steady,* and

Rage represented an affirmation, an anthem, a rallying cry to anyone who had ever felt kicked in the teeth and counted out.

> *So he picks up the gang at the usual places,*
> *To hear the soundtrack of their lives.*
> *Yeah they're rollin' downtown,*
> *To hear that rock 'n' roll music.*
> *Well it may not save the world,*
> *But it helps them survive.*
> *And the rock and' roll rebels are riding tonight,*
> *Cruisin' 'til daylight again.*
> *Yes, they're rockin' this town,*
> *For the time of their lives,*
> *Wishin' this night'd never end.*

ROCK & ROLL REBELS, 1987

We recorded the album at my Nichols Canyon studio which the
guys dubbed Phantom Sound. Michael Wilk is incredibly creative
when it comes to writing. He can go all day long coming up with
new riffs and ideas. Rocket's really good at finding his own part
that nails the song down just right. The three of us wrote most of
the ROCK & ROLL REBELS album. Once we had a satisfactory tape,
Ron Rainey began pitching it to the labels.

Ron Rainey: *I had been trying to sell MCA on the band because that
was where their back catalog was. Steppenwolf's catalog sales were
staggering in the Eighties. Most of the albums had been off the
market for a number of years but when they started putting them out
on CD, people were buying them all like hotcakes, in the hundreds of
thousands each year. But I couldn't get an answer out of them. Two
weeks after we signed a K-Tel deal for their independent Qwil label, a
former MCA Records A and R man now with Capitol Records made
an offer for the band. He had recognized the potential of the band
and liked the new stuff but couldn't convince MCA. When he moved
over to Capitol, his first priority was to get John Kay And
Steppenwolf. I nearly fell through the floor but I couldn't get them out
of the K-Tel deal. It was totally frustrating.*

In order to push the album we had to hire five or six independent promotion people as well as a public relations firm. The album became the number one most added rock and roll record for two weeks running in *R 'n' R* magazine, which was impressive enough to warrant interest from Atlantic Records who offered to buy up our contract with K-Tel. But they weren't biting. Unfortunately K-Tel's Qwil label was too small to break the record nationally, nor was the label willing to come up with a promotional budget necessary to compete with the major labels. It was disappointing because we had so much of ourselves in that record.

That notwithstanding, 1987 did have its high points. With our own publicist working for us for the first time in many years, our media exposure increased considerably. It was gratifying to see us on national television once again, performing new material as well as the familiar hits, stating our case in interviews on *Entertainment Tonight*, *CNN Nightly News*, *MTV,* and so on. The good people at Farm Aid also called again. This time we found ourselves in Lincoln, Nebraska before over 80,000 at Farm Aid III performing during daylight hours so we had the pleasure of watching the crowd enjoy it. By the time we launched into *Born To Be Wild* the audience was total bedlam. Another perfect moment.

Next day it was back on the road — theaters, county fairs, festivals. We went out with Alvin Lee (of Ten Years After) as special guest artist and The Byrds' Roger McGuinn on solo acoustic twelve string guitar as opening act. With a trimmed down unit traveling was a bit easier. We eventually acquired our own bus and started traveling in comfort. We were still logging an amazing number of miles each year across North America, Europe, and for the first time in Japan. We've evolved into a tight, efficient unit that gives maximum bang for the buck. Our crew knows exactly what needs to be done and generally see to it that when we walk on stage, things are what they should be. Because of them we're able to give the audience a top notch show. To accomplish this requires hard, demanding work, often coupled with physical discomfort and sleep deprivation. We are fortunate to have a dedicated group that takes pride in what it does. Chris Bray, our production manager, has been with the crew the longest, followed by Doug Adams our sound engineer. Jerry Sumner and Tyler Lockett alternated as stage managers these past few years, with Steve Heinz as our lighting director and transportation coordinator completing the team.

Considering our longevity, we should not be as successful as we are, particularly with the bogus band that got in the way. But it's due to the fact that we're professional entertainers who want to give a good show that starts on time with good lights and sound.

I get a certain satisfaction from the fact that our little organization, with smoke and mirrors and a handful of people, manages to do what other acts do less effectively with much more money and many more people. That's why it's still fun, successful, and lucrative. Much of this attitude developed during the bogus band fiasco when I learned to focus on what was really important and how I was going to accomplish it.

You can see a variety of acts of our vintage who are a mere hulk of their former selves. I've tried to see to it that we can be thought of or mentioned in the same breath as someone with an album on the charts. I don't have any patience with anything other than the way we do it at this stage of my career. I've done enough sound checks in my life where I don't need them to be any longer than absolutely necessary. When it's show time, the tape starts and 'boom boom boom' everybody knows there assigned places and we're on stage. I like that sort of 'mission control, launch count-down' approach. Everybody is keenly aware of what they are doing and it's like a well-oiled machine most of the time. I minimize the things that have absolutely nothing to do with what happens from the moment the first note is struck on stage until the last one is played. I want to show up twenty minutes before the show and be rolling out ten minutes after the last encore. That means I maximize that amount of time on the road that is my private time.

The other guys have their way of coping with the road. They're younger so they prefer to hang around afterward and soak in the adulation and the spoils. I know the high you experience — it's going well, the crowd's response was great, so afterward it's the pickin's. For me, the drawbacks of this side of the rock 'n' roll lifestyle far outweigh the amount of fun that I could have. I'm allergic to smoke so for me to hang out in a bar, suck in a lot of smoke and drink alcohol (which I know will be rough on my pipes for the next show), is out of the question. I'd rather go back to the hotel and wind down reading a little bit or watching something on the news and wait for my metabolism to slow down. I can be asleep within ninety minutes of a performance. I can cut that feeling off and let it subside without getting me into trouble. Because I get up early in the morning, come midnight I quite naturally start to slow down and I'm ready to sleep. I adhere to that as religiously as I can because I like to be up all day to do work on the bus. I'd rather be in good physical and mental shape and I get more satisfaction out of making sure that everything is running right.

I like the appreciation of the music, but I don't need the adulation and the ego stroking afterwards. I've grown out of that. As long as they're friendly and mean well, I don't mind taking time to sign autographs or chat with fans. I feel I owe them a lot. However I don't consider that as an obligation on my part. My obligation is to write songs that mean something to me and hopefully to them, then to give the best performance I can manage hoping they will go home saying, "I paid good money, I got a good show. I like these guys and their music." After that, my life reverts to being my life.

My contemporaries from the earlier years often ask me why I keep touring several months each year. I get antsy being in the same place after awhile. I miss performing if I'm in the studio recording or writing for too long. In a way, the process of all this keeps me younger than I would otherwise feel, I'm convinced of that. There's an energizing experience that takes place when I'm out there and focused on the performance. When I'm on stage for that seventy-five or ninety minutes, that period is going to either make or break that day, particularly when we have some new tunes to do. Then it's as good as it's ever been.

The road gives me a view of the world from the ground level. It's my picture window on daily life in many ways, on the bus, in the hotel, meeting people. I need it as a stimulus for my writing to observe and experience other things. The road has a routine to it and a certain predictability, but it is also a surprise package. After 26 years, not a year goes by that we don't play places we've never been before. It also makes me very appreciative of what I have at home when I return.

Quite frankly, I don't give a rat's ass if we ever get another hit. What I do care about is that we can put out good albums that are successful enough for the guys in the band to make a comfortable living and get the recognition they deserve. Having a hit is really a double-edged sword. People who tend to buy hits are fickle. They come and go. Generally speaking, the people who supported us in the early years bought every album and knew what Steppenwolf was about. They were not the ones who bought *Born To Be Wild* as a single and expected everything we did to be the same. I don't really have to prove anything to anybody at this point. I would be quite content to continue being comfortably successful on my own terms rather than jump on that treadmill again. All that would result in is a demand on my time and an invasion of my privacy, which has become increasingly important to me. I don't need it ego-wise and I don't need it financially. But it is absolutely imperative that we continue to have new material. And it's rather pointless to have new material unless you are also able to get it out for sale, whether it sells a half million or not.

Ron Rainey: *John Kay is one of those people who is a star. He has this star quality. He's in tremendous shape and he's as good a front man as it gets. He's now taken on an elder statesman sort of role. He's a rarity, an honest man in a business that isn't always honest. He's a man of his word and if he makes a commitment, he lives up to it. John's a very dedicated guy, extremely professional. This is not a very forgiving business and he's had to claw his way into any respect he has today.*

Unfortunately, in this business, the public is also not very forgiving and it's rare that they allow an artist to re-invent himself. There was a particular sound they expected. As he matured, John thought his audience would mature with him but they didn't. They still come out because they want to hear those songs, the ones they remember and identify with.

Bill Cooper: *John Kay is legitimately the only guy that can do Born To Be Wild. He is the voice. Without the lead singer, you can't pull it off. So many people saw him do it, the image, the sunglasses. In the eyes of the public, he is Steppenwolf.*

Shawn Kay: *I remember when I was still a little kid going to his shows*

*and being proud of my father but intimidated by the audience. I
was very close to the Beach Boys through my friend Carney Wilson
and they were so clean cut while here was my Dad in black leather,
microphone stand held high in the air doing Born To Be Wild. But
what really got me was looking around at the crowd. There were
always a lot of bikers in the audience. These weren't the kind of
people I associated with my father. He never lived the biker lifestyle.
A friend of mine came down to my parents' place and saw my Dad
driving a tractor around spreading gravel on the driveway. He
seemed surprised at that. "Born To Be Wild and your Dad's
driving a tractor?" People think he drives around the yard in a
Harley. It bothers me that the only image people have of my father
is* Born To Be Wild *and* Easy Rider. *I would like him to be
recognized for his other songs as well.*

I've sung *Born To Be Wild* and *The Pusher* enough times to last a
lifetime, but as long as people get off on them and we get back that
energy from the audience, I still get excited about singing them.
But I don't want those songs to blind people to the fact that we
have others which are equally good. I wouldn't be where I am
today if songs like *Born To Be Wild* or *Magic Carpet Ride* didn't have
a constant rebirth in movies, television shows, commercials and
compilations exposing them to a second and third generation of
rock 'n' rollers. The fact is that those songs are often the spark of
ignition in an audience. To come out as a retro-act and get the
audience digging your newer material along with the old is going
against the odds. But we've managed it. We felt that our newer
material was strong and the feedback we receive from our fans
confirms that. Some of the most rewarding experiences of the past
few years were when people came up after the show or wrote us
letters wanting to know where they can buy *Rocket Ship* or *Make
The Best Of What You've Got* which aren't even released yet. What
is also very gratifying is to see the reaction to *Rock 'n' Roll War*
from a recent album, people singing along, crying, hugging.

By the late 1980s, Jutta and I had tired of life in Los Angeles and
were ready for a change. We decided to look around in the Nashville, Tennessee area. I had traveled through there many times over
the years and had pleasant recollections of the countryside and its

people. To some extent I was attracted by the region's musical history. Shawn was grown up now, living on her own and working in the management end of the music business. Jutta and I contacted a friend, Kevin Lamb, in Nashville whom I had befriended during my Muscle Shoals recordings in 1978 and flew to Tennessee to view some properties. After a couple of visits we found what we were looking for, a secluded property with acres of wooded rolling hills on a private lake. In October of 1989, after having sold our Nichols Canyon home the previous May for more than ten times what we had paid for it originally, we moved out to Franklin, Tennessee, a few short miles south of Nashville. Soon after moving in I had a recording studio constructed by the lake a short stroll from the house. The tranquility of the setting, nestled amid the trees and hills, brought with it an inner peace for me. This was truly my retreat from the road, my sanctuary, my own little world where there are no semi-trailers in the parking lot waking me up at five-thirty in the morning. It was one of the best decisions we ever made.

Jutta Maue-Kay: *John likes to be more at home now. He still enjoys going out on the road but on a more comfortable pace and not such long intervals. He's learned to relax. He's been in this business long enough to see that it all comes around. You're up and you're down. As long as he still enjoys it and can make a decent living at it and tuck some money away for the future, no more is needed. He's very content with who he is and where he is.*

He's started going to guitar circles with musician friends in the neighborhood. He needed those times because he was so focused on the business end of it that it took the fun out of it. Since we've moved out here friends like Radney Foster and John Hiatt along with others get together and play their songs for one another. John really enjoys those times. He gets out his National steel guitar and plays the blues and songs which have not been recorded. These people appreciate him as a songwriter and performer.

Shawn Kay: *My father has changed a lot since moving to Tennessee. He's much more cheerful and relaxed. Now he comes home when he has breaks in the tour, whereas he didn't do that before. He really seems to enjoy being home. He's also more involved in our*

family as a whole. I really feel closer to him than I ever have before.
When I was in my teens we didn't communicate very well. Mom
was always the mediator between us. She and I are extremely close.
Now Dad and I talk more comfortably. I'm very lucky to have
parents who have been married more than twenty-five years and
still love each other, perhaps more now than ever. It's very rare,
especially in the music industry.

I know my father is happier in Tennessee than he was in Los
Angeles. Besides the slower pace and friendlier people, there also
seems to be a stronger appreciation for musicians and songwriters
here. He enjoys meeting and playing with other artists whom he
respects.

My parents have a beautiful home in the country. It's my
father's sanctuary. After twenty-five years of working so hard I
think it's wonderful that he can relax and enjoy it, at least until he
goes back on the road.

Hand in hand with the move to Tennessee came the RISE AND SHINE
album. Whereas ROCK & ROLL REBELS was about surviving, overcom-
ing adversity, RISE AND SHINE concerned itself with going past that to
the next level, turning our energy and attention to the world. That
album was a call to arms to end the greed, overcome the cynicism,
and start making positive contributions where they were needed.
Much of the music was written on the bus throughout 1989. I wrote
the lyrics in my living room in Tennessee while the studio was being
finished. The backdrop for much of that writing came from the
nightly television news. That November I watched the Berlin Wall
come down and I was completely shattered. I followed the events as
they unfolded daily: the demonstrations in Dresden and Leipzig, the
refusal of the army and the police chief to bring out the troops,
Gorbachev coming for the celebration of the East German regime
but failing to give Honneker the go ahead to stop the demonstrations. It was, for me, a personal catharsis. Jutta and I stood together
in our living room weeping, watching in disbelief.

Think of the shattered lives, think of the broken hearts,
Think of the battered dreams of families still torn apart.
Wall of bitter tears, Wall of crying pain,

Wall of chilling fear, you will never keep me here.
For I shall crawl right down through that Wall.
Then came the day when I had my chance to pay,
My respects to the names on that Wall.
I saw the wooden crosses, saw the bloody stains,
Saw the gruesome pictures of all the ones that died in vain.
Wall of countless victims, Wall of endless shame,
Had just one thing gone wrong I might have joined that list of names.
And I cried for all who died there at the Wall.
Oh, I recall weeping at the Wall.

Turned on the news in November '89.
I could not move, I could not speak.
Something was burning up in my eyes,
Something wet ran down my cheek.
All those laughing faces, all those tears of joy,
All those warm embraces of men and women,
Girls and boys.
Sisters and brothers dancing,
All singing freedom's song.
God, if only I could be there,
To shake your hands and sing along.
Oh I, I would climb right up on that Wall,
And join you all dancing on the Wall.
Tear it down, right down to the ground.

THE WALL, 1991

I had been to Germany several times on tours with Steppenwolf but I had never gone to the Berlin Wall. When I finally visited the Wall in 1991, I was moved far more than I had anticipated. I went to Checkpoint Charlie and through the museum where photographs were displayed showing various escape methods people had devised to get to freedom. A lot of 'what if's' crowded my mind. What if my father had not died during the war, would we have stayed in East Germany? What if my mother had not taken me as a baby from East Prussia as the Russians moved in? What if my eyesight hadn't been bad and I hadn't required the kind of medical care only available in the West? What if my mother had not snuck me across the border when she did? What if she had waited a few months, or even a year? Would we have been able to escape then? If I had stayed in the Eastern side of the Wall, would I have become one of those names scrawled on the Wall?

Watching the events in Berlin unfold in front of me, I longed to be there, to join the thousands who were celebrating the end of that symbol of oppression that haunted my childhood. That experience infused me with a tremendous elation, a reaffirmation that the world was not just going to go down in a Cold War deadlock. There was hope and belief in changing the world for the better. The following year I had my chance to carve out my own piece of the Wall while once again touring Germany. We played near what was left of the Wall and it was a moving experience.

Jutta Maue-Kay: *The collapse of the Berlin Wall affected John more than me. He was crying as he watched. He was in the middle of writing the song* The Wall *when it happened. It was very moving for him. I was born in West Germany, so I accepted the two Germanies as the way it was because of the war. But it's different for those from East Germany like John. When he visited the museum at Checkpoint Charlie and saw the ways people tried to get out and the names, it tore him up. Like he says in the song, "If just one thing had gone wrong. . . ." That song made me cry the first time I heard it.*

When we went to Berlin after the Wall was down, John was out there buying all these souvenirs from East German police, articles from Russian uniforms and little pieces of the Wall.

Michael Wilk: *We played John's song* The Wall *in Germany. I hit the low note and let it hang there in the air to create the ambience. Then John broke into German to explain that he had been born in East Prussia during the war and had lived in East Germany. He told his whole story and the audience just sat there hushed. Then we played the song. When the Kennedy speech came on in the middle, it just blew everybody away. The whole effect was absolutely killer. That song is not just some bullshit song, it's real, it's a piece of art.*

The RISE AND SHINE album was written from this positive point of view: 'life is worth living and fighting for.' The album is dedicated to those people who, during the darkest times of the 1980s, were my inspiration and is intended as a word of encouragement to them.

We recorded RISE AND SHINE at my studio in Franklin, Phantom Sound South, and released it on the IRS label. Besides *The Wall*, another centerpiece of the album was *Rock 'n' Roll War* about the Vietnam War and one soldier's attempt to come to terms with it years later. In concert, the song never fails to elicit an emotional response, especially from the veterans who often attend our shows. It's also been used at Vietnam War Veterans support group meetings.

Although sales figures for RISE AND SHINE weren't earth shattering, it has become my third favorite album, ranking right up there behind the first and SEVEN albums. With the exception of some of my solo projects, it is also the first album in many years where I felt that every song, having written the words and melodies myself, was genuine, heartfelt. RISE AND SHINE is something I can point to and say, "This is a quality piece of work.".

The issues I addressed in some of the songs on RISE AND SHINE recall the spirit of the Sixties. As a spokesman for those ideals, I'm sometimes asked what am I doing to advance the cause now that I've achieved a degree of comfort, success, and financial stability. Like most of us, I'm affected by the rather common affliction of being busy running my own life, but Jutta and I do make financial contributions to the organizations we believe in and whose agendas we want to advance, whether it's Amnesty International, the ACLU, Greenpeace, People for the American Way, or Zero Population Growth. These organizations are run by people who are willing to give of themselves over to something they believe in. The least we can do is give them the means with which to buy the suit of armor and weapons required to continue the fight. I try to participate in the local grass roots issues that concern the environment. As a human being on this planet I have a responsibility to become part of the solution rather than the problem. And as a writer, I continue to speak my mind on issues that I feel are important.

When I'm prompted by such questions to look back at my life and career, I recognize that I'm, still striving to strike a balance between my family life and my creative self, between my obligations to Jutta, Shawn, and my mother and my ties to my band mates, past and present.

Jutta and I have lived through the ups and downs of my profession and have become closer because of the experiences we endured together. My love for her grew from the initial physical attraction into a far more encompassing love that is not only romantic or sexual but also complementary. She is my best friend, my other self, the missing gap in my own personality. She is a soul mate.

Jutta Maue-Kay: *We had a lot in common in the first place when we met but we have really become best friends. We talk a lot and that is one of the most important things in a relationship. Maybe because he was raised by his mother he always understood me as a woman and tried to understand what I felt and help out. We just had something that both of us were well aware does not come along every day. We give each other room to be ourselves. But no matter where he is on tour, John calls me every night.*

My mother moved back to Germany in 1976 because she had family over there. She still missed my father and probably always will. When she retired from her job, she knew she wouldn't often be seeing her friends from work and reverted back to the old country in her mind. Her health was adversely affected by living in LA. She contracted a mild form of emphysema from the smog and suffered from bronchitis frequently. She suffered a mild stroke a few years ago but is still a strong woman. We talk on the phone and I visit every time I'm touring Germany. Shawn worked in Ron Stone's office and for Van Halen's management in LA before moving out to Nashville where she now lives on her own, and works for a record company owned by one of the nicer guys in this business.

During the early 1990s Ron Hurst, Chris Bray, and Michael Wilk all made the move to Nashville as well, along with our tour manager Charlie Wolf. Larry Byrom is based in Nashville and has established a flourishing career as a studio musician working with artists like Travis Tritt, Kenny Rogers, and Clint Black. Nick St. Nicholas runs Rose Artists Management out of Oxnard, California, and as a born-again Christian, performs Christian rock. Goldy McJohn currently plays in a club band in Seattle. After leaving

Steppenwolf, Michael Monarch formed Detective, releasing a couple of albums on Led Zeppelin's Swan Song label. He's still living in Hollywood, pursuing a country music songwriting career in the duo, Stevens and Monarch. Rushton Moreve was killed in a car accident in the late 1970s. I had not seen him for several years after he was dismissed from the band until I ran into him at a gig in LA. He seemed more mature by then and perhaps regretful for his ill-conceived actions that resulted in his firing. Eighteen months later he was dead.

Bill Cooper: *I ran into Rushton a year or more after he was out of the band. I was leaving the studio to go next door where we stored guitars and I found Rushton walking past the bus stop just outside the door. I recognized him and asked how he was doing. We had been holding onto his gold record for the* STEPPENWOLF THE SECOND *album because no one knew how to get hold of him, so I gave it to him, he said thanks, and headed off down the street with it. It was strange.*

Gabriel Mekler was killed in a motorcycle accident around the same time. He was a very special person in the Wolf story and a dear friend in those early days. I only wish we had stayed closer in the latter years. Jay Lasker also passed away some years later. Mars Bonfire (Dennis Edmonton) continues to live out near the desert in California, still writing songs and traveling. *Born To Be Wild* remains the most in-demand song in the entire MCA publishing catalog, so Mars' income seems pretty secure.

Ron Rainey and I parted company amicably in the early 1990s when I decided to take the management reins into my own hands, assisted by the very capable Charlie Wolf. Ron continues to work in artist management. In those rough rebuilding years, Ron was one of the few people who saw any potential in what I was attempting to do, and for his belief in me, I shall always remain grateful. Richard Podolor and Bill Cooper still operate American Recording Company at a new location in Woodland Hills with a state-of-the-art, forty-eight track facility. Morgan Cavett came to work for legendary songwriter Johnny Mercer in the 1970s and managed Mercer's substantial publishing holdings as well as producing at various studios. We still see each other whenever I'm in LA. Steve Palmer is currently involved in video production in LA, and his brother Michael still plays, as does Bobby Cochran. Jerry Sloan also lives in Southern California and offers personal management services. After almost nine years on the road with us, Rocket Ritchotte left John Kay And Steppenwolf at the end of 1993, his place admirably taken by Steve Fister of Nashville.

Solveigh Schattmann now resides in south Florida where she organizes holiday junkets for German tourists. My old motorcycle-riding sight saving class buddy Stan King is still in Toronto working for a piano company. Whenever I'm through that area we talk on the phone and catch up with each other's lives. Penti Glan, from the first John Kay Band, keeps busy as a studio drummer in Toronto and New York. Hugh O'Sullivan never managed to shake loose his personal demons and took his own life in the 1980s. Keyboard player Andy Chapin, who replaced Goldy on the HOUR OF THE WOLF album, always hated touring. Unfortunately, it was a touring accident that took his life. He was in Rick Nelson's band when their plane crashed in 1981. Lisa, Andy's widow, eventually married Jerry Edmonton and the two settled down in the Santa Ynez Valley to operate a photo studio and raise horses. Jerry and I remained business partners in Steppenwolf Productions Inc. and, although retired from active playing, he continued to share in the profits of our early successes and my work on the road.

In late November 1993, on a stretch of highway just west of Santa Ynez, Jerry was killed in a car accident after he missed a turn and spun off onto the shoulder. The news was simply devastating for me and I was deeply saddened by it. He had been my partner in many ways and I had often gone to him for his valuable opinions and advise. During the bogus Wolf period he and I leaned on each other for moral support and became closer friends. He was a talented and special human being without whom Steppenwolf would not have been what it was. I'll miss him. May he find peace on the other side.

The last time Jerry and I talked, he was considering attending Wolf Fest. As editor of *The Howl*, our Wolfpack fan club newsletter and a long time Steppenwolf fan, Charlie Wolf decided to organize a fanfare style event that would allow Wolfpackers from across North America and as far away as Germany and Holland to get together and share their affection for The Wolf. In March 1994, many of our most faithful supporters and friends congregated in Nashville for a weekend event. They brought their Steppenwolf memorabilia, their families, video cameras, and tape recorders. In addition the band and crew, Larry Byrom and Bobby Cochran were also on hand and joined me for a "John Kay Unplugged" session. The event gave me the opportunity to spend some time with these fans and let them know how much they were appreciated. It was a family-like atmosphere and I hope it becomes an annual event.

Despite turning fifty in 1994, I've never considered retirement. I think I'll always have my hand in music in some way. Going out with Steppenwolf depends on how long the fun or the demand lasts. In this business you never know when it'll stop. I would like to diversify and possibly due a solo blues album or solo acoustic album of songs that are too personal to put under the Steppenwolf umbrella. I may even want to do a little lecture tour work. I know enough about this business that a lot of younger people just learning the ropes may be able to benefit from my experiences. I wouldn't mind doing some acoustic performances now and then with perhaps another guitar player just as a way of keeping another side of what I do active. But that's more in addition to rather in place of. I figure I'll do at least another five years on the road. Besides, we have too many new projects in the works to quit now. We recorded numerous performances during our twenty-fifth anniversary tour in 1992 which will be released as a double "LIVE AT TWENTY-FIVE" CD. A video anthology and song book featuring transcriptions of twenty Steppenwolf songs are also in the works.

Early in June 1994 I returned to my old home town of Arnstadt, Germany to perform a benefit concert. Nothing could have prepared me for what took place that day. The concert was arranged by a local promoter as a kind of celebration of "The Little Boy from Arnstadt Who Had Made It Big in America" with proceeds going to a local home for the handicapped. What it became for me was a rollercoaster ride of emotions. Arriving in Arnstadt, I was brought to the town square where, to my surprise, several faces from my past awaited. A month earlier, the local newspaper ran a story requesting anyone who remembered Joachim Fritz Krauledat as a young boy almost fifty years earlier to come forward. Two elderly women responded, both relatives of the Kranz family who had given shelter to my mother and me at the tannery on Obere Weisse. There in the town square these two women greeted me warmly and presented me with photographs of the tannery and of Else Kranz. Along with them was a man named Gerd Tappert who had been my childhood friend when we played together in the streets near the tannery. His grandfather owned a clock making shop, and Gerd produced a tattered photograph of the two of us on his grandfather's step, me in little britches and my round, tinted glasses. But the most startling revelation was yet to come. My host, the local promoter, next introduced me to an elderly gentleman standing amid the old friends and reporters, my Uncle Franz Krauledat. Now 74 years old and living nearby, he had been the second youngest of the seven brothers in my father's family, five of whom, my father included, died during World War II. Apparently I had seen him once when I was three but had no recollection of him. Meeting Uncle Franz along with his daughter (and my cousin) Ursula brought a flood of emotions and I found myself fighting back the tears. Here I was in the town where I first learned of my father's death and in front of me was someone who was the closest blood relative to my father still alive on this earth. Ursula told me that both her children, now grown up, were born with the same sight affliction as me. All my life I had believed, as had my mother, that my eye deficiency was a birth defect but it occurred to me for the first time that perhaps my eye problem was hereditary.

Our host later took us on a guided tour of the town, showing us where the tannery had stood and recent renovations since reunification. Arnstadt is about to celebrate its 1000th anniversary, the oldest town in Thuringen, and has preserved much of its historical character right down to its cobblestone streets. When we stopped in a market square, I was informed that in this very spot the first silent candle-light vigil against Honneker's East German communist regime had taken place. News of the event spread to neighboring town and cities, including Dresden and Leipzig, where international attention was soon gained and the tide of change could not be halted.

At sunset we played the best concert of our German tour before 3,500 people. I addressed the crowd in German, telling them the story of my childhood life in Arnstadt. Throughout the performance I was bombarded with recollections. Lying in bed later that night, I found myself trying to come to terms with everything that had happened that day. How strange the course of my life had been to bring me back 45 years later to this little town to find a branch of my family tree. The circle now seemed complete.

Once when I was interviewed during the early Steppenwolf days, I was asked to state my goal in life." To achieve prolonged periods of contentment," I replied. Sometimes I wake up in the morning, take a look around and cackle at my good fortune in life. I'm one of the luckiest people I know. Sometimes Jutta and I sit outside in the evening and look out at the sunset over the lake. After awhile I start to grin and say to her, "Not too shabby, eh?"

Dues are non-deductible, you got to pay,
But dreams are indestructible and won't fade away.
So make your move, make your mark, don't wait your turn.
Get a life, then give a little back to the world.
Ain't no use in sighin', make the best of what you got.
Don't be silent, agitate, make the best of what you got.

MAKE THE BEST OF WHAT YOU GOT, 1992

When I look over my shoulder at the past, I see a lot of 'what if's' and many incredible moments I've enjoyed along the way. My life reads like a Hollywood script. A kid born in Germany during the war who can't see worth a damn standing in front of his mother's tailoring mirror with a cardboard guitar dreaming of being the next Little Richard. What are the odds of having that dream come true?

A couple of years back, Jutta and I were at the Hyatt House on Sunset Boulevard in LA. We were on our way down in the elevator when we stopped at a lower floor, the door opened and in walked Little Richard himself with two of his attendants dressed to the nines. He had the makeup, the hair, the silk suit, looking every inch a star. Here was my first rock 'n' roll idol. As we all stepped out of the elevator, Little Richard turned to me and said, "Aren't you John Kay?" I answered, "Yes," thrilled that the one and only Little Richard had recognized me. "I don't care what anyone says, you've got one of the best voices in rock 'n' roll. Bruce Springsteen ain't got nothing on you!" Little Richard and his entourage then stepped into a stretch limousine and off they went. Coming from the man who inspired me to pursue a rock 'n' roll fantasy that became a life-long magic carpet ride, Little Richard's praise left me beaming.

Striking an "up yours" pose (left to right: Rocket Ritchotte, Michael Wilk, John Kay, and Ron Hurst), 1985.

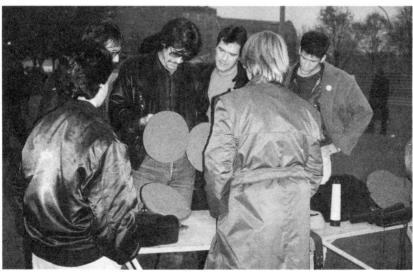

Haggling over the price of East German army uniform hats at the site of the fallen Berlin Wall during our RISE & SHINE *tour, 1990.*

Greeting my Uncle Franz (my father's brother) for the first time since I was four years old during our June 1994 tour of Germany, where we played to an enthusiastic crowd in my old home town of Arnstadt.

Jutta, Shawn, and John shortly before we moved from LA to the hills of Tennessee, where (as a friend of ours put it) you only hear the occasional nut fall from a tree — or two oars breaking the surface of the lake.

361

*Readers are invited to contact
John Kay & Steppenwolf
for tour schedules,
Wolfpack fan club membership,
and any other information:*

John Kay & Steppenwolf
*P.O. Box 1435
Franklin, Tennessee
37064 U.S.A.*

CREDITS

PHOTOGRAPHS

Unless otherwise credited here, all photographs, clippings, memorabilia, and album jackets reproduced in this book are from the collection of John Kay. We are pleased to acknowledge the following artists, individuals, and agencies for their cooperation in supplying photographs:

Ed Careff:	262
Morgan Cavett:	119, 149 (top)
Henry Diltz:	207, 230 (bottom), 231, 260
David Warner Ellis:	334 (top)
Amy Etra:	361 (top)
John Exley:	back cover, 13 (top)
Tom Gundelfinger:	6, 208, 232, 278, 279, 301 (top)
Uwe Jens Igel:	360
Kathy McCarthy:	12
McCarthy & Teal:	230
Gerry Miskolczi:	149 (bottom)
Jutta Maue-Kay:	182, 359 (bottom), 361 (bottom)
Nathan Pyle:	302 (top)
Randee St. Nicholas:	336
Sony Music:	179 (top)
Lorrie Sullivan:	302 (bottom)
Herbie Wothington:	334 (bottom)
Neil Zlozower:	front cover, 358 (bottom)

DISCOGRAPHY

THE SPARROW

Singles:

Tomorrow's Ship / Isn't It Strange
(Columbia 43755) 1966

Green Bottle Lover /
Down Goes Your Love Life
(Columbia 4396) 1966

Square Headed People / Twisted
(Columbia 44769) 1969

Albums:

John Kay And The Sparrow
(Columbia 9758) 1969

Twisted
Baby Please Don't Go
Bright Lights, Big City
Good Morning Little School Girl
Square Headed People
Green Bottle Lover

Goin' To California
Down Goes Your Love Life
Can't Make Love By Yourself
King Pin
Chasin' Shadows
Isn't It Strange

The Best of John Kay & Sparrow*
(Columbia CK 53044) 1993

Twisted
Square Headed People
Bright Lights, Big City
The Pusher
Goin' Upstairs
Tomorrow's Ship
Goin' To California
Green Bottle Lover
Too Late

Goin' To California
Good Morning Little School Girl
Hootchie Kootchie Man
King Pin
Baby Please Don't Go
Isn't It Strange
Twisted
Tighten Up Your Wig
Can't Make Love By Yourself

STEPPENWOLF

Singles

A Girl I Knew / The Ostrich
(ABC-Dunhill 4109) 1967

Sookie Sookie / Take What You Need
(ABC-Dunhill 4123) 1968

Born To Be Wild / Everybody's Next One
(ABC-Dunhill 4138) 1968

Magic Carpet Ride / Sookie Sookie
(ABC-Dunhill 4161) 1968

Rock Me / Jupiter Child
(ABC-Dunhill 4182) 1969

It's Never Too Late / Happy Birthday
(ABC-Dunhill 4192) 1969

Move Over / Power Play
(ABC-Dunhill 4205) 1969

Monster / Berry Rides Again
(ABC-Dunhill 4221) 1970

Hey Lawdy Mama / Twisted
(ABC-Dunhill 4234) 1970

Screaming Night Hog / Spiritual Fantasy
(ABC-Dunhill 4248) 1970

Who Needs Ya' /
Earschplittenloudenboomer
(ABC-Dunhill 4261) 1970

Snow Blind Friend / Hippo Stomp
(ABC-Dunhill 4269) 1971

Ride With Me / For Madmen Only
(ABC-Dunhill 4283) 1971

For Ladies Only / Sparkle Eyes
(ABC-Dunhill 4292 1971

Born To Be Wild / Magic Carpet Ride
(ABC-Dunhill 1433) 1970

Born To Be Wild / The Pusher
(ABC-Dunhill 1436) 1970

Monster / Rock Me
(ABC-Dunhill 1444) 1970

Straight Shootin' Woman /
Justice Don't Be Slow
(MUMS ZS8 6031) 1974

Get Into The Wind / Morning Blue
(MUMS ZS8 6034) 1974

Smokey Factory Blues / A Fool's Fantasy
(MUMS ZS8 6036) 1974

Caroline / Angeldrawers
(MUMS ZS8 6040) 1974

Albums

Steppenwolf*
(ABC-Dunhill 50029) 1968

Sookie Sookie
Berry Rides Again
Born To Be Wild
Desperation
A Girl I Knew
The Ostrich

Everybody's Next One
Hootchie Kootchie Man
Your Wall's Too High
The Pusher
Take What You Need

Steppenwolf The Second**
(ABC-Dunhill 50037) 1968

Faster Than The Speed Of Life
None Of Your Doing
Don't Step On The Grass, Sam
Magic Carpet Ride

Tighten Up Your Wig
Spiritual Fantasy
28
Disappointment Number (Unknown)

Lost And Found By Trial And Error
Resurrection

Hodge Podge Strained Through A Leslie
Reflections

Steppenwolf At Your Birthday Party**
(ABC-Dunhill 50053) 1969

Don't Cry
Chicken Wolf
Round And Down
Sleeping Dreaming
She'll Be Better
Cat Killer
God Fearing Man

Happy Birthday
Lovely Meter
It's Never Too Late
Jupiter Child
Rock Me
Mango Juice

Early Steppenwolf**
(ABC-Dunhill 50060) 1969

Power Play
Goin' Upstairs
Tighten Up Your Wig

Howlin' For My Baby
Corina Corina
The Pusher

Monster**
(ABC-Dunhill 50066) 1969

Monster (Suicide, America)
Power Play
Fag
From Here To There Eventually

Draft Resister
Move Over
What Would You Do

Steppenwolf Live**
(ABC-Dunhill 50075) 1970

Sookie Sookie
Tighten Up Your Wig
Draft Resister
Corina Corina
From Here To There Eventually
Magic Carpet Ride
Born To Be Wild

Don't Step On The Grass, Sam
Monster
Power Play
Twisted
Hey Lawdy Mama
The Pusher

Steppenwolf Seven**
(ABC-Dunhill 50090) 1970

Ball Crusher
Fat Jack
Foggy Mental Breakdown
Snow Blind Friend
Earschplittenloudenboomer

Forty Days And Forty Nights
Renegade
Who Needs Ya
Hippo Stomp

Steppenwolf Gold
(ABC-Dunhill 50099) 1971

Born To Be Wild	Rock Me
Hey Lawdy Mama	Magic Carpet Ride
It's Never Too Late	Who Needs Ya
Sookie Sookie	The Pusher
Jupiter's Child	Screaming Night Hog
Monster	Move Over

For Ladies Only**
(ABC-Dunhill 50110) 1971

For Ladies Only	I'm Asking
Shackles and Chains	Tenderness
The Night Time's For You	Jaded Strumpet
Sparkle Eyes	Black Pit
Ride With Me	In Hopes Of A Garden

Rest In Peace
(ABC-Dunhill 50124) 1972

The Ostrich	Your Wall's Too High
Don't Step On The Grass, Sam	Desperation
Renegade	Foggy Mental Breakdown
Hippo Stomp	Take What You Need
Everybody's Next One	None Of Your Doing

Sixteen Greatest Hits**
(ABC-Dunhill 50135) 1973

Born To Be Wild	It's Never Too Late
Rock Me	Hey Lawdy Mama
Move Over	Who Needs Ya
Snow Blind Friend	Ride With Me
Magic Carpet Ride	The Pusher
Sookie Sookie	Jupiter's Child
Screaming Night Hog	For Ladies Only
Tenderness	Monster

Slow Flux
(MUMS PZ33093) 1974

Gang War Blues	Children Of The Night
Justice Don't Be Slow	Get Into The Wind
Jeraboah	Straight Shootin' Woman
Smokey Factory Blues	Morning Blue
A Fool's Fantasy	Fishin' In The Dark

Hour Of The Wolf
(Epic PE33583) 1975)

Caroline
Two For The Love Of One
Hard Rock Road
Another's Lifetime

Annie, Annie Over
Just For Tonight
Someone Told A Lie
Mr. Penny Pincher

Skullduggery
(Epic PE34120) 1976

Skullduggery
Rock 'N' Roll Song
Life Is A Gamble
Sleep

I'm A Road Runner
Train Of Thought
Pass It On
Lip Service

Reborn To Be Wild
(Epic PE34382) 1977

Straight Shootin' Woman
Another Lifetime
Smokey Factory Blues
Get Into The Wind
Skullduggery

Hard Rock Road
Mr. Penny Pincher
Caroline
Gang War Blues
Children Of The Night

Born To Be Wild — A Retrospective*
(MCA D2-10389) 1991

Twisted
Sookie Sookie
Your Wall's Too High
The Pusher
Don't Step On The Grass, Sam
Rock Me
It's Never Too Late
Move Over
Snow Blind Friend
Screaming Night Hog
Tenderness
I'm Movin' On
Children Of The Night
Caroline
Ain't Nothin' Like It Used To Be
Rock 'N' Roll Rebels
The Wall

Good Morning Little Schoolgirl
Everybody's Next One
Born To Be Wild
Desperation
The Ostrich
Magic Carpet Ride
Jupiter's Child
Monster
Hey Lawdy Mama
Who Needs Ya'
For Ladies Only (edited)
Ride With Me
My Sportin' Life
Straight Shootin' Woman
Live Your Life
Born To Be Wild (live)
Give Me News I Can Use

JOHN KAY

Singles:

I'm Movin' On / Walk Beside Me
(ABC-Dunhill 4309) 1972

Somebody / You Win Again
(ABC-Dunhill 4319) 1972

Moonshine / Nobody Lives Here Anymore
(ABC-Dunhill 4351) 1973

Easy Evil / Dance To My Song
(ABC-Dunhill 4360) 1973

Give Me Some News I Can Use / same (mono)
(Mercury 74004) 1978

Albums:

Forgotten Songs And Unsung Heroes
(ABC-Dunhill 50120) 1972

Many A Mile
You Win Again
Bold Marauder
Walkin' Blues
I'm Movin' On

Walk Beside Me
To Be Alive
Two Of A Kind
Somebody

My Sportin' Life
(ABC-Dunhill 50147) 1973

Moonshine
Drift Away
My Sportin' Life
Giles Of The River
Sing With The Children

Nobody Lives Here Anymore
Heroes And Devils
Easy Evil
Dance To My Song

All In Good Time
(Mercury 1-3715) 1978

Give Me News I Can Use
That's When I Think Of You
Ain't Nobody Home In California
Ain't Nothing Like It Used To Be
Show Me How You'd Like It Done

The Best Is Barely Good Enough
Say You Will
Hey, I'm All Right
Business Is Business
Down In New Orleans

Lone Steppenwolf*
(MCA 25167) 1987

Easy Evil
Many A Mile
Sing With The Children
You Win Again
Nobody Lives Here Anymore

Walkin' Blues
Drift Away
My Sportin' Life
I'm Movin' On
Somebody

JOHN KAY AND STEPPENWOLF

Albums

John Kay And Steppenwolf Live In London
(Mercury 6437 147) 1981 (released only in Australia)

Sookie Sookie	Give Me News I Can Use You
Hot Night In A Cold Town	Ain't Nothin' Like It Used To Be
Magic Carpet Ride	Five Finger Discount
Hey Lawdy Mama	Business Is Business
Born To Be Wild	The Pusher

WolfTracks*
(Allegiance AV434) 1982 (also released as an audiofile recording by Nautilus — NR 53)

Time	None Of The Above
You	Every Man For Himself
Five Finger Discount	Hold Your Head Up
Hot Night In A Cold Town	Down To Earth
For Rock 'n' Roll	The Balance

Paradox
(Attic Lat 1191) 1984 (released only in Canada)

Watch Your Innocence	Nothing Is Forever
You're The Only One	The Fixer
Give Me News I Can Use	Only The Strong Survive
Ain't Nothing Like It Used To Be	Slender Thread Of Hope
Tell Me Its All Right	Circles Of Confusion

Rock & Roll Rebels*
(Qwil NU 1560) 1987

Give Me Life	Rock & Roll Rebels
Hold On (Never Give Up, Never Give In)	Man On A Mission
Everybody Knows You	Rock Steady (I'm Rough And Ready)
Replace The Face	Turn Out The Lights
Give Me News I Can Use	Rage

Rise And Shine*
(IRS 82046) 1990

Let's Do It All	Time Out
Do Or Die	Rise And Shine
The Wall	The Daily Blues
Keep Rockin'	Rock 'n' Roll War
Sign On The Line	We Like It, We Love It

* available on CD
** available on CD from MCA

ACKNOWLEDGEMENTS

The authors would like to extend sincere 'thank you's' to everyone who agreed to be interviewed for this book or who, in some manner, provided assistance toward its completion. Special thanks go to the following who went above and beyond the call of duty: Charlie Wolf, for all his support and encouragement; Ron Rainey, for getting the ball rolling in the first place; Bill Weeks, Steppenwolf fan extraordinaire, for his invaluable assistance with the discography; Morgan Cavett, Tom Gundelfinger, Henry Diltz, Bill Cooper, and Sony/CBS for their photographs; Jay Kenoff (Kenoff and Machtinger); Bob Hilderley (Quarry Press); Mike Hamilburg; Lisa McCrohan; Kevin Donnelly (Nite-Out Entertainment, Winnipeg); Marc Coulavin (Canadian Music Network); Gerry Miskolczi (All That Rocks); Bill Munson; Lanora Loyd (Encina Lodge, Santa Barbara, CA); Frederick Carsted and Esmé Keith for various translations and spellings.

Extra-special thanks to Jutta Maue-Kay and Harriett Einarson for their tireless support and constructive criticism. Also, thanks to Shawn Kay and to Matt and Lynsey Einarson for their enduring understanding and support.